To Fritz & Lucy

On the occasion of Fritz's
induction into the America's Cup
Hall of Fame @ St Francis
Yacht Club October 14 2005,
Congratulations

Halsey C. Herreshoff

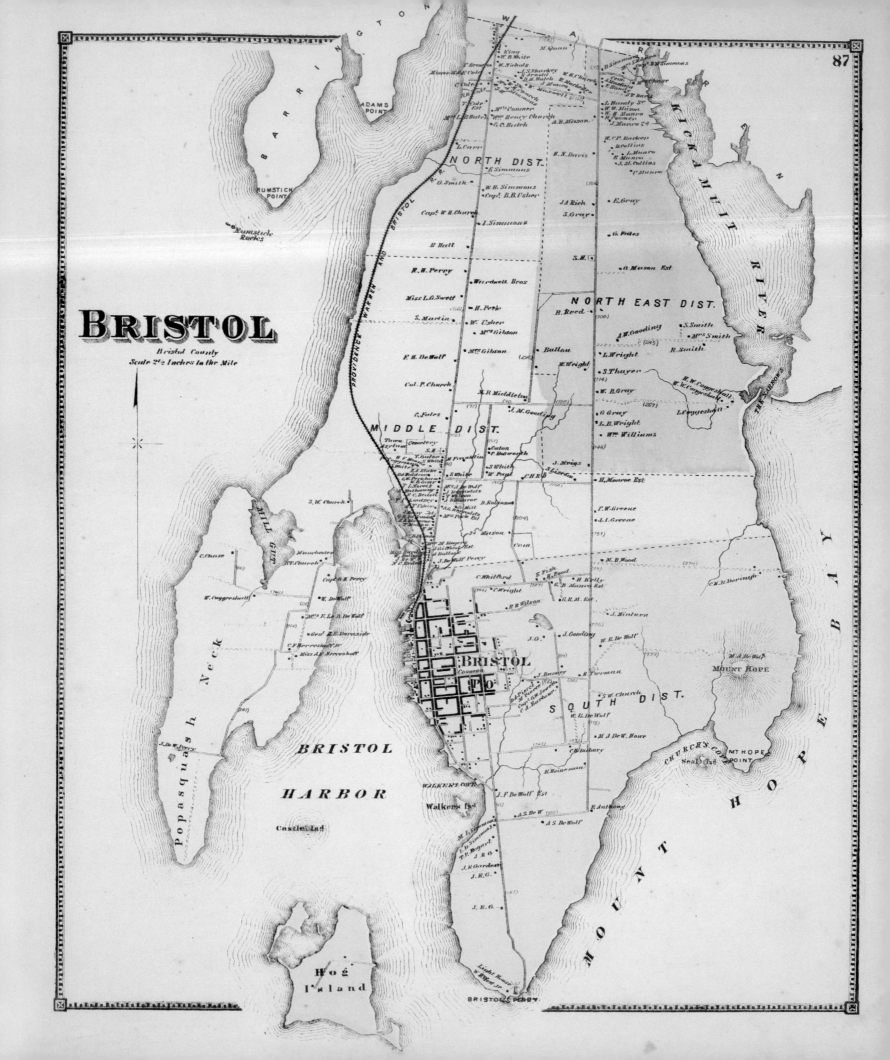

Herreshoff OF BRISTOL

A Photographic History of America's Greatest Yacht and Boat Builders

MAYNARD BRAY
and CARLTON PINHEIRO

HERRESHOFF MARINE MUSEUM • BRISTOL, RHODE ISLAND

Published by Herreshoff Marine Museum
One Burnside Street (P.O. Box 450)
Bristol, Rhode Island 02809-0450

Second edition

Herreshoff of Bristol, the second edition, was designed and
set in Minion by Gilbert Design Associates in Providence, Rhode Island.

The book was printed by Reynolds DeWalt Printing on Garda Silk Text
and bound by Acme Bookbinding.

ISBN 0–9710678–2–1
Library of Congress Control Number: 2005927840

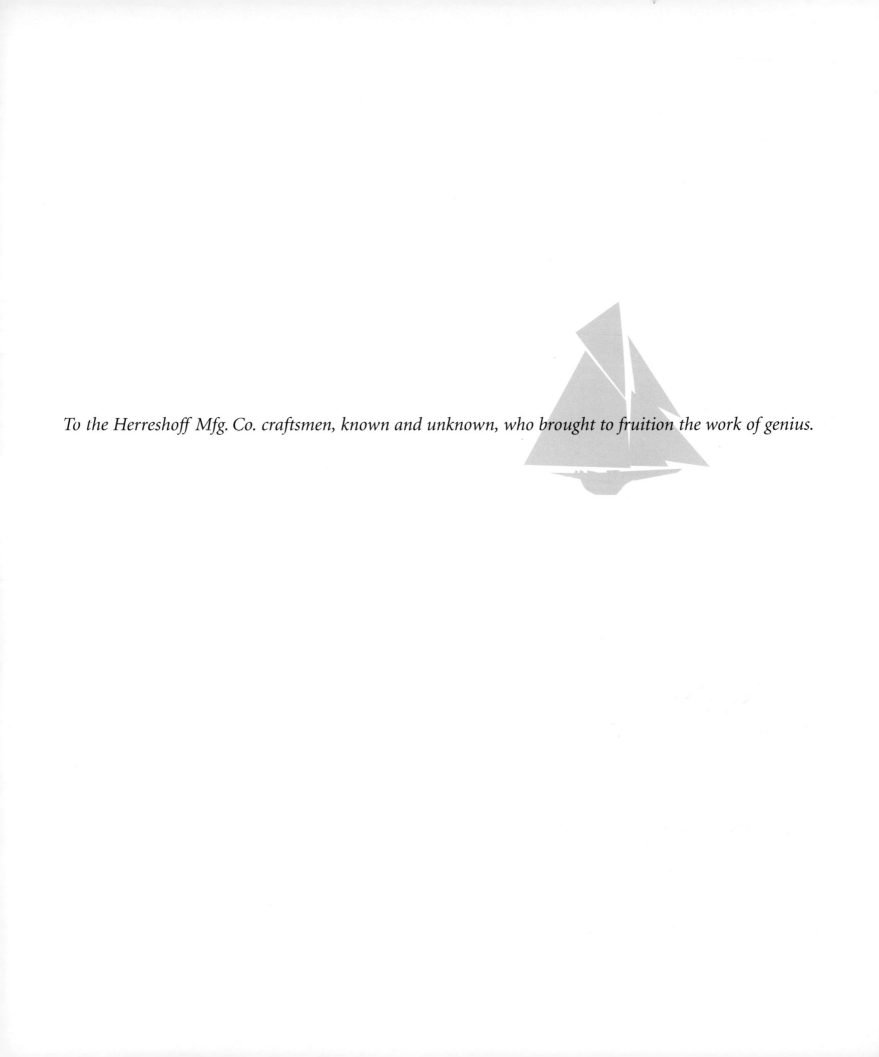

To the Herreshoff Mfg. Co. craftsmen, known and unknown, who brought to fruition the work of genius.

A Dedication to

WILLIAM DAVIS TAYLOR

Grandson of General Charles H. Taylor, reviver of the Boston Globe in 1872, Wm. Davis Taylor served as its publisher from 1955 to 1977. His highly successful career was matched by his dedication to civic causes in Boston. He was a founder of both the U.S.S. CONSTITUTION Museum and the Head of the Charles Regatta.

At age six, Dave Taylor was taught to sail by Captain Bill Martin in Marion, Massachusetts. In 1914, his father, Wm. O. Taylor, was encouraged by Robert W. Emmons, a family friend and later, an owner of the Herreshoff Manufacturing Company, to purchase one of the original Herreshoff 12½-footers (HMCo #746).

As Dave told the story, his father was keen to send NGH the prerequisite number of orders to start production on the 12½ design.

So, on a train ride from Boston to the Cape, he proceeded to "button-hole" each of his friends in turn in the carriage, and upon arriving on the Cape, called my grandfather to place the first orders!

Dave learned to sail his 12½-footer, PEGGY (named for his late sister) with a "very tender hand." Thus began his life-long reverence for Herreshoff boats. The Taylor family also owned the Herreshoff launch MARGARET and the Buzzards Bay 30, NOTOS.

Wm. Davis Taylor was a Life Member and Trustee of the Herreshoff Marine Museum. His personal friendship, leadership on the Board and generosity to the Museum has enhanced both my life and that of other Trustees. His contribution is fittingly memorialized in this fine book.

HALSEY C. HERRESHOFF
President
Herreshoff Marine Museum

Introduction

IT IS HIGHLY gratifying to write this introduction to *Herreshoff of Bristol* on the occasion of its second edition, now in the twenty-first century, about one hundred years after the greatest triumphs of the Herreshoffs and their Herreshoff Manufacturing Company. Sadly, since publication of the first edition in 1989, Carlton J. Pinheiro has passed away. We greatly miss him both for his expertise and for his sterling character that so favorably guided his tenure as curator of the Herreshoff Marine Museum. Fortunately, Carlton's widow, Lianne Pinheiro, carries on his wish for perfection in anything done—especially for this book. We are grateful that co-author Maynard Bray continues to be active in reviewing editorial content and other issues for this important second edition.

The book conveys the facts and feel of the signal accomplishments of the Herreshoffs of Bristol. From the earliest years of organized sailing, Herreshoff yachts led the way in design, construction, and performance. The daring of J. B. Herreshoff teamed with the genius of his brother Nat forged a legend that grows with the perspective of this age.

Authors Maynard Bray and Carlton Pinheiro put flesh on the bones of the legend. Using previously unpublished photographs, they weave the historic mosaic of innovation, craft, and glamour associated with magnificent creations of the Herreshoff Manufacturing Company. From fast steamers, to exquisite small craft, to handsome schooners, to America's Cup winners, the reader is provided both precise information and the aura of this remarkable Yankee enterprise.

Best of all, perhaps, is that through this book, we are led to appreciate the intellect, method, and ethic that produced the world's best in yachting over many decades commencing more than a century ago. For, while it is natural for each succeeding generation to build on accumulated knowledge and developed materials, we have to be both awed and humbled by the techniques and results conveyed in the images and text of these pages.

My gratitude for this portrayal is enhanced by my special window for observation of my grandfather, Nat Herreshoff, afforded by the mirror of my own father, Sidney Herreshoff. I cherish the memories of working along with him on designs and development projects. Like his famous father, Sid Herreshoff possessed a genius for seemingly infallible engineering insight. His total honesty extended way beyond ethical matters to a purity of technical objectivity. Moreover, he possessed a serene but dynamic confidence unfettered by the slightest tinge of vanity. Many times I observed him boldly modeling a fine hull form or reducing a complex engineering problem to the most basic of elegant solutions. This truly had to be Captain Nat's way also; it is the only possible explanation for the prodigious accomplishments wrought by him and the marvelous workmen of the Herreshoff Mfg. Co.

My pulse quickens at the recollection of that special warmth of feeling accompanying successful launchings at "The Shop" during its final years. As a small boy in 1937, I was present with my family for the arrival of T. O. M. Sopwith's ENDEAVOUR II in preparation for the final J-boat America's Cup races. These are choice memories now perpetuated by the yachts and memorabilia on permanent display at the Herreshoff Marine Museum on the original site of the Herreshoff Mfg. Co. in Bristol, Rhode Island.

It is wonderful through the medium of this volume to link that special past to our modern-day sport of sailing. Yachting now keeps vibrant the traditions of seamanship, competition, and camaraderie of the past. Our accomplishments and pleasure in the sport grow with understanding of the boats and people of the earlier age of development led by the Herreshoffs.

I truly believe that "there is nothing quite like messing about in boats." Best of all is the satisfaction to invent boat designs, craft the product, and then to sail one's own creation to victory. Nat Herreshoff did this for seventy-five active years spanning the "Golden Age of Yachting." In this volume, as never before was possible, the reader may join him vicariously to view the Bristol adventures of creation, competition, and satisfaction.

HALSEY C. HERRESHOFF

Preface

THIS BOOK came about because both authors were passionately interested in the Herreshoffs and their boats, and because of a unique collaboration between the Herreshoff Marine Museum and WoodenBoat Publications, Inc. Although the idea of someday creating a book lurked in our minds (as with most people who pursue historical research), the inspiration for a book of this nature was provided by Halsey Herreshoff, in 1987. His cousin Katherine's glass-plate negatives had recently been donated to the Herreshoff Marine Museum, and murals made from them constituted a new exhibit there. Halsey asked if WoodenBoat would consider producing a book using these negatives. The answer was yes, but it was foreseen that the proposed book, if limited to only those images—wonderful as they are—would be pretty thin. Halsey then offered all of the museum's photographic holdings, including the family albums.

With several thousand negatives, prints, and snapshots to sort through, and with many of the images undated and unidentified, we had a fairly daunting task, in spite of our general familiarity with the boats, scenes, and people. The first culling resulted in about 800 candidates. Over the next year, they were reduced in number to about 300 images, and our research and caption-writing dwelt upon these. (Carlton, a Bristol native, concentrated on the people and local history, while Maynard, a boat builder and maritime historian, focused on the boats.) With the help of Llewellyn

Howland III, Jon Wilson and his wife Sherry Streeter, the book was then organized into chapters and a final picture selection made. From here on, our work involved editing and rewriting our independent captions into a unified and essentially chronological story which would match our established photo sequence. Tempting though it was to include photos from other collections, we have, with only one or two exceptions, limited the images to those that are in the collection of the Herreshoff Marine Museum.

The research itself, based to a large degree upon what was shown in the photographs, proved to be an absorbing study and kept us ever inspired with new discoveries about the Herreshoffs and their boats. We, and you as readers, owe a debt of gratitude to Katherine Kilton Herreshoff, Thomas P. Brightman, N. G. Herreshoff, Jr., and Agnes M. Herreshoff, who recorded with their cameras so much of what went on. In many, many instances, their pictures have turned folklore into fact. So, too, are we grateful to those who have spoken with us or written of the Herreshoff Mfg. Co., its methods, its boats, and its people. The notes left by NGH himself have been invaluable. Conversations with Sidney Herreshoff, Tom Brightman, Charlie Sylvester, L. Francis Herreshoff, and Carl Haffenreffer, for example, have been priceless, and the information they conveyed has supplemented the sources listed in the bibliography.

In a book that contains so many dates, dimensions, and proper names, there are bound to be errors. We take full responsibility for them, and welcome corrections and comment for inclusion in future editions. As for the particulars, LOA, the abbreviation for length overall, has two different meanings these days. Throughout this book, however, LOA means length of hull meas-

ured on deck, excluding appurtenances such as bowsprits and booms. These are the definitions accepted by *Lloyd's Register of American Yachts* and *The Register of Wooden Boats*. In gathering the particulars for each of the pictured boats, we have had to make some judgment calls where one source of information conflicts with another. For example, the Herreshoff Construction List for sailing craft shows the contract date for most of the boats, but contains no indication of what the completion date was. Construction went along quickly at Herreshoff's, and in most cases, the boats were completed in the same year that they were ordered. But for large craft ordered late in the year, the Construction List may show, say, 1912 when *Lloyd's Register* shows a 1913 date. If it seemed to make sense to use the later date, we have done so.

As publisher of the first edition, Jon Wilson of WoodenBoat pulled out all the stops to achieve top quality. This book's contents were greatly enhanced by two very fine editors: Jane Crosen (a patient chaser of proper fact and grammar) and Louie Howland (an enthusiastic and knowledgeable guiding light). Nick Whitman worked unbelievable darkroom magic in reproducing photos that were faded, yellowed, and, more often than not, without the "snap" that the subject cried for.

Herreshoff Marine Museum rather than WoodenBoat Publications, Inc. became publisher for this second edition and arranged to have its cost subsidized by two donors, thus enabling an overall redesign and update without compromising the book's quality. As with the first edition, we feel fortunate at not being asked to cut corners because of cost.

A new team was assembled, led by Halsey Herreshoff. He appointed HMM Development Director James Russell to work out the text revisions with us, and a new layout with the book's designer. Upon James's departure, the reins were passed to HMM Curator John Palmieri whose thoughtful suggestions and attention to detail we much appreciate. It's been a pleasure to work with these gentlemen, and gratifying to know that we all wanted the best possible result.

When what proved to be a false start with a European co-publisher had to be abandoned, our friend and colleague Ben Mendlowitz helped smooth out the bumps and get the project off on a new track. We deeply appreciate his assistance.

We also wish to acknowledge and thank Jon Wilson of WoodenBoat Publications for loaning the very same photographic prints used in the first edition. Without those Nick Whitman images, achieving comparable quality in this second edition would have been extremely difficult and a great deal more expensive.

As with Sherry Streeter, who created the book's original design, we've been fortunate in having a skilled and understanding designer to work with. Understandably, the Museum wanted this second edition to look different from the first, and we feel made a good choice in selecting Gilbert Design Associates. As authors, we're grateful to have been included in the redesign.

MAYNARD BRAY
LIANNE PINHEIRO
January 2005

CARLTON J. PINHEIRO
In Memoriam

*C*ARLTON J. PINHEIRO, the late Curator of the Herreshoff Marine Museum, was co-author of Herreshoff of Bristol. *He would have been delighted to see this book printed in the brilliant new volume of 2005. Sadly, Carlton passed away on July 23, 2000; his passing leaves an irreplaceable void at the Museum. During his many years as curator of the Herreshoff Marine Museum, Carlton accomplished much more than can be fully appreciated.*

From early childhood, Carlton, a Bristol boy, had a fascination for things Herreshoff. He studied the Herreshoff Manufacturing Company, its great yachts, and the methods of Captain Nat and J. B. Herreshoff. Carlton collected Herreshoff artifacts, even furniture formerly at Captain Nat's house "Love Rocks," as well as many items that he donated or displayed at the Museum.

Carlton's lectures were legendary. Exact, precise, innovative, and laced with humor or irony, Carlton always had his audience sitting on the edge of their seats. As he would sometime adopt the role of Captain Nat to enhance readings or dialogue, we marveled at the similarities of modest manner and conservative hirsute appearance. Many remarked, how with age, Carlton's appearance grew even more like Captain Nat's. This was not quite coincidental; Carlton greatly admired Captain Nat and enjoyed appearing more and more like him.

He was the unquestioned authority on historical facts, the precise and diligent master of the Museum's Collection, and above all the magnificent face of this institution. Always friendly, ever helpful, Carlton was generous to anyone who sought help or showed interest at the Museum.

Carlton was much more than that. He inspired devotion, precision and care about the Collection, the activities of the Museum, and service to our Museum visitors. This had great impact upon members, volunteers, and visitors from around the world. Always the perfect gentleman, intelligent, eager for life, and possessing a special sense of humor, Carlton meant a great deal to me personally at the Museum. I was proud to share work and adventures with him.

HALSEY C. HERRESHOFF
*President, Herreshoff
Marine Museum*

*C*ARLTON was a good friend, passionate about many of life's offerings, and with a particular passion for things Herreshoff. That's how I made his acquaintance more than 20 years ago. Being a Bristol native, his interest lay with the local Herreshoff history and people, while mine centered on the technical aspects of the boats themselves. We complemented each other perfectly and coincidentally, discovered that we each had a son named Nathanael.

Carlton's modesty tended to keep his name from being as widely recognized as it should have been, but to those who knew him, he was pure gold: an eagle scout, a URI graduate, a fondly remembered high-school teacher of literature, a father of two fine sons, a wonderful lecturer with wit and wisdom, and restorer of prize-winning antique autos. As Curator of the Herreshoff Marine Museum, he wrote fine articles for the HMM Chronicle and most important to you, the reader, co-authored with me this book. It's no exaggeration to say that without Carlton's help and insight, Herreshoff of Bristol would have come out severely lacking, if at all. I'll miss Carlton and so will many others—especially his wife Lianne who loved him and gave him such wonderful companionship and comfort right up until the end; and, of course Halsey Herreshoff, with whom Carlton worked so closely to help build and operate the Herreshoff Marine Museum.

MAYNARD BRAY
Adapted from the Editor's page of WoodenBoat

The Principal Photographers

AGNES M. HERRESHOFF
(1884–1965)

N. G. Herreshoff's daughter became interested in amateur photography about 1901. At this time, with a rather simple Kodak camera, she began to chronicle family life—cruises, picnics, and the daily activities at Love Rocks. Over the years, she became quite proficient, and her photographs show a remarkable ability for composition. Her numerous family albums have provided considerable insight into the daily lives of the Herreshoff clan.

KATHERINE KILTON HERRESHOFF DEWOLF
(1871–1954)

John B. Herreshoff's daughter became interested in photography in the early 1890s when her father gave her a camera. By the turn of the century, she was recognized as one of the best amateur photographers in Bristol. As she was a constant companion to her blind father, her camera subjects, for the most part, reflect a fondness for yachting and the work at the shop, but many of her photographs also show a great ability with pastoral subjects. In 1901, recently widowed, she arranged a handsome book of souvenir photos of Bristol after receiving advanced instruction in photography from Mr. Walter J. Tubbs, a professional Bristol photographer. Mr. Tubbs also taught her to paint with watercolors on photographs. The mutual photographic interests of pupil and teacher resulted in their marriage in 1902.

Tom Peckham Brightman
(1882–1978)

Tom Brightman, a second-generation Herreshoff employee, began work at the Herreshoff Mfg. Co. in 1901. Shortly there-after, he began to take pictures with a little 3-A folding camera. This activity came to the attention of JBH, and young Brightman was called into the office. Suspecting that he would be fired for taking pictures on the job, Tom was surprised when JBH engaged him to take pictures of one of his automobiles that he wanted to trade for a launch. On the basis of Tom's pictures, the trade was made, and JBH subsequently asked Tom to take pictures of the yachts built at the shop. JBH provided Tom with a 5-by-7-inch Press Graflex outfit (it cost about $400) which included a twelve-plate magazine for the glass plates. Tom used it for forty years, finally trading it in for a 3½-by-4¼-inch Speed Grafic, later to be supplanted in World War II by a 4-by-5-inch Speed Grafic. Tom rose quickly in the shop hierarchy and was instrumental in organizing the Haffenreffer purchase in 1924. After 1924, he was a highly respected junior executive, serving as manager of the company. When the Herreshoff Mfg. Co. closed after World War II, Tom went to work at the Heustis Machine Co. in Bristol and remained there until he retired in 1973 at the age of ninety. In 1976, he returned to work at Heustis on a part-time basis, continuing there until his death at ninety-six years of age.

Nathanael G. Herreshoff, Jr.
(1888–1926)

NGH's son Nat graduated from Bristol High School and attended M.I.T. for two years, followed by a year's study of electricity at the General Electric Company in Lynn, Massachusetts. About 1910 he took employment at the Herreshoff Mfg. Co., where he specialized in electrical matters. His interest in photography led to his taking pictures of the affairs of the company, and, along with Tom Brightman, he set up a darkroom in one of the shop buildings. As a member of the Bristol Naval Reserve Company, at the outbreak of World War I, he was assigned to the gunboat u.s.s. MARIETTA. After three months' service, he received an honorable discharge from the U.S. Navy and enlisted in the photographers' unit of the Aviation Corps of the United States Army. In this service he further honed his photography skills and specialized in aerial photography. When the Herreshoff Mfg. Co. was auctioned in 1924, he accepted a position with the Cranston Worsted Mills of Bristol. He died in 1926 at the age of thirty-eight.

Contents

R-Class sloop
GAME COCK
of 1925
(see page 163)

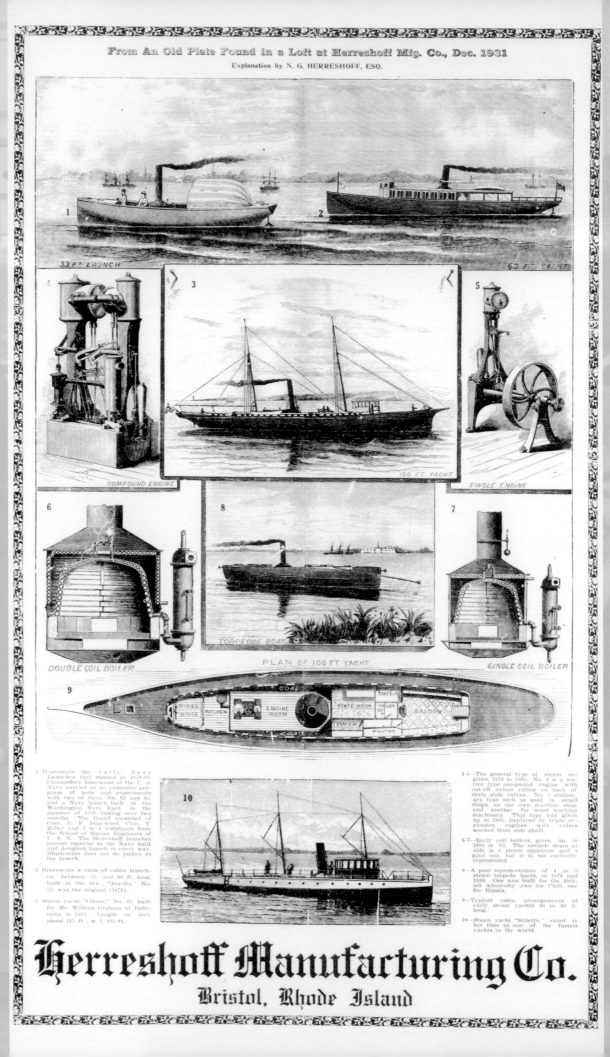

From An Old Plate Found in a Loft at Herreshoff Mfg. Co., Dec. 1931

Explanation by N. G. HERRESHOFF, ESQ.

33 FT LAUNCH

63 FT YACHT

COMPOUND ENGINE

100 FT. YACHT

SINGLE ENGINE

DOUBLE COIL BOILER

TORPEDOE BOAT

SINGLE COIL BOILER

PLAN OF 100 FT YACHT

WHEEL HOUSE — KITCHEN — ENGINE ROOM — STATE ROOM — TOILET — SALOON — STATE R. — PANTRY — COAL

1 — Represents the early Navy Launches that started in 1879-80. Commodore Isherwood of the U. S. Navy carried on an extensive program of tests and experiments with two of them, No. 62 and 63, and a Navy launch built in the Washington Navy Yard, in the summer of 1880, lasting over two months. The Board consisted of Com. B. F. Isherwood, Com. T. Zeller and 3 or 4 assistants from the School of Marine Engineers of U. S. N. The Herreshoff launches proved superior to the Navy built and designed launch in every way. Illustration does not do justice to the launch.

2 — Represents a class of cabin launches, between 55 and 68 ft. long, built in the 80's. "Javelin," No. 52, was the original (1879).

3 — Steam yacht "Steam," No. 65, built for Mr. William Graham of Baltimore in 1880. Length on deck about 115 ft.; w. l. 105 ft.

4-5 — The general type of steam engines, 1879 to 1885. No. 4 is a marine type compound engine with cut-off valves riding on back of main slide valves. No. 5 stationary type such as used in small shops, as our own machine shop and another for wood working machinery. This type was given up in 1885. Replaced by triple expansion engines with valves worked from side shaft.

6-7 — Early coil boilers, given up in 1881 or '82. The verticle drum at side is a steam separator and a good one, but it is not correctly represented.

8 — A poor representation of 4 or 5 steam torpedo boats, in 1879 and 1880. One was built for the British Admiralty, two for Chili, one for Russia.

9 — Typical cabin arrangements of early steam yachts 80 to 90 ft. long.

10 — Steam yacht "Stiletto," rated in her time as one of the fastest yachts in the world.

Herreshoff Manufacturing Co.

Bristol, Rhode Island

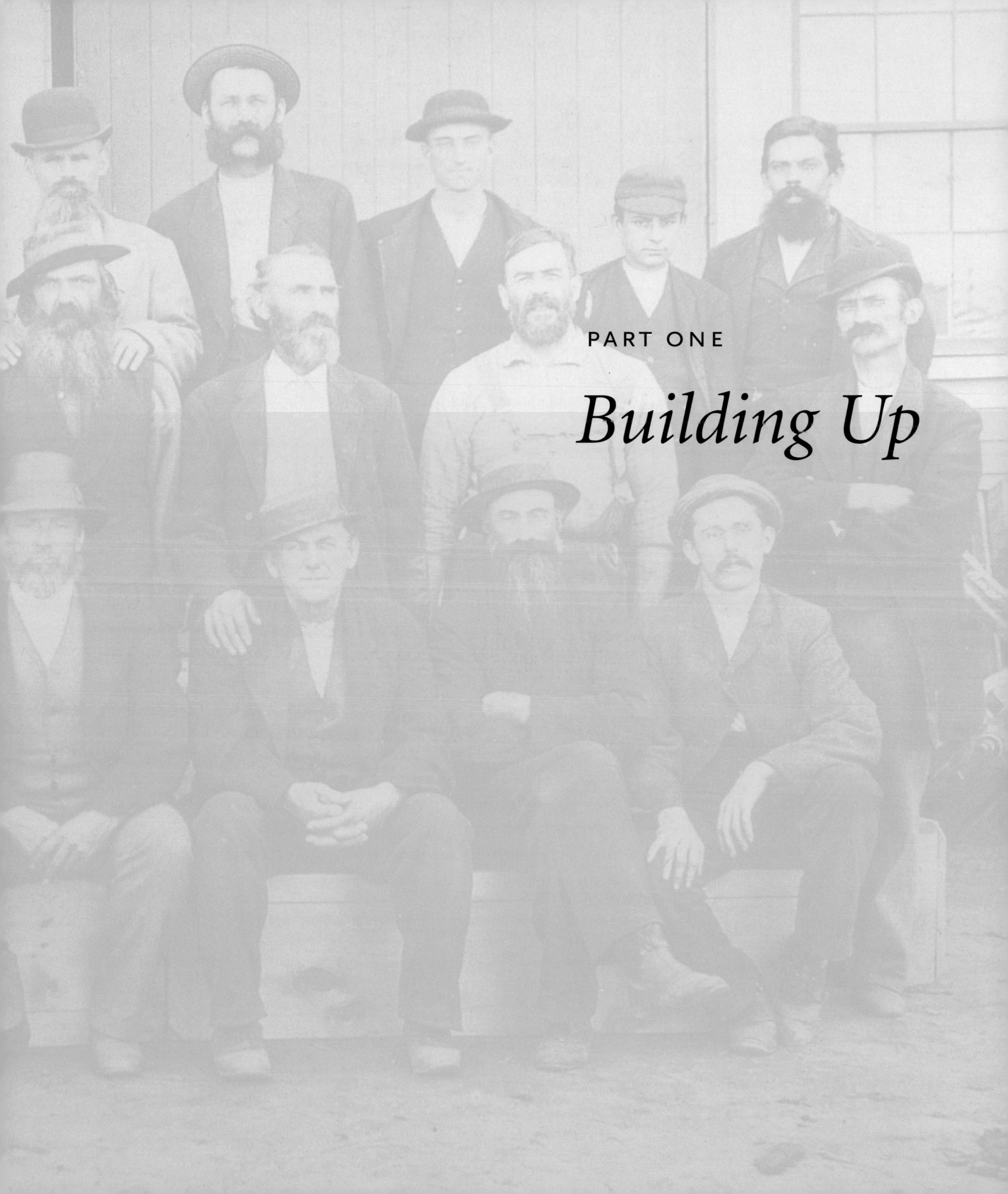

PART ONE

Building Up

CHAPTER I

The Old Tannery

Herreshoff Boatbuilding to 1878

L ONG BEFORE there was a Herreshoff Manufacturing Company, the Herreshoffs were building, sailing, and racing boats. Charles Frederick Herreshoff, Sr., whose large family included John Brown Herreshoff and Nathanael Greene Herreshoff upon whom this book dwells, owned a series of cruising catboats named JULIA (after his wife) with which he inspired and instructed his sons. Racing became a favorite family pastime, and, as the boys themselves commenced to build and race similar boats of their own, the name Herreshoff became well known in Narragansett Bay waters for skilled sailing and fast boats. SPRITE, whose 1859 origin is described in Chapter XI, was one such craft.

For John Brown Herreshoff (JBH), who as a teenager became totally sightless, success at business became an obsession. He settled on boatbuilding as a career, and, as he prospered, he came more and more to utilize the natural talent of his younger brother, Nathanael Greene Herreshoff (NGH), in preparing the designs for hulls and rigs, as well as steam power plants. Before NGH was thirty, yielding to this sibling pressure and creative opportunity, he joined with JBH in forming the Herreshoff Mfg. Co.

In the post-Civil War years there was no shortage of work, especially with the flourishing of fishing, yachting, and the United States Navy—all within a few miles of Bristol. Although, ultimately, the Herreshoff brothers' worldwide reputation grew from the design and building of fast sailing yachts, other types—steam yachts, commercial vessels, and naval craft—were equally important products of the early days.

THIS 1864 PAINTING by Charles
DeWolf Brownell shows the Herreshoff
homestead on Hope Street, Bristol—the
waterfront location that would, by the century's end, become world famous as the
Herreshoff Mfg. Co.

Boatbuilding began in the shoreside
building known as the "Old Tannery"
with the family-owned catboats METEOR
(1856–1857) and SPRITE (1859–1860). Within
a few years, JBH would start in business as
a boatbuilder in the Old Tannery.

In a 1934 penciled recollection, NGH
noted that the old building was said to
have been a nail factory at one time, but
was used as a tannery for tanning leather
and in turning out harnesses and saddles
before the Herreshoff purchase in 1856.
The building was about 32 feet by 55 feet.

It had two floors, the upper one supported
from the roof so that the lower level was
clear of posts. The structure was strongly
built of pitch-pine timbers, from which resin
would ooze in the hot weather. In the winter, a good-sized stove kept the western part
of the lower floor warm. The eastern section was partitioned off by hanging canvas.

Charles DeWolf Brownell (1822–1901),
a Bristol native with a fondness for local
subjects, was trained in the Hudson River
School style of painting. Although educated
for the law, he eventually turned his attention toward art and studied in Europe. He
was a friend and neighbor of the Herreshoff
family when he resided in Bristol.

John Brown Herreshoff
in 1865, at age 24

THIS STUDIO PORTRAIT of JBH, made in 1865 for the Herreshoff family album, is the earliest-known photograph of him.

John Brown Herreshoff (1841–1915) was the fourth child of nine children born to Charles Frederick and Julia Ann Herreshoff, and the first of four children to have defective eyes. When JBH was about seven years old, a cataract formed on one eye, and he lost the sight of it. His other eye was still useful, however, and he was able to attend school in Bristol. After school and in the summer recesses, the youthful JBH showed considerable business enterprise and built several small boats and a rope walk. In 1856, just after his fifteenth birthday, he was accidentally struck in his good eye with a stick while playing with his brother Charles. As a result, he became totally blind.

JBH's determination to work soon overcame his affliction. Later that same year, with the help of his father, John completed the building of the 12-foot sailboat METEOR, which had been in process when he lost his sight. He built a number of boats after METEOR, and in 1863, at the age of twenty-two, he was employing several workmen to help in his boat-construction business. In 1864 he formed a partnership with Dexter S. Stone. (Stone, a Brown University graduate from Providence, Rhode Island, was a yachtsman who had cruised with the Herreshoff brothers for several seasons.) Although JBH was incapacitated for several months in 1864 with a severe attack of typhoid fever, the firm of Herreshoff & Stone produced a large number of small catboats, fishing boats, and an order of yawlboats for South American buyers. Many of these boats were modeled by the blind JBH with the help of his father; some were modeled by his brother Nat, then a teenager.

THIS FORMAL studio photograph was taken on June 1, 1865. Nat Herreshoff (1848–1938) attended Bristol High School from 1861 to 1865. The school, known as the "Old Academy," was located at the west side of the Bristol Common. There were fifty-two students in the four grades at the school, twenty-three boys and twenty-nine girls. The course of study included arithmetic, algebra, botany, United States and general history, geometry, philosophy, chemistry, physiology, Latin, grammar, and English literature.

The same year this photo was taken, young Nat turned out his first designs, HAIDEE I, a 25-foot LWL sloop for Dr. S. Powell, and POPPASQUASH, a 16-foot catboat, for Charles F. Chase. In a recollection written in the summer of 1933, Captain Nat (as NGH was often called) stated that HAIDEE I "was my first design, and she proved very satisfactory." Later sold to Edward Burgess (who would himself become a highly respected yacht designer) and renamed FANCHON, she built a reputation as a prizewinner.

During the summer, after graduation, Nat Herreshoff made the models for the boats that Herreshoff & Stone would build for the spring of 1866. These included FANNIE I, a 21-foot LWL catboat; and HAIDEE II, ARIEL, and VIOLET, all 35 feet LOA and 32 feet LWL.

Nathanael Greene Herreshoff in 1865, at age 17

THESE ARE the earliest photographs that have yet come to light showing the site of the Herreshoff Mfg. Co. Each is one of two almost-identical views forming a stereopticon pair, which, when inserted in a hand-held stereoscope viewer, combine to give the observer the effect of depth.

The upper photograph was taken looking south from the beach at the intersection of Summer (now Burnside) Street and Hope Street, just after the Civil War. The small shore building in the center was owned by Captain Lawless, whose homestead was on the east side of Hope Street. Old Bristolians often refer to this area as "Fort Rounds." The Old Tannery building can be seen to the right, with a catboat tied to the wharf.

The lower photograph was taken, no doubt, by the same unknown photographer at the same time. It looks northward from the Love Rocks shore at the foot of Walley Street. The Love Rocks land would become the site of NGH's home, built in 1883 and described in Chapter XIV. At the time of the photograph, JBH was building boats in partnership with Dexter Stone.

The photographic card is inserted into a stereopticon to provide the viewer depth perception

Two views of the Old Tannery, 1866 upper: looking south lower: looking north

THE OLD TANNERY building on the shore (abutting the Hope Street house occupied by the Charles F. Herreshoff family from 1856) had its own stone wharf and was ideal for the boatbuilding purposes of the Herreshoff family. The Herreshoff Mfg. Co.'s South Construction Shop would eventually be built on the land occupied by the tannery and would become the birthplace of many America's Cup defenders. The wharf still stands today and is part of the Herreshoff Marine Museum complex. The Herreshoff homestead, built about 1800, was purchased by Julia Lewis Herreshoff in 1863 and passed down to Norman F. Herreshoff, who bequeathed it to the Herreshoff Marine Museum in 1990.

On the back of this photograph is a penciled notation by NGH, dated October 1934, which describes the scene: "This photo was taken in the late fall of 1866 and shows the waterfront property owned by my father, Charles F. Herreshoff. The Old Tannery is, at this time, occupied by his son John B. Herreshoff and his partner, and is used for the building of yachts and fishing craft. The 33-foot-waterline yacht CLYTIE is about ready for launching; that will make room for building the schooner SADIE, 47 feet waterline. On the wharf, in the foreground, is my father; next to the left is my brother John with his partner at the time, Dexter S. Stone; more to the left is my older brother James. On the shore at the extreme right is my youngest brother, Julian, who is eleven years old, with three toy boats. Hauled out on the bank next to the shed is my father's catboat JULIA III; next south is the 39-foot-waterline yacht QUI VIVE, owned by Thomas Clapham; then comes the catboat FANNIE I, which was built by John for Captain Benjamin Gibbs. Beyond FANNIE are several purse and seine boats of the menhaden fishery. Under CLYTIE's stern are shop foreman Edward Thompson (left) and William Thatcher. In the back center is the old Burnside Rifle Factory (with an office in the northwest corner), at this time occupied by John and his partner for their steam sawmill on the ground floor and on the second floor for building small boats."

The Herreshoff & Stone partnership was short-lived. In early 1867 it was dissolved, and JBH carried on business alone until 1878. During these years he continued building boats, using a hired crew and getting help from various family members, especially his father and his brothers NGH and James.

As the boats JBH built increased in length (remember that these were the post-Civil War boom times), he added to the Old Tannery, reached farther into Bristol Harbor with launching ways, and erected temporary shelters over the larger vessels which, because of their size, had to be built outside the shop.

The Old Tannery
and the Herreshoff
homestead, 1866

S ADIE was modeled by JBH and his father in 1866. The sail plan and all drawings were made by NGH while he was a student at the Massachusetts Institute of Technology. Originally built for and by JBH as a schooner, SADIE was rerigged by him in 1868 as a sloop. This 1875 pencil drawing by George Phillips (a draftsman at the Corliss Steam Engine Co. in Providence, and a close friend of NGH) shows SADIE as a sloop carrying the New York Yacht Club burgee at the masthead and JBH's private signal at the mainsail peak.

As a schooner, SADIE sailed in the first regatta of the Boston Yacht Club on June 17, 1867, and won in the first class. In the second class of that same regatta, the first three yachts—CLYTIE, VIOLET, and KELPIE— had been built by JBH. The winner in the third class was the Herreshoff catboat FANNIE. On September 8, 1869, SADIE weathered the Great Gale in East Greenwich Cove, with JBH and NGH on board. Later that year, she was sold to Benjamin Franklin Burgess, older brother of Edward Burgess.

Although JBH built many sailing craft such as SADIE before the Herreshoff Mfg. Co. was formed in 1878, none were assigned hull numbers and none appear in the Herreshoff Mfg. Co. construction record. Herreshoff power craft (that is, steamers), on the other hand, are included in the record regardless of when built.

The centerboard yacht SADIE of 1867, rigged as a sloop
LOA 50'5"
LWL 47'0"
Beam 16'0"
Draft (centerboard raised) 5'0"

THE SITE IS Common Fence Point at the head of the Sakonnet River, a few miles southeast of Bristol. Seine boats are in the foreground.

SEVEN BROTHERS was built for the seven Church brothers of Sakonnet, who owned a fish-processing plant making fertilizer. The vessel's function was to tow the net-carrying, open seine boats to and from the fishing grounds, and then, after assisting in encircling, pursing up, and loading a school of ever-plentiful menhaden, to bring them to the fish plant. SEVEN BROTHERS was the first of her type. Her layout, with

machinery aft, pilothouse forward, and fish-hold between, became standard for the so-called "pogy boats" for years afterwards, even though the boats grew considerably larger. JBH's shop built the engine, a simple, single-cylinder unit with 11-inch bore and 12-inch stroke, as well as the hull. Both engine and hull were designed by NGH.

The menhaden steamer SEVEN BROTHERS at her owners' dock

HMCo #3, 1870
LWL 65'0"
Beam 14'7"
Draft 5'10"

LIGHTNING's 50½-inch-diameter coil boiler, which had been recently patented, and her two-cylinder steam engine show clearly in this 1876 photo. Both were built by JBH's yard, as was the hull itself.

LIGHTNING was an easily driven double-ender whose huge (38-inch-diameter), slow-turning propeller was located abaft the rudder, although both were unusually close to amidships She is what was known as a "spar torpedo boat," meaning that the torpedoes were carried and set from the ends of long poles rather than being self-propelled, as we know them today. LIGHTNING was designed to sneak up close to an enemy vessel, running silently and in the dark of the night, and deposit a lit torpedo next to her hull by means of the spar, then back away

quickly before it exploded. This was hazardous business, of course, and with the advent of so-called "automobile" torpedoes that could be "fired" from a distance, spar torpedo boats became obsolete. Given the 1876 technology, however, LIGHTNING was effectively thought out. She was low, dark, and relatively quiet, not easily seen or heard. After a "hit," her backing-down acceleration must have been a head-snapper, and with a pointed stern and the rudder in the wash of the big propeller, LIGHTNING's speed and maneuverability while going backward were exceptional. According to NGH, LIGHTNING made 20 m.p.h. on trials and on one run got up to 21.5 m.p.h. This was while going forward; but the speed astern must have been about the same. The Herreshoff Mfg. Co. construction log shows five more spar-type torpedo boats in the four years following LIGHTNING: one for England, one for Russia, and three for Chile and Peru.

Brother James is given universal credit for designing the once-famous Herreshoff

Safety Coil Boiler, used for a while in every steam-powered craft that the Herreshoffs built. Its chief virtues were its compactness and its ability to get up steam in a hurry. Whereas other boilers of the day took perhaps an hour after light-off until they'd make enough steam to get a boat underway, the coil boiler took under five minutes. These patented coil boilers appear to have been a real selling point for the early Herreshoff steamers, and they were used exclusively by the Herreshoffs until about 1883, being manufactured in a variety of sizes. What killed the coil boiler was the high cost of manufacture. The "coil" was a continuous length of piping with a gradually increasing diameter which had to be formed entirely by hand. It was also impossible mechanically to clean the scale from the inside surface of the coils; in time, the scale buildup so lowered the boiler's efficiency that a replacement boiler (or at least the coil) was needed. Eventually, the Herreshoffs abandoned coil boilers in favor of more conventional ones, designed by NGH.

LIGHTNING, the
United States Navy's
first torpedo boat
in Newport waters

HMCo #20, 1876
LWL 57'0"
Beam 6'0"
Draft 3'0"

Estelle was built for Cuban insurgents; immediately after sea trials, however, she was seized and tied up by the United States government. She was eventually sold to other owners. Estelle could raise steam in her Herreshoff-patented coil boiler so fast that the revenue cutter Dexter had to keep up a head of steam even while anchored, in case Estelle made a break and Dexter had to give chase.

Estelle's building and subsequent trials were truly remarkable achievements —the result of youthful exuberance, a flair for organization and business, the ability to orchestrate a big job, sound design and engineering, and good basic seamanship. Estelle was a bigger vessel, by far, than any JBH had ever built. He, nevertheless, convinced the New York lawyer who represented the owners that he could do it and was awarded the contract, which contained a bonus for early delivery. The little family boatyard was not equipped to build Estelle's hull, and JBH therefore farmed out the entire hull construction to Job Terry in nearby Fall River, Massachusetts, after getting NGH (who was working full-time at the Corliss Steam Engine Co.) to build the half model and prepare the plans. To make the schedule, NGH hired a draftsman to prepare the finished drawings for the engine. The engine was, of course, steam driven, having two cylinders (or a so-called compound engine) with bores of 12 and 21 inches and a stroke of 24 inches. It was built well and fast by the Rhode Island Locomotive Works in Providence. The boiler was built by the crew in JBH's boatyard, and its tapering, circular coils of steam piping required some very sophisticated hand forging.

With work going on simultaneously in several locations, with business arrangements to be made, with deliveries and in-house work to supervise, JBH must have been busy indeed. How long did it take to build Estelle? Only a few months. JBH got the job in early May, and the hull was ready in early September. The machinery was installed in October (after the hull was towed to Bristol), and trials took place in November.

With a bit of imagination, one can see JBH in his mid-thirties, NGH still in his twenties, with a pick-up crew, probably of family members and yard workers, conducting sea trials on this 120-foot-long vessel. Her contract speed was to be 16 m.p.h. (over a three-hour full-speed trial); she made the speed and ran continuously for twice that time. Here, in the slightly edited words of NGH, is the story of a portion of the sea trials: "In turning the south end of Goat Island, the rudder, which was a bronze casting, gave out and was completely lost, but we didn't stop—only to anchor a few times to get the vessel on course—then started ahead. When east of Prudence Island, we took in tow a Bristol sloop-yacht about 30 feet long, and she steered us to our home anchorage."

About a month later, after the rudder was replaced, NGH wrote: "John [JBH] was anxious to make the speed trial called for in the contract, so the boat could be turned over to her owners, and with parleying with the heads at Washington, this was arranged for. The morning was favorable with light westerly and northerly wind. I had charge of running the boat and the machinery. I think my brother Charles did most of the steering. I do not recollect the engineer, but

William Terry and assistant were firemen. Raymond Perry and Dr. Neylan were guests. The owners were represented by their attorney and a cutthroat-looking Spaniard, who was supposed to take charge of the craft when turned over. The captain and several armed men from the Dexter were also with us.

"The start was made in the afternoon, and we ran moderately with natural draft up the Sound as far as Faulkners Island, turned, and ran back at full speed using the blower, or jet, in the stack. We ran into the Bay, and made over the contract speed of 16 m.p.h. The boat was accepted by the agent and paid for, and was immediately seized by the United States Treasury, part of the engine taken, and tied up at a wharf in Bristol in charge of a shipkeeper."

The Spanish government heard about Estelle and was sufficiently impressed to order a gunboat, Clara (HMCo #39), with an identical power plant, the very next year.

The magnitude of the Estelle project, and the awareness that there could be others like it, precipitated the brothers' forming of the Herreshoff Mfg. Co. in 1878. All subsequent boatbuilding was carried out under the new organization's auspices.

The steamer
Estelle at right,
under guard of the
Revenue Service
cutter Dexter in
Bristol Harbor

HMCo #35, 1877
LOA 120'0"
Beam 16'0"

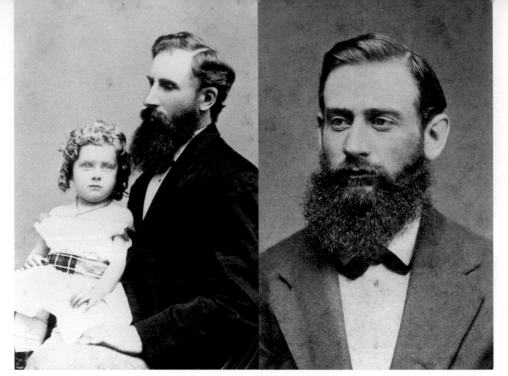

John Brown Herreshoff
and his daughter
Katherine Kilton Herreshoff,
about 1874

Nathanael Greene Herreshoff,
about 1876

JBH MARRIED Sarah Lucas Kilton (1837–1906) in 1870. Katherine, or "Katie," was the only child born of this marriage, which ended in divorce in the late 1880s. In this portrait, she was about three years old.

Katie and her Papa enjoyed a close relationship, with the young girl acting as the eyes for her blind father on walks about the Herreshoff shops and on trips to purchase materials. Katie's devotion to JBH remained undiminished during his lifetime. When Katie's own daughters were born in the late 1890s, JBH showed strong affection for the little girls and relished the time he spent with them.

ABOUT 1869, after completing a special three-year course in mechanical engineering at M.I.T., Nat Herreshoff secured employment as a draftsman at Corliss Steam Engine Co. in Providence. This company had the reputation of being the foremost steam-engine builder of the period. In addition to his design and drafting work, NGH also inspected and adjusted Corliss-built engines after they were set up at their final destinations. In 1876 he was placed in charge of the installation and running of the massive Corliss steam engine that supplied power for the nation's Centennial Exhibition in Philadelphia. This photograph of him in his late twenties was probably taken at about the time of his important work for the 1876 Centenary.

While at Corliss, NGH devoted much time evenings and weekends to designing yachts and steam engines for his brother John. For a short time when on leave during the summer of 1877, he went into the catamaran-building business full-time on his own.

"IN 1875, while still with Mr. Corliss but ever thinking of sailing craft," wrote NGH, as quoted in *The Eastern Yacht Club Ditty Box,* "I conceived the idea of making a double-hulled sailing boat, by which great stability could be obtained with little weight and easy lines. To make the thing practical in a seaway, I devised a system of jointed connections between the hulls and intermediate structure that carried the rig, so the hulls could pitch and dive independently with but little restraint. These catamarans would sail very fast, and would make 20 m.p.h. on a close reach, also 8 m.p.h. dead to windward. For actual sailing, I enjoyed these craft more than any other I ever owned."

NGH produced seven catamarans, starting in 1875 with AMARYLLIS, built by JBH's boatyard crew. Two years later, after patenting his design, NGH went into business for himself, offering catamarans in three sizes: a 20-footer for three to four persons, a 25-footer for five to six persons, and a 32-footer for seven or eight, "these to be furnished complete with anchors and cables, storm jibs, built of the best material, and guaranteed." The endeavor proved unsuccessful, and only three more catamarans were built under this arrangement. Their cost was higher than anticipated, and, after a brief return in the fall of 1877 to the Corliss Steam Engine Co., NGH joined his brother to form the Herreshoff Mfg. Co.

LODOLA was NGH's final catamaran, and he claimed she was the best of the lot. She was built—along with two others— by the Herreshoff Mfg. Co. in its early years. After using LODOLA for three-and-a-half seasons and reaching the age of thirty-five, NGH decided to try more conventional sailing craft. His first cat-yawl, CONSUELO, came out in 1883, the first year of his marriage, but it was several years before he disposed of his catamaran LODOLA.

LIGHT WEIGHT was far more critical to the performance of a catamaran than to that of any of the other boats NGH had sailed, and he became almost evangelical in describing the virtues of cruising with light and simple gear (this philosophy was recorded in an 1877 article in *The Spirit of the Times*). He was most upset with the Centennial Regatta race committee when they disqualified his AMARYLLIS on the grounds that the race she'd just won was for cruising boats—and that AMARYLLIS lacked cruising accommodations. In those days, NGH considered a boom tent, such as shown here, to be a perfectly acceptable cabin. Notice, by the way, how the boom has been raised extra high to serve as a ridgepole. Notice also the neat furls, especially in the jib.

Both of these photos were posed, and put to use in promoting NGH's short-lived catamaran-building business. Although never widely accepted in their day, the NGH catamarans could really sail! On one cruise, NGH did 18 m.p.h. over a measured course, and another time he was sure he hit 22 m.p.h. The work at the Herreshoff Mfg. Co., however, soon became too demanding for continued catamaran development, and no more were built until the company's twilight years, when NGH was well into his retirement.

A boom tent made catamaran cruising possible

One of several catamarans built about 1877 to NGH's patented design

13

CHAPTER II

Manufacturing for Steam

Herreshoff Mfg. Co. Power Vessels, 1878–1897

WHEN JBH AND NGH joined forces in 1878, they concentrated wholly on the design and building of steam-powered vessels—and the fledgling Herreshoff Mfg. Co. was soon off and running. Although the Herreshoff Mfg. Co. was new, the Herreshoff brothers were far from being neophytes. Already, JBH had put together a boatbuilding facility and a crew and had well over a decade's experience in turning out a wide variety of craft on his own. NGH, on the other hand, after his nine years at the Corliss Steam Engine Co. and his earlier training at M.I.T., had become an exceptionally skilled designer of steam-power plants. The Herreshoffs also had the use of a unique coil boiler, invented and patented by their elder brother James, which, because of its light weight and quick warm-up, gave them a distinct advantage over other builders.

NGH wrote: "I reluctantly resigned from the Corliss Steam Engine Co. on December 31, 1877, and took up designing and drafting for John. I gave up a salary of $1,400 per year and took one of $1,000, but I decided the business could be built up and there was prospect of better times in John's business if certain rules were adhered to. I therefore made a verbal agreement with John that if I joined him, our entire efforts would be given to business: that John's indebtedness should be settled as soon as possible; that we should borrow no money and that any capital needed must come from earnings, and that new tools or expansion of plant should also be from earnings.

"Our object would be to turn out the very best work possible and deal only with those who appreciated and could pay for good, honest work.

"John stood up to our verbal agreements, and with his wonderful business ability, and my designing and superintending of the work turned out, we very soon put new life [into the operation and initiated] a new era as the Herreshoff Mfg. Co."

JBH, ever the business opportunist, quickly saw Navy work as a significant source of income, and he successfully pursued torpedo-boat contracts.

For both the brothers, turning out craft of superior performance was a primary goal, and that meant light weight in both the hulls and their power plants. Quality and sophistication also became a Herreshoff trademark, as did the high cost of their products. High-speed steam yachts and naval craft, for owners who could afford the very best, became the company's chief output—to the near exclusion of the commercial craft that were built in earlier times.

For a dozen years after its formation, the Herreshoff Mfg. Co. focused on steam-driven craft, and during that time—that is, until 1890—only three small sailboats were built for customers outside the Herreshoff family. Let's look now at two decades of manufacturing for steam.

THESE YACHTS are evidence of the activity of the brothers' newly created partnership. The photograph was taken from Hope Street, looking across the harbor toward Poppasquash Point, on an unusually calm day. On the left, sailing past the wharf, is the catboat JULIA (the fourth of that name), skippered by Charles F. Herreshoff, Sr. The big dark-hulled, schooner-rigged cabin yacht at the end of the dock is probably the 105-foot LURLINE, built elsewhere, here to pick up her new Herreshoff Mfg. Co. steam launch. In front of LURLINE is the 47-foot steam launch KELPIE. Tied alongside the wharf is KITTATINNY, a white-painted, open launch with peaked stern, irreverently christened by the employees "the Giant's Bathtub."

The waterfront of the Herreshoff Mfg. Co. in its first year in business

KELPIE
HMCo #43, 1878
LOA 47'0"
Beam 6'10"
Draft 2'10"

KITTATINNY
HMCo #41, 1878
LOA 60'0"
Beam 6'0"
Draft 2'6"

The steam launch WAIF
HMCo #37, 1878
LOA 30'0"
Beam 6'9"
Draft 2'10"

O N N E W Y E A R ' S D A Y, 1878, the Herreshoff Mfg. Co. came into being. Entering WAIF in the Independence Day festivities that year, with steam up and the propeller turning, was one way of announcing the fact.

The trailer allowed WAIF to be drawn by horses through the streets of Bristol as a float in the "Trades Procession" of the parade. The photo shows a vertically staved yellow-pine coaming and a huge, square-tipped propeller, 27 inches in diameter, according to Herreshoff Mfg. Co. records. Three other open launches like WAIF had already been built shortly before the Herreshoff Mfg. Co. was formed, all with the same Herreshoff coil boilers and 3½-by-7-inch engines.

H ERRESHOFF steam power plants had first come to the attention of government officials through the spar torpedo boat LIGHTNING (HMCo #20), which the Navy had ordered in 1876, and by the performance of the big steamer ESTELLE (both are shown in Chapter I). The Navy's respect for Herreshoff power plants seems to have further increased with its testing of LEILA, which the Herreshoff Mfg. Co. made available, fully crewed, at no cost, apparently for promotional purposes. The Navy's comprehensive report* (issued June 3, 1881) speaks in glowing terms of both machinery and hull: "The steam yachts of the Herreshoff Mfg. Co. have long been celebrated for their high qualities. They are remarkable for the lightness of their hulls and machinery, for their economy in fuel, for the excellence of their design, materials, and workmanship, for their speed, for the extreme rapidity with which steam can be raised from cold water, and for their safety and freedom from accidents; all of which qualities have been progressively developed by a very long, costly, and intelligent experience, the practice of this company being to experiment thoroughly and accurately with its work, and to avail itself of the knowledge thus acquired.

"The Herreshoff steam yachts are modeled and engined for speed alone, the purpose being to obtain the highest possible speed while allowing large cabins for the comfortable accommodation of a considerable number of persons. LEILA is about three years old, and has been in constant service in Chesapeake Bay, Long Island Sound, and Narragansett Bay, without repairs or showing any signs of weakness or change of form, notwithstanding the rough weather encountered and the high speed at which she has always been driven.

"For steam-cutters, launches, gunboats, torpedo-boats, vedette boats, yachts, dispatch boats, small rams for littoral warfare, and small sloops of war, the Herreshoff boiler is very greatly superior to any other known to the undersigned. It is the safest,

simplest, lightest, and cheapest, and possesses so great a balance of advantages that,
in our opinion, none other can be put in
competition with it."

LEILA was first owned by William
Graham of Baltimore, Maryland, who traded
her in two years later for a larger Herreshoff
steam yacht. In 1882, after the Navy's test,
the Herreshoff Mfg. Co. sold LEILA to a
party from Toledo, Ohio. Her rig was

removed before she left for the Great Lakes,
and one of her masts became the flagpole at
NGH's Love Rocks home, where it served
for more than a half-century.

---

* "Report of a Board of United States Naval
Engineers on the Herreshoff System of Motive
Machinery as applied to the Steam Yacht LEILA
and on the Performance of that Vessel," prepared
by the Bureau of Steam Engineering, Navy Dept.,
and published by the U.S. Government Printing
Office, 1881.

The Herreshoff crew,
about 1880

IBIS JR.,
a steam launch

HMCo #45, 1878
LOA 30'0"
Beam 5'0"

I N CHARACTERISTIC attitudes and
dress of the period, a group of twenty-
five employees pose for a photographer
outside one of the shop buildings. Many of
the men stayed at the Herreshoff Mfg. Co.
all their working lives, coming as youths
and remaining three, four, or five decades.
Often, two generations of a family were
employed simultaneously.

This crew worked a six-day week,
and the regular working hours were from
7:00 a.m. to 6:00 p.m., with a recess of one
hour from 12:00 to 1:00. Many of the workmen lived near the shop, and most ate their
lunch at home. The shop bell was rung at
five minutes to 7:00 a.m. and five minutes
to 1:00 p.m. as a signal to assemble; it was
rung at noon and 6:00 p.m. as a signal to
stop work. Smoking was allowed only
between noon and 12:55 p.m., in the Blacksmith Shop and the Boiler Shop.

I BIS JR. was the first of three identical
open, double-ended, steam-powered
launches built in the Herreshoff Mfg. Co.'s
first year. She was shipped to England to
serve the steam yacht IBIS. In fact, she was
personally delivered by NGH and JBH,
along with a few of the Herreshoff Mfg. Co.
crew, who, on the same steamer, were taking
a new torpedo boat to the British Royal Navy.

As a larger boat's launch, IBIS JR. was
fitted with lifting eyes forward and aft so she

could be hoisted on davits. Light weight was
beneficial, if not crucial, for a proper davit
boat; this photo and others show IBIS JR.
as having the delicate elegance for which
the Herreshoff Mfg. Co. became famous.
With a double-acting 2½-by-5-inch steam
engine and a 20-by-30-inch propeller (both
of NGH's design), IBIS JR. had a speed
of about 13 m.p.h.

John Brown Herreshoff
at age 40, in London,
England, 1881

ABOUT 1880, the English naval authorities decided to replace the small torpedo boats they had been using with steel-hulled, launch-type vessels of greater versatility. John Samuel White of Cowes was the most successful of the private builders who had been invited to compete for the construction of these new "vedette" boats. His boats attained a speed of 13.3 knots.

When the Herreshoff brothers learned of the demand for these boats, they sent a proposal to the British Admiralty stating that the Herreshoffs would supply vedette boats that were not only superior in speed, but better in other respects as well. The Herreshoffs received a reply stating that if their vedettes were capable of 14 knots, the Admiralty would purchase them. On July 16, 1881, two Herreshoff vedettes landed in England and were taken to Portsmouth for trial. These boats were 48 feet in length, 9 feet beam, and 5 feet depth, exactly the same as White's. The Herreshoff Safety Coil Boiler made them much lighter, and after a lengthy series of trials, the Admiralty found in favor of the Herreshoff boats. Not only did they make the required 14 knots, they actually made 15.5 knots; the White vedette used for comparison only made 12.6 knots.

So successful were the trials that the Admiralty immediately gave an order to the Herreshoffs for two pinnaces (open boats known as launches in America), which were shipped to England in October 1881. JBH and Katie accompanied the pinnaces to England, and this portrait was taken during their stay in London; the pinnace (shown below) was photographed in Portsmouth, England. Trials for the pinnaces began at once, and the Herreshoff boats made 9.25 knots to the White's 7.3 knots. The triumph of the Herreshoff boats so pleased the English authorities that they accommodated the blind JBH by concluding the trials, cutting the red tape on the reports, and paying the bill, all within the short space of ten days.

One of the two 48'
pinnaces built by
the Herreshoff Mfg.
Co. for the English
government, 1881

HMCo #74–75
LOA 48'0"
Beam 8'10½"
Draft 4'10"

G LEAM was considered sufficiently representative of Herreshoff steam yachts to have been selected for a contemporary Herreshoff Mfg. Co. advertising brochure.* GLEAM was one of several steam yachts built for William Graham of Baltimore; he paid for her in part by trading in his earlier Herreshoff yacht, LEILA.

It was through building yachts for Graham that the Herreshoffs became acquainted with William Young, who first appeared at the Herreshoff Mfg. Co. to be Graham's representative, while his yachts were being constructed. This went on for a dozen or so years during which Young, in spite of his role as a potential adversary, became a fast friend of NGH and his family. Young was some twenty years older than NGH and continued to visit the Herreshoffs, even after his last official work of supervising BALLYMENA's construction in 1888 was complete. It was during one of his later visits to Love Rocks, in 1899, that he died. In later correspondence, NGH speaks of his high regard for Mr. Young. This kind of praise was rare from NGH. Unfortunately, little more is known about William Young.

* The brochure is reproduced in the book *Yachts by Herreshoff*, Herreshoff Mfg. Co., Bristol, Rhode Island, 1935. It is also reproduced opposite page one in this book.

The steam yacht GLEAM at the Herreshoff Mfg. Co. dock

HMCo #65, 1880
LOA 112'0"
Beam 15'3"
Draft 6'7"

CAMILLA was a passenger launch in which occupants could choose between sitting under the open canopy forward or within a windowed day cabin aft. Lifelines encircling the forward and after decks indicate that passengers ventured out on deck occasionally. Just how the lovely double-ender resting on CAMILLA's awning is launched or hoisted is a bit of a mystery; the usual davits are nowhere in sight. Built for Dr. J. G. Holland (editor of *Scribner's Monthly*), CAMILLA was powered by a compound, condensing 6-by-10½-by-10-inch engine with a 51-by-47-inch coil boiler supplying the steam.

The steam launch CAMILLA at Bonnie Castle Pier on Alexandria Bay

HMCo #72, 1881
LOA 60'0"
Beam 8'4"
Draft 4'4"

Employees of the
Herreshoff Mfg. Co.,
March 1882

Fɪғᴛʏ-ɴɪɴᴇ ᴇᴍᴘʟᴏʏᴇᴇs of the
Herreshoff Mfg. Co. are gathered for
this professional portrait outside the Boiler
Shop at 28 Burnside Street. Although some
of the office staff are in the picture, the
Herreshoff brothers are absent.

In the 1880s, the Herreshoffs were
paying the highest boatbuilding wages in
Rhode Island, and first-rate craftsmen made
up the work force. A majority of these arti-
sans were second- and third-generation
Yankee boatbuilders who brought with
them the cumulative experience of their
maritime ancestry. Herreshoff Mfg. Co. was
known to have an unusually cooperative
work force. Some of the workers were

known to each other by the work they performed—"Charlie Copper," "Charlie Paint"—
or by their appearance—"Big John," "Black
Charlie." Many employees were related,
either by blood or by marriage, and a large
percentage of them belonged to Bristol's
fraternal societies. Shared memberships in
St. Alban's Lodge of Masons, the Odd
Fellows, and the Babbitt Post of the Grand
Army of the Republic helped to contribute
to a congenial and productive working
atmosphere. The fine work of these men
gave the young company a considerable
advantage over the other yacht-building
concerns in the 1880s.

RATHER THAN having the usual long deckhouse, NGH raised MAGNOLIA's sheer for headroom under the deck itself—an unusual and rather good-looking configuration for a Herreshoff steam yacht and a natural outcome of the vessel's very shallow draft. An exquisite Whitehall-type owner's gig is hanging from davits, where it can be easily lowered for use at the boarding platform.

MAGNOLIA was built for comfort rather than speed, her twin screws giving her a speed of only 11.5 m.p.h. Nevertheless, with this, the first of the powered houseboats, owner Fairman Rogers of Philadelphia enjoyed a number of winter trips to southern waters.

The steam yacht
MAGNOLIA
anchored in Newport,
Rhode Island

HMCo #104, 1883
LOA 99'0"
Beam 17'7"
Draft 4'9"

PERMELIA was the second steam yacht of this name in as many years. Both were built for Mark Hopkins of Port Huron, Michigan. Onboard for this photo may be Hopkins, accompanied by his wife and daughter. They sit under the afterdeck awning, while the professional crew stand forward—the cook, engineer, and fireman near the mast, the skipper by the pilothouse, and a deckhand on the foredeck.

PERMELIA carries a pair of tenders hoisted on davits and has a boarding platform and stairway rigged for the owner's convenience. Her so-called "light schooner rig" is extremely neat, with track and metal slides, instead of the usual jaws, connecting the gaffs to the masts. The one-hundredth power craft completed by the Herreshoff yard, 100 feet in length, PERMELIA even carries the number 100 on her pilothouse nameboard.

She's functional, yes, but beautiful? Probably not to the modern eye—not even, perhaps, by the standards of the day. Herreshoff's reputation was not enhanced by the aesthetics of these early craft. The great early-twentieth-century yacht designer Clinton Crane, for example, has stated that, in his opinion, Herreshoff steam yachts were extremely homely but were light and easily propelled, and therefore economical. For some, this pureness of function was beauty enough—although of another kind.

PERMELIA,
HMCo #100,
posed for portrait
off Newport,
Rhode Island

HMCo #100, 1883
LOA 100'0"
Beam 12'6"
Draft 5'9"

The steam launch
HENRIETTA
HMCo #133, 1886
LOA 48'0"
Beam 7'6"

IT APPEARS that five of these launches, looking much like stretched-out Whitehall rowing boats, were built by the Herreshoff Mfg. Co. HENRIETTA was the first, built for publisher Norman Munro, who returned the following year for the fast steam yacht NOW THEN and the year after for the even faster and larger 138-foot SAY WHEN.

The photo shows HENRIETTA to have a molded sheerstrake, docking bitts forward and aft, and the usual steamboat canvas awning to keep the sun out and the coal dust from settling on the passengers. With an open cockpit and democratic seating, HENRIETTA was no doubt used as a passenger-carrying ferry in some sheltered water area.

CLARA HERRESHOFF (1853–1905) was the daughter of Algernon Sidney DeWolf and the granddaughter of Professor John DeWolf, a noted chemist and member of the faculty of Brown University. She was the granddaughter, on her mother's side, of Governor Byron Diman of Rhode Island, and was descended from six of the MAYFLOWER Pilgrims and from eight of the first settlers of Bristol. She married Nathanael G. Herreshoff on December 26, 1883.

Clara Herreshoff was much admired for her gentle and generous manner, and had many friends in Bristol. The employees of the Herreshoff Mfg. Co. and their families held her in particularly high regard, as she devoted herself to their welfare in times of illness and hardship and would visit them with baskets of food. She preferred to keep her acts of charity secret, but knowledge of her generosity was widely known. Clara Herreshoff was not only a wonderful mother, but, according to her children, a most patient and understanding wife. How fortunate Captain Nat was to have had a mate who realized the importance of his work and his need to spend long hours in the model room at Love Rocks.

Horticulture, especially the raising of flowers, was her great passion, and she was a most skillful gardener. This skill she passed on to her daughter Agnes, who maintained her mother's garden at "The Farm" (the DeWolf family estate on Griswold Avenue, Bristol, inherited by Clara) until the 1960s.

Mr. And Mrs. Nathanael
G. Herreshoff
(Clara Anna DeWolf),
September 22, 1884

ABOUT 1885, after his separation from Sarah Kilton Herreshoff, JBH moved from the 20 Burnside Street house (shown in Chapter III) to the new residence he had built at 64 High Street, Bristol, at the head of Burnside Street, an easy walk from his office. Here, in the southwest parlor of that new home, he is being read to by his niece, Miss Julia Herreshoff (1864–1942). Miss Julia was the daughter of Charles F. Herreshoff, Jr., of Poppasquash Point, and often read to her Uncle John when she visited him in town. In her later years, Miss Julia resided at the family homestead at 142 Hope Street. She was a familiar figure to the townspeople as she navigated the old streets in her brass-radiator Model T Ford.

At the time this photograph was taken, JBH's daughter Katie was a sophomore at Bristol High School (her school chums called her "Kittie") and lived here with her Papa.

JBH furnished his home in the Victorian style. He did, however, possess and display some fine examples of Colonial American furniture which he could authenticate by feeling the tool marks on the wood with his sensitive fingers. Some of the contemporary furniture in JBH's home was made at the Herreshoff Mfg. Co., and several of these pieces still exist. The Bristol Historical and Preservation Society, for example, has a secretary on display, and the Herreshoff Marine Museum owns a paneled china display cabinet.

John B. Herreshoff
at home, 1887

As youths, JBH and NGH were obsessive in their drive to have the fastest sailboats on Narragansett Bay. As businessmen and yacht builders they were no less eager for speed. It was quite in character for them to have built for themselves an exceptionally fast boat like STILETTO just as soon as their new company could afford it. By 1885 they had built enough long and narrow steamers to have arrived at the lightest-possible hulls and steam plants with the most horsepower per pound. STILETTO, carrying a Herreshoff-built compound steam engine and Herreshoff patented safety boiler of the so-called square type, embodied this experience and would demonstrate to the world just how well these Herreshoff creations performed.

With STILETTO, the Herreshoffs challenged the reigning Hudson River speed queen—the huge passenger steamer MARY POWELL—and won, knowing full well that the race would make national headlines. STILETTO's 1885 win became front-page news in the New York papers, and the name Herreshoff was spread far and wide across the country as builders of the fastest steam yachts—yachts that would make an astonishing 26 m.p.h.

The steam yacht STILETTO's record-breaking speed brought the Herreshoffs nation-wide publicity

HMCo #118, 1885
LOA 94'0"
Beam 11'0"

VAMOOSE underway

HMCo #168, 1890
LOA 112'0"
Beam 12'7"

W ILLIAM RANDOLPH HEARST'S
VAMOOSE was probably the fastest
steam yacht in the country when new, wrote
L. Francis Herreshoff. Others must have
thought so as well, because VAMOOSE was
the only boat that showed up for the
American Yacht Club's 90-mile race from
Race Rock in Fishers Island Sound to the
club's Rye, New York, station. (The Mosher-
designed NORWOOD, the only other entry,
was damaged by grounding while en route.)

VAMOOSE was built primarily for
speed; comfort was a secondary consideration. For power VAMOOSE carried one of
the huge NGH-designed, Herreshoff-built,
quadruple-expansion steam engines that
turned a 52-inch-diameter propeller; she
claimed a speed of better than 27 m.p.h., and,
like STILETTO and JAVELIN, underwent a
rite of passage by racing the Hudson River
steamer MARY POWELL.

Here, as VAMOOSE runs past photographer Bolles's camera for an underway

portrait, her owner's party are on the afterdeck under the canopy. A bicycle is lashed
to the rail near the stern. She is steered
from the deckhouse by a vertical-shaft
wheel. Crew's quarters are forward. Boiler,
engine, and auxiliary machinery are amidships. The galley is aft, along with rather
spartan accommodations for the owner.

A ride on VAMOOSE must have been
novel and thrilling: the wind in your face,
a virtually unobstructed view, comfortable
rattan chairs on the very long and narrow
uncluttered close-to-the-water deck, where,
thanks to a nearly silent steam power plant,
the loudest sound was the snapping of the
flags. Newspaper publisher Hearst surely
enjoyed his new toy as she flashed along,
leaving other boats in her wake.

VAMOOSE spent only a short time in
East Coast waters before being shipped to
San Francisco on the deck of a steamer.

W ITH THE much-heralded speed of
their personal steam yacht STILETTO,
the Herreshoffs began to enjoy a widespread reputation for steam yachts that were
fast as well as efficient. As a result, orders
came for boats like JAVELIN—boats that
could do close to 30 m.p.h. JAVELIN did
about 26 m.p.h., and she, too, took on the
MARY POWELL and won.

JAVELIN was ordered by newspaper
publisher William Randolph Hearst on July
26, 1890. Before completion, Hearst changed
his mind and ordered a larger yacht, which
was to become VAMOOSE. On January 26,
1891, the Herreshoff Mfg. Co. sold the partly
finished JAVELIN to E. D. Morgan, who took
delivery about six months later. (Morgan,
during the same period, also took delivery
of the cat-yawls GANNET, PELICAN, and the
famous 46-foot LWL sloop GLORIANA.)

JAVELIN was composite-built with
mahogany planking over a steel framework,
and, like STILETTO and VAMOOSE, was
given a kind of turtleback deck shape which
limited the usable space but added to the
rakish appearance. On the dock, beyond
JAVELIN in the photo, are the Herreshoff
Mfg. Co.'s first set of sheerlegs and its
steam-yacht coaling station.

JAVELIN at the
Herreshoff Mfg. Co.
dock

HMCo #164, 1890
LOA 98'0"
Beam 10'6"

KATRINA, a small steam yacht

HMCo #163, 1890
LOA 73'0"
Beam 9'0"
Draft 3'10"

As THE RACY and rather handsome KATRINA backs away from the dock, one has a good view of her features. Lifelines enclose her deck. She can be boarded either forward or aft through gates in the lifelines; access to the cabin is by sliding companionway (the cabin windows can be lowered as shown to admit fresh air below deck). Crew's quarters, forward, are entered through a hatch (the one upon which the white-coated man is standing). Chairs on the afterdeck are for the owners, who sit protected by the usual canvas canopy. Steering is by a horizontal-shaft wheel located just forward of the smokestack.

KATRINA's tender—one of the plumb-stemmed, raking-sterned Coquina models —is lifted and lowered with only a single davit. The photo shows the boarding gangway lying on the foredeck along with fenders and docklines; presumably, this clutter will soon be stowed away now that the boat is away from the dock.

THIS STUDIO portrait of NGH was made at the time of his emergence as a world-class designer. Considered by many to be the best portrait of Captain Nat in his middle years, it was kept in a small oval frame in the bedroom at Love Rocks. (*The Yachtsman's Annual Guide and Nautical Calendar* for 1894 featured a page with photographic portraits of prominent American yacht designers grouped between the spokes of a ship's wheel; NGH is featured at the hub in a similar pose.) According to his grandson, Nathanael G. Herreshoff III, "Captain Nat was always well dressed and wore a beard from the time he was a teenager. He had brown hair, a red beard, and greenish-brown eyes."

Nathanael G. Herreshoff, about 1894

CHAPTER III

The Shops

A Look at the Herreshoff Mfg. Co. Facilities, 1878–1897

WITHIN THREE OR FOUR years after the Herreshoff Mfg. Co. was founded, the Herreshoff brothers began transforming the yard from the "make-do," mostly open-air shipyard shown at right, into a first-class manufacturing facility properly housed against the New England weather, where the work of building boats and their steam power plants could be accomplished both efficiently and well. The rapid expansion resulted in a totally changed scene along the Hope Street waterfront, a scene dominated by the two imposing North and South Construction Shops and the wharves, ways, railways, and smaller buildings that went along with them.

Less apparent in most of the photographs, but equally vital to the Herreshoff Mfg. Co.'s well-being, were the shops that ran inshore and up Burnside Street. These started with the old three-story Burnside Rifle Factory building, which was leased by JBH in 1864 and refitted for building small boats. Most of the other buildings were constructed new, having been designed by NGH for their respective purposes. It was within this complex that boilers, steam engines, castings and forgings, and, ultimately, sails and upholstery were produced.

JBH and NGH had been lucky in having deep water right in front of the Herreshoff homestead, and in being able to acquire the adjoining land for their needed expansion. By the mid-1890's, when both Cup defenders and Navy torpedo boats were alternately under construction, the Herreshoff Mfg. Co. work force numbered about 300 men. The yard's many new shops enabled a large percentage of this work to be done inside, where the necessary tools were close at hand and there was protection from inclement weather.

THIS PHOTOGRAPH was taken from the south side of the Herreshoff Mfg. Co.'s wharf, looking north toward the town of Bristol and the head of Bristol Harbor. Although much of the shoreline north of the construction shop has changed since 1882, some of the buildings depicted can be recognized today.

The vessel under construction is the 126-foot schooner-rigged steam yacht ORIENTA (HMCo #89), for Jabez A. Bostwick of New York. (Incidentally, Bostwick, a Standard Oil magnate, became the chief backer of naphtha launches and the first manager of the Gas Engine & Power Co.,

which produced them.) Although the wharf appears to have been greatly expanded from the 1866 photos shown in Chapter I, the Old Tannery still serves as the yard's shop.

Because of her size, ORIENTA has to be built outside, and the A-frame-supported temporary canvas shelter over her gives only scant protection from sun, wind, and rain. Next year, however, as shown on the next page, a spacious new two-story workshop, later to be known as the South Construction Shop, will be built on the side of the venerable Old Tannery building.

The catboat JULIA IV, being sailed home by her owner, Charles F. Herreshoff, Sr., about 1883

THE BRAND-NEW South Construction Shop can be seen just ahead of JULIA's mast, while alongside the Herreshoff Mfg. Co. docks, several recently launched steam yachts can be seen. The prosperity that two of his sons were achieving right here at home must have brought forth a feeling of considerable pride in Charles Frederick Herreshoff, Sr., as he sailed past.

Sailing was the elder Herreshoff's chief pleasure. Charles Frederick, Sr., had expert knowledge of Narragansett Bay and enjoyed racing, and his boats were always kept in top condition, in readiness for any "scrap" with similar catboats owned by Bristol sailors.

Each of the four JULIAS used a shifting ballast box on wheels and tracks. NGH recalled: "This affair was cleverly designed and arranged.... The box was of oak and filled with lead.... It ran on cross tracks and was controlled by ropes at each side, and had a strong toggle with notches forward and aft to hold the box either amidships or at either side, as desired; foot pedals with gear released the toggle from the notches when [the ballast box] was to be shifted.... It was generally expected to shift the ballast just as the tack was made so it would roll downhill."

IN THIS EARLY (pre-1900) shop-interior photo the 45-foot steam launch XANTHO (HMCo #99) is being decked, while JBH stands by (at right) and NGH confers with a workman (at left).

The presence of the Herreshoff brothers in the building shops was not unusual. NGH made two daily tours of inspection. On these tours, he not only observed all of the work in progress, but also made suggestions regarding the improvement of that work. Often on his morning tour he would sketch ideas on small pieces of paper for the foremen; on his afternoon tour, he would see the concept implemented. JBH, frequently accompanied by his daughter Katie, and later by his granddaughter Katherine, would tour the shops from time to time, stopping to ask what work was in progress and sometimes inspecting it with his hands, offering encouragement to the men as he moved through the shops.

In this photo, the timber molds from previous jobs lie stacked against the south wall, and along the north wall opposite is a full-length workbench. Second-level balconies run along each side above, and the two traveling cranes are evident overhead.

The idea for overhead cranes (and, no doubt, for other features of the Herreshoff Mfg. Co. plant as well) may have come from the shops of the Corliss Steam Engine Co. Although the original purpose of the cranes was to facilitate the building of steam yachts (the cranes were used for hoisting boilers and engines aboard awaiting hulls), they soon became a vital part of the Herreshoff wooden hull-building process, in which the hulls of all but the largest yachts were framed and planked upside down, then, by use of the cranes, turned over for completion.

The removable floor panels that can be seen toward the water end of the new shop provide additional shop floor space, but will be given up later, after a railway and its cradle are installed. Later, too, the North Construction Shop and its connecting, roofed-over space will penetrate this shop's north wall and cut off some of the natural light now apparent.

THE HOUSE in the foreground—
now 20 Burnside Street—was the
home of Mr. and Mrs. John B. Herreshoff
and daughter Katherine from 1874 until the
mid-1880s. Katie can be seen riding her tri-
cycle on the dirt sidewalk in front of the
fenced-in yard.

The adjacent building (with the
Herreshoff Mfg. Co. sign above the third-
floor windows) was the first Burnside Street
property acquired by JBH, purchased from
Civil War General Ambrose E. Burnside,
who manufactured carbines there for the
U.S. Cavalry during the period before the
war. This building and the one farther up
the street were used by the Herreshoffs for
engine and boiler construction. In 1882,
the Herreshoff Mfg. Co. office occupied
part of the lower floor of the large building;
it was entered through the door that can
be seen close to the sidewalk.

That large building, 22 Burnside Street,
looks today almost as it does in the photograph. The company bell (just behind the
flagpole) was moved into the Museum in
1977, and the flagpole and sign are gone;
all else remains the same.

After JBH moved out of the house in
1885, it was altered to accommodate a new
office on the ground floor and a drafting
room on the second floor.

The first residence of John B. Herreshoff and the Burnside Street shops of the Herreshoff Mfg. Co., 1882

JBH WAS A FANATIC when it came to tools and machinery, always procuring the latest and best that were available. His passion is evident from this photo—and from the astonishing inventory that appeared in the bidders' catalog that came out in 1924 when the plant and its contents were put up for auction.

NGH was the more conservative of the two brothers, but he, too, saw the benefits of a well-equipped facility. The existence of the Machine Shop meant that the Herreshoff Mfg. Co. could produce steam engines and related machinery every bit as efficiently as they could build the boats themselves.

The three-story shop shown here was built in the winter of 1896–1897 as an addition to the old Burnside Rifle Factory building shown on the facing page. It measured 113 feet by 70 feet, with a 25-foot overhead clearance. In it were the same type of traveling cranes as in the boatshops, only here they were used for moving heavy machinery rather than hulls. The lathes, drill presses, milling machines, shapers, etc., were all powered by a single Herreshoff-built steam engine, which drove leather belts through the overhead shafting that can be seen in the photo.

All of the Herreshoff Mfg. Co. shops were well lighted, with plenty of windows and white-painted interiors. Conceptually, the layout shown here is much the same as in the boatshops: the main floor is for assembly, and the wings are for building the pieces.

Inside the Herreshoff Mfg. Co. Machine Shop, in the late 1890s

GANNET and VAMOOSE in the North Construction Shop, May 1891

GANNET is one of two cat-yawls ordered and built in the fall of 1890 for E. D. Morgan; she and her slightly smaller sister PELICAN are described more fully in Chapter V. VAMOOSE, a fast 112-foot steam yacht built for William Randolph Hearst, is featured in Chapter II. Until the discovery of NGH's diary for 1890–1891, it had been assumed that this photo was of PELICAN, taken just before her launching in the fall of 1890. With the new information, however, it becomes clear that PELICAN was already completed before VAMOOSE was set up.

These were busy times for GANNET's owner, who can be seen talking to NGH over that boat's bow. Morgan's new 71-foot sloop GLORIANA, built in the South Construction Shop, had been launched on May 6 and sailed for the first times on May 19 and 20. His fast new 98-foot steamer JAVELIN, which can be seen behind VAMOOSE, is well along, and in the previous September he had taken delivery of the 48-foot launch

KATYDID. GANNET will be launched on June 4, and on June 12, GLORIANA will start for New York, where Morgan and NGH will demonstrate her astonishing speed.

As for VAMOOSE, her Thornycroft-type boiler sits in the shop's Hope Street doorway, waiting to be hoisted aboard on May 25. It will furnish steam for the NGH-designed, five-cylinder, quadruple-expansion engine (one of only five built) that will drive VAMOOSE at a near-30-m.p.h. clip.

At this time, the 164-foot-by-39-foot North Construction Shop is nearly new, having been built in 1888–1889, and it much resembles the South Construction Shop in size and layout. Like the Herreshoff-designed yachts, the shop is lightly but thoughtfully built: 4-by-8-inch wall studs, 2-by-8-inch rafters in 20-to-30-foot lengths, 1¼-by-6-inch collar beams, and 2-by-10 inch floor beams. It took the place of a smaller shop that had stood on the site for a short time.

THE NARROW BEAMS of these two boats allowed them to be set up side by side for completion. Chances are that the hulls were built in the far end of the shop (where the big catboat SAYONARA can be seen upside down, in the standard Herreshoff hull-building position), then moved back here, near the shop's water end, for convenience in launching.

DRUSILLA (right), a bright-finished fin-keeler for E. D. Morgan and described in Chapter V, appears to be about com-plete, while the long, narrow steam yacht LOTUS SEEKER—her bulkheads fitted and her deck already laid—is having her coamings installed. Her sheerstrakes are of harder wood than the planking below them and have not yet been painted. (Had this been a sailing hull, the sheerstrakes might have been varnished.)

In winter, the Herreshoff Mfg. Co. shops were heated with steam and lit, during those dark days, by gas. Gaslights and brackets can be seen in the photo.

LOTUS SEEKER and DRUSILLA in the North Construction Shop, 1892

Two unidentified schooner-rigged steam yachts, dark-hulled and recently launched, are being fitted out; the one in the foreground lies against newly driven pilings that have bark still partly in place. A third steam yacht is hauled out and covered with canvas just south of the South Construction Shop.

The simple layout of these early steam yachts, their narrow beam, and the elegant workmanship are evident in the boat in the foreground. The starboard davits on this vessel have been swung inboard so as not to hit the wharf, and the small boat they normally carry has been lowered to the deck. The spars, lashed to the after handrail, are probably boat booms, to be rigged out from the vessel's sides when at anchor for tethering the small boats when they lie alongside.

About twenty years after the 1866 photo of the Herreshoff & Stone yard shown in Chapter I, and a decade or so after the formation of the Herreshoff Mfg. Co., the two main waterfront buildings known as the North and South Construction Shops were in place, giving the yard its familiar and distinctly businesslike appearance. NGH, who designed these construction shops (as well as the other Herreshoff Mfg. Co. buildings that would come into being as the company expanded), drew from his experience with the Old Tannery, in which, as a youth, he'd taken part in building a number of boats. The floors of the North and South Construction Shops, like that of the Old Tannery, were below street level and extended westward out over the water. Both shops were fitted with opening skylights in their roofs. At the seaward ends, for launching vessels, each had a pair of big doors that swung outward, as well as a third door above them.

The North and South Construction Shops viewed from the southwest, about 1890

THE BEARDED gentleman swimming is Lewis Herreshoff (1844–1926); the girl in the bathing costume and in mid-leap is probably Katie Herreshoff. The little boy is unknown.

Although sightless from his youth, "Mr. Lewis," as he was called by Bristolians,* was a physically active and powerful man. He often crewed with his older brother, John, in sailing races for their younger brother, Nat. Lewis, like JBH, could sail a boat well to windward by feel alone. In 1874 he accompanied NGH to Europe, where they cruised along the Mediterranean coast and the rivers and canals of France, Germany, Belgium, and Holland. In Europe, Lewis assisted NGH in the building of two small sailboats, L'ONDA and RIVIERA.

Lewis took pride in walking about the family property unassisted, and in managing the family homestead. He was fond of rowing, with someone to steer, and had a passion for swimming. Many Bristolians were taught to swim by Mr. Lewis. He sometimes would allow non-swimmers to hold onto his powerful back to accustom themselves to the water and to the motions of swimming. The townspeople cherished his congenial nature and friendship.

Trained in music in Europe, Lewis entertained his family and many friends with his skillful playing of the piano. He also wrote well, using both the conventional typewriter and the Braille writer, and contributed articles about the Herreshoffs and aspects of yachting to various publications, including a chapter in the Badminton Sports Library book *Yachting* (London, 1894). He wrote about the Herreshoff catamaran TARANTELLA for *The Spirit of the Times*, a popular sporting and recreation magazine, in 1877. Although this article was credited to NGH, he denied it, claiming in a July 9, 1936, letter to yachting historian William P. Stephens, "The story of the

cruise of the TARANTELLA to Hyde Park-on-Hudson, to which he [Lewis] improperly attached my name, was not by me but by my brother Lewis. He was fond of writing, but I am not."

---

* The Herreshoffs of NGH's generation were always called "Mr. _____" or "Miss _____" by townspeople as a token of respect, as they were regarded as aristocracy. This term of address extended to the next generation in "Mr. Sid," "Miss Agnes," "Mr. Clarence," etc.

Swimming off the Herreshoff South Wharf in the 1890s

CHAPTER IV

Trials and Triumphs

Military Craft, 1878–1897

T HE RELATIONSHIP between the United States Navy and the Herreshoff Mfg. Co. could be an absorbing study in itself. Beginning in 1876, when JBH's yard built the spar torpedo boat LIGHTNING, Navy contracts (as well as those from other government agencies, such as the Coast Survey) came in steadily for two decades and at times amounted to a fair share of the Herreshoff Mfg. Co.'s revenue. Torpedo boats were a specialty, and after LIGHTNING there were several others for foreign governments. There were also smaller cutters and launches, and "machinery only" contracts. Performance—that is to say, speed, reliability, and economy of operation— were, of course, high on the Navy's list of priorities, and performance is what the Herreshoffs had always specialized in. It was a natural alliance.

JBH was never backward in going after business. As already mentioned in Chapter II, in the fall of 1880 the Herreshoffs put the steam yacht LEILA at the Navy's disposal in order to show off her capability. They later sold their fast personal steam yacht STILETTO to the Navy and converted her as shown on the facing page. Thus, when the U.S. government, in its late-nineteenth-century rush toward imperialism, sought a vast naval expansion and the need for an entire fleet of torpedo boats arose, the Herreshoff name was high on the list of bidders. The Herreshoff Mfg. Co. built six torpedo boats to four different NGH designs for the U.S. Navy between 1890 and 1897.

Had NGH not been the consummate marine engineer, as capable at designing boilers and steam engines as he was designing hulls and propellers, it is doubtful whether a relatively small yard like the Herreshoff Mfg. Co., with its one-man engineering department, could long compete in the face of increasing technical sophistication. But the Herreshoffs did indeed stay in the running—in design as well as construction—and their share of the Navy's rapidly growing volume of warship contracts increased dramatically in the mid-1890's.

October 6, 1896, when JBH returned from Washington, D.C., with con-tracts for two 100-footers and a 140-footer—all torpedo boats—signaled a cresting of Navy work for the Herreshoff brothers. After completing these contracts, they bid on no more government work of that magnitude. Navy inspectors had begun disputing certain aspects of the work; the vessels themselves were becoming increasingly complex; and, perhaps most important of all, these big torpedo boats were tying up the shop for many months, crowding out major yacht work which was more to the yard's liking and certainly better suited to NGH's autonomous approach to designing.

STILETTO had been a signal design for the Herreshoffs—the powerboat equivalent of their revolutionary sailing yacht GLORIANA of 1891. As a yacht (Chapter II), STILETTO had become nationally famous for her great speed—and her reputation did not escape the notice of the military. She was purchased by the Navy in May 1888. A short time later, with the deckhouse removed and armament added, she became an experimental torpedo boat.

STILETTO was stationed at Newport for many years, engaged in the business of testing torpedoes—and an ever-present reminder of the name Herreshoff. In fact, the Navy's torpedo station being based in nearby Newport—only a short run by boat from Bristol—was a distinct advantage for the Herreshoffs. The officers stationed there couldn't help but be aware of Herreshoff steam yachts as they came and went from the Bristol yard.

The ex-steam yacht STILETTO in military garb, after she was purchased by the Navy

L AUNCHES LIKE this one used to be an anchored vessel's primary link with the shore, transporting officers, crew, and messages back and forth in the days before radio communication and elaborate docking facilities. In those days, steam plants were the only mechanical power available, but most were too large for launches. The compact Herreshoff engines and coil boilers were an exception, however, and the Navy became so interested in them that it ran trials on this launch and her sister, HMCo #63, comparing them with the nearest equivalent Navy design. The Herreshoff version proved superior.

The folding canvas top, known as a "melon canopy," was supported on steambent wooden bows that pivoted from a common pin. This same canopy design, but with the open end facing aft, showed up on later Herreshoff launches built for pleasure.

A small steam launch built for the U.S. Navy

HMCo #62, 1880
LOA 33'0"
Beam 9'0"
Draft 4'0"

A MONG THE alterations made to STILETTO by the Navy, besides the built-in torpedo tube, was the addition of davits for retrieving torpedoes.

STILETTO remained in naval service at Newport for over thirty years, until World War I.

STILETTO, firing an "automobile" torpedo, about 1890

HMCo #118, 1885
LOA 94'0"
Beam 11'0"

CUSHING, the Navy's "Seagoing Torpedo Boat No. 1," ready for plating, 1889

Although the wooden-hulled spar torpedo boat LIGHTNING of 1876 (Chapter I) was the Navy's first-of-type, she was primitive compared to the sleek, new NGH-designed CUSHING, which came out in 1890. She is shown here in frame, as her workers stand to face the camera.

The framing, deckbeams, bulkheads, and other steel structure were galvanized for longer life in a seawater environment. The wooden ribbands shown were temporarily bolted to the frames to stiffen CUSHING's skeleton and hold it fair until the hull was partially plated.

CUSHING being launched from the South Construction Shop, January 23, 1890

BAD WEATHER delayed launching a day, but, once waterborne, CUSHING's twin-screw power plants were ready for operation. Her engines were tried on the afternoon of this same day.

Dock trials for CUSHING

TWO SEPARATE steam power plants gave CUSHING some 2,000 horsepower. Here, the after boiler is steaming away while a crowd observes from the dock; the thick pall of smoke suggests a full head of steam.

This photo was probably taken on the afternoon of launching day. CUSHING's sea trials started five days later on January 29, 1890, and lasted through March; the more than two dozen trial trips occupied much of NGH's time that spring.

An early set of the ever-present sheer-legs show at the end of the dock in the background, and the structure at the right is the means by which steamers took on coal.

THE FULL-LENGTH awning seems a
bit out of place on a fighting ship, but,
as with steam yachts, it helped keep the
soot off this new vessel of the Navy's "Great
White Fleet." The standard Herreshoff
stock anchor (in chocks on the foredeck) is
unusual as well; one might expect a heavy
Navy anchor housed in a hawsepipe on such
a craft instead of an anchor of yacht origin.

While the tipped-back profile of the
bow and stern reflect naval tradition of the
day, the highly crowned deck may have come
from NGH; it was a feature of the contemporary fast, non-military Herreshoff steamers such as VAMOOSE and JAVELIN.

CUSHING was equipped with two of
the largest and most powerful steam engines
ever produced by the Herreshoff Mfg. Co.;
similar ones had been in use for the past
year or two on the Herreshoff steam yachts
BALLYMENA and SAY WHEN. NGH designed
these as five-cylinder quadruple-expansion
engines, each with two low-pressure cylinders that measured nearly 2 feet in diameter. CUSHING's speed at sea trials matched
STILETTO's of about 26 m.p.h.

CUSHING in
drydock, probably
in Providence,
March, 1890

HMCo #152, 1890
LOA 138'0"
Beam 15'0"
Draft 10'0"

Like the earlier CUSHING, MORRIS was fitted with two steam engines and two boilers. Here, she's steaming on a single boiler, as indicated by the steam coming out of her after stack and a weather cloth over the forward one.

The Herreshoff Mfg. Co. built five torpedo boats for the Navy in the mid-1890s in three different sizes, all designed by NGH. Besides MORRIS, there were two larger vessels, PORTER and DUPONT, and two smaller ones, TALBOT and GWIN.

Other builders besides Herreshoff were engaged in designing and building torpedo boats, as the United States had a lot of catching up to do. By the end of 1896, England, France, Russia, Italy, Germany, and Japan *each* had huge torpedo-boat fleets of well over a hundred boats. England and France had over 250 each! This was the eve of the Spanish-American War, and Spain outnumbered the United States with fifty-six torpedo boats to our twenty-one. (Before 1895, the United States had only two torpedo boats, one of them, of course, being CUSHING.)

Because neither the mission nor the ideal torpedo-boat design had yet been worked out, and because there was such an urgency for operational boats, private yards such as the Herreshoff Mfg. Co. were awarded contracts for the design as well as the construction. Other designer/builders included Bath Iron Works, Union Iron Works, Columbian Iron Works, Harlan & Hollingsworth, and the Gas Engine & Power Co. Together with the resultant non-standardization—and, in fact, compounded by it—was a general lack of properly trained operating personnel. For the U.S. Navy's torpedo-boat program, the mid-1890s were a time of chaos.

In spite of the prevailing uncertainty, all five Herreshoff torpedo boats of this period found great favor, especially MORRIS, whose size was considered an advantage over larger, more costly vessels—and over the smaller ones as well, which had comparatively limited range, accommodations, and speed. Following are two endorsements:

"I have had charge of repairs to the torpedo-boat fleet, eleven boats all told. After many hours spent on each of these boats, I am of the opinion that the MORRIS is the ideal type...."
—R. M. Watt
    Assistant Naval Constructor
    (excerpted from *SNAME Transactions*, 1898)

Torpedo boat
MORRIS

HMCo #190, 1897
LOA 140'0"
Beam 15'6"
Draft 5'9"

"It has been my good fortune to see practically every torpedo boat in four or five foreign navies and to study the various types somewhat superficially. I unhesitatingly give it as my opinion that the DUPONT, the PORTER, and the MORRIS, built by Herreshoff, are the three best boats of their type in the world.... Herreshoff is as much a master in boatbuilding in general as Edison is in the field of electricity.... It is only a grief that Herreshoff does not build all our boats or that we do not copy his models and fittings.... To me personally, the outlook is very gloomy."
—Lieutenant A. P. Niblack, U.S.N.
　(excerpted from *SNAME Transactions*, 1898)

In spite of their unqualified success with torpedo boats and the lamentations of some of the Navy personnel, JBH and NGH pulled out of further work of this magnitude with the Navy. It was not until the Herreshoff Mfg. Co. passed to other owners that this situation changed. During the world wars, well over a hundred vessels were built by the Herreshoff Mfg. Co. for the armed services.

Torpedo boat GWIN
(TALBOT, HMCo
#192, was identical)

HMCo #191, 1897
LOA 100'0"
Beam 12'6"
Draft 5'3"

Torpedo boat
PORTER (DUPONT,
HMCo #185,
was identical)

HMCo #184, 1895
LOA 175'6"
Beam 17'6"
Draft 6'9"

CHAPTER V

The Age of Gloriana

Herreshoff Mfg. Co. Sailboats, 1878–1897

I T WASN'T UNTIL the 1890s that the Herreshoff Mfg. Co. began building sailing yachts in any great numbers. Before that, for the company's first dozen years, steamers and their engines and boilers dominated production. Soon after 1891, however, beginning with the success of the 46-foot Class sloop GLORIANA (shown on the facing page) and the astonishing publicity she received, the demand for Herreshoff sailing yachts increased dramatically.

Although it went unrecognized at the time, the shiftover actually began in 1890 with the building of the cat-yawls PELICAN and GANNET for E. D. Morgan, a self-indulging sportsman and future commodore of the New York Yacht Club whose yachting fleet already included a 130-foot schooner and a 186-foot steam yacht. Well pleased with the first cat-yawl, launched and sailed in the fall of 1890, Morgan continued patronizing the Herreshoff Mfg. Co., purchasing the fast steamer JAVELIN and ordering GLORIANA the following spring. In the fall of 1891, he became intrigued with NGH's new fin-keeled sloop DILEMMA and promptly commissioned the building of DRUSILLA, a larger version.

From 1891 on, the Herreshoffs were immersed in orders for sailing craft. WASP, a second 46-foot Class sloop, followed GLORIANA, and the huge steel-hulled sloop NAVAHOE came a year later in early 1893. This was an America's Cup year, and with Edward Burgess no longer alive (he died in 1891), two of the syndicates turned to NGH for their boats. The first, COLONIA, was launched on May 15; VIGILANT, the second, was launched on June 14. VIGILANT's success begot the contract for DEFENDER in 1895. Sandwiched between in the off year of 1894 were the big 20-Rater sloops NIAGARA and ISOLDE.

Smaller sailboats were filling the shops as well. Before GLORIANA came out in 1891, the Herreshoff Mfg. Co. had built only ten sailboats, all under 30 feet LWL, four of the ten being for the Herreshoffs themselves. In the next six years, the company built seventy-four sailboats, not even counting the big ones just mentioned.

"For the racing season of 1891, nine 46-footers were built, five from Burgess designs, and one each from the drafting boards of Herreshoff, Paine, Fife, and Wintringham. Of all this fleet, GLORIANA was easily the best. She closed the season with the remarkable record of eight first prizes without a defeat."
—George A. Stewart, from the book *Representative American Yachts*, photographed and published by Henry G. Peabody, Boston, 1891

GLORIANA
captured on film
by Henry Peabody,
August 7, 1891

CLARA and
COQUINA,
N.G. Herreshoff's
personal yachts,
about 1890

CLARA
HMCo #402, 1887
LOA 35'0"
LWL 29'6"
Beam 9'1"

COQUINA
HMCo #404, 1889
LOA 16'8"
LWL 15'9"
Beam 5'0"

The Herreshoff Mfg. Co.'s transition from steam to sail, and the subsequent evolution of Herreshoff sailboats into two distinct types, can be traced, in part, from these personal boats of NGH, shown here drying sails in the tranquility of a Bristol morning.

CLARA was built in 1887 as a replacement for the smaller but similar CONSUELO of 1883, which NGH had been persuaded to sell. From CLARA sprang the near-sister cat-yawls of E. D. Morgan (PELICAN and GANNET, already mentioned), then GLORIANA, WASP, VIGILANT, and the other Cup defenders through 1914, the nine great metal-hulled Herreshoff schooners, and the other major sailing yachts designed by NGH. Stemming also from CLARA were a variety of practical mid-sized cruiser/racers, many around 30 feet LWL, such as the New York 30s and the Bar Harbor 31s.

COQUINA's progeny, on the other hand, were day boats that one person could handle. COQUINA was NGH's most-used boat, and his diaries indicate that she was underway often, even in winter, for single-handed outings and for family sails as pictured in Chapter X. Following the building of COQUINA in 1889, NGH produced dozens of different day-boat designs. DILEMMA, for example, NGH's prototype fin-keeler of 1891, was followed by many more of the same type but ranging widely in size and appearance. There was a variety of knockabouts both with and without small cabins, of which KILDEE and COCK ROBIN, shown on the following pages, were the first. Sonder boats and the 18-foot, 21-foot, and 25-foot Classes for Massachusetts Bay and Long Island Sound were others. Best known today are the one-design classes, such as the Buzzards Bay 15s and S-boats. All of NGH's day boats were simple and easy to handle, and some were stunningly beautiful as well.

CLARA was similar in hull design to the English pilot cutters of the period, but carried batwing sails with full-length battens in her original cat-yawl rig. This feature, however, was not used again. Even after thinning down the battens and kerfing their forward ends for more flexibility, NGH considered that sails like this, which were inspired by sailing-canoe rigs, were too bothersome in their adjustment to incorporate into another boat. It wasn't long before he outfitted CLARA with conventional gaff-headed sails.

CLARA was beautifully built and had some features that were quite unusual in her day—features such as outside ballast held on in part by bronze keel straps, a double-planked hull, lift-off companionway doors, metal hanging knees in lieu of sheer clamps in way of the deckhouse, and a specially designed anchor windlass and steering gear. These would appear repeatedly in subsequent Herreshoff sailboats.

Following the custom of his father, NGH named the boat for his wife. The Herreshoffs sailed CLARA until 1890. During that time, Captain Nat experimented with the sail plan and derived much pleasure from entertaining friends on board. In this photograph, taken while anchored in Newport Harbor, the designer is with Lucian Sharpe of Providence, whose family was in the toolmaking business, and who, with his brother Henry, would soon purchase a boat of his own. The Brown and Sharpe Company of Providence made a number of precision tools of NGH's design for use in his model room.

Mr. and Mrs. Kerry Geraghty of San Diego, California, donated CLARA to the Museum and the boat has been subsequently restored to its original form.

N. G. Herreshoff
and Lucian Sharpe
aboard CLARA,
about 1888

NGH FAVORED the cat-yawl rig for his designs of the late 1880s, possibly because he'd sailed so much in catboats as a youth and appreciated the value of a mizzen for cruising. In his later years, however, after a lifetime of experience with all kinds of rigs and hull shapes, NGH concluded that cat-yawls like ALICE and CLARA had their drawbacks. The combination of the plumb stem and a heavy mast way forward made the boats pitch unmercifully at times, which is why he gave their successors PELICAN and GANNET some forward overhang. His subsequent designs, for the most part, had masts that were farther aft, as well as overhanging bows, a now familiar configuration, which proved to be the best cure for this hobby-horsing.

ALICE was built for brother Charles on the molds of the 1876 catboat GLEAM, but with some alterations. NGH records that ALICE proved to be a very fast craft that could beat any boat on Narragansett Bay. Although she was an outside-ballasted centerboarder when built, ALICE later became a pure keelboat. Her rig was also changed so that she carried a bowsprit and jib, along with a smaller mainsail. Her mast was moved aft some as well, and with these changes, she proved both stiffer and less lively in a seaway. ALICE, much weathered from age and neglect, is now at the Museum.

GLORIANA's story has become an American yachting legend, and any good book on yachting history contains the tale. Briefly, here's what happened, first in the words of E. D. Morgan, who had her built.

"When the 46-foot Class was gotten up by the New York Yacht Club, I said I would build a boat, so I went with all haste to Bristol and laid the proposition before Nat Herreshoff, who told me to come back in about two or three weeks and he would show me what he planned. Again I made the trip to Bristol and found the plans for the GLORIANA, 46 feet waterline and 70 feet overall. My hopes were so high for her that Mrs. Morgan felt apprehensive that I might have a dreadful disappointment. There was no disappointment about GLORIANA, however. I sailed her in eight races that summer and won every one, except when Nat Herreshoff sailed her one day for me when I was under the weather. She not only did what was expected of her, but she revolutionized yacht designing."

And in the words of NGH: "In launching, ways had to be built, as she was the first deep-draft craft constructed by the Herreshoff Mfg. Co. To save expense, I devised a single ways no wider than the yacht's keel (about 24 inches), and she slid down over it.

"After the trial, we found we had to put a system of diagonals under her deck to keep it from working. There were no other changes except a pair of truss shrouds at each forward quarter to keep the thrust of the gaff from bending the mast.

"She was completed and went to New York in time for the June races, and was successful from the start. Mr. E. D. Morgan sailed her in her first race, and I sailed her in the several that followed that season, all of which she won—over the most notable class of that era." [Note the conflict between this and Morgan's account of who did the sailing;]

"GLORIANA's design had much longer overall length and fuller, more rounding waterlines at each end than was usual, giving a longer body for sailing, and the long ends very much decreased the tendency to

Charles Herreshoff Jr.'s cat-yawl, ALICE

HMCo #405, 1889
LOA 29'6"
LWL 26'6"
Beam 11'0"
Draft 2'8"

'hobbyhorse'; consequently, she was a much faster and better boat in a seaway."

And in the eyes of the *Forest and Stream* reporter, before the races: "Her model is unlike all the rest of her class, and as seen afloat, she is by no means remarkable for beauty. The forward overhang is not only very long, but lacks grace and symmetry, the topsides are round and full, and the counter long, wide, and flat. The topsides are plain white from waterline to planksheer, and there is not a line of carving or gilding to relieve the full, heavy look of the boat. On deck and below, however, two points are noticeable. The workmanship is good, and the predominating consideration has been utility rather than style."

After the races: "The best construction of all the American boats was that of the Herreshoff craft GLORIANA, with steel frames and straps and a part double skin, the hull being very light. Although a weakness in the deck developed on the first trial, it was soon remedied, and the yacht has sailed through the season without a breakdown…. GLORIANA was the only one of the class which was ready in time and at the same time was well handled throughout the season…. As old racing men, the Herreshoffs were fully aware of the great advantage of early and thorough preparation and of regular and skillful handling, and as the results prove, they took no chances, but reduced everything in advance to a mechanical certainty."

After laying her up afloat for the winter off his Newport estate, E. D. Morgan—perhaps fearing defeat by WASP, the new 1892 Herreshoff 46-footer—sold GLORIANA before her second season. In other hands, her useful life spanned some eighteen years.

GLORIANA at the Herreshoff Mfg. Co. dock, with workmen aboard. Scupper streaks indicate that it's been awhile since her topsides have been scrubbed.

GLORIANA in a floating drydock, held upright only by a single strut on each side

HMCo #411, 1891
LOA approx. 71'0"
LWL 46'0"
Beam 13'0"
Draft 10'6"

The fin-keeled sloop DRUSILLA under reduced sail in Newport Harbor, about 1892

HMCo #417, 1891
LOA 52'0"
LWL 34'4"
Beam 9'6"
Draft 8'10"

IN 1891, besides setting the yacht-racing fraternity on its ear with the revolutionary sloop GLORIANA, NGH designed the first fin-keeler, the 25-foot LWL sloop DILEMMA (HMCo #412), which is preserved at the Mariners' Museum in Newport News, Virginia. (A fin-keeler consisted of a scow-like, shallow-bodied hull from which hung a thin vertical, steep plate with a heavy, streamlined lead casting fastened along its lower edge. This short keel, located near the middle of the boat, combined with a spade or pendant-type separated rudder aft of it, resulted in an extremely quick-turning—and therefore exceptionally sporty—boat.) The Herreshoff Mfg. Co. built fin-keelers throughout the 1890s. Other builders soon followed suit, and as a type the fin-keelers became popular all up and down the East Coast.

There were large Herreshoff fin-keelers as well as small ones. DRUSILLA, built for E. D. Morgan, was on the large side. She was

a disappointment as a racer, however; even NGH admits it: "A failure as a racing craft. Did well to windward, but hopelessly beaten off the wind." It seems that she was designed especially for afternoon sailing, and therefore was made wider and shallower than most fin-keelers. This gave her initial stability and therefore more comfort from sailing with less heel. With more stability from hull shape, she was given a lighter-than-usual ballast casting, or bulb. The ballast keel proved too light (there was insufficient stability in a breeze) and was replaced with a heavier one which provided the needed stability but caused the boat to float deeper in the water, added considerable wetted surface, and caused her to be dead when sailing off the wind.

If DRUSILLA wasn't much of a racer, she was even less of a cruiser. Although she had 52 feet of deck length, her hull lacked depth under the flush deck for anything like full headroom. Other than having

two settees and an enclosed toilet room, DRUSILLA's interior was empty.

DRUSILLA's dark hull, even though double-planked, shows its plank lines, indicating the evils of a heat-absorbing dark topside color and, it would seem, the close of a tough sailing season. Scupper streaks and scum along the waterline also suggest the end of the season, and tell something of Newport's dirty waterfront as well. Certainly industrial pollution from installations such as the colliery in the background made good boatkeeping difficult.

The deeply reefed mainsail indicates that it had been blowing hard outside earlier in the day, although the harbor breeze has now moderated. Battens, used then, as now, to prevent a sail's leech from curling, are external and are tucked under loops sewn onto the sail along seam lines. DRUSILLA was designed with a bowsprit, but is not carrying it today; instead, the jib is tacked down to the stemhead.

NIAGARA and her sistership ISOLDE (HMCo #450) were the largest of NGH's fin-keelers. Both were designed under the prevailing Length-and-Sail-Area Rule, which encouraged long, overhanging bows and sterns and shallow-bodied hulls. After sailing trials in Bristol, NIAGARA's keel was unbolted and removed, and keel, hull, and rig were shipped to England, where the boat's racing record became legendary, vindicating both her designer (whose Cup defender VIGILANT had put in a mediocre performance in those waters the previous season) and her skipper, John Barr, who had not fared well in the THISTLE–VOLUNTEER matches of 1887. NIAGARA's owner, Howard Gould, who had been part owner of VIGILANT during her 1894 English campaign, must have been pleased as well.

Although NIAGARA was well designed, built, managed, and sailed, certainly part of her speed must be credited to her new crosscut sails, invented by NGH only a few months earlier. Handling sails aboard NIAGARA kept the crew busy, since, in tacking, there were the running backstays, three headsail sheets, and the topsail to tend; only the mainsheet was immune, being rigged (although strangely, it appears) to be self-tending. Under certain conditions, such as running before a following wind and sea, the helmsman surely had his hands full as well; because, in spite of her 65-foot length on deck, NIAGARA steers with a tiller.

NIAGARA's double-planked hull was originally varnished above the waterline, as this photo shows. Its outer layer was Honduras mahogany and was set off by the lighter hue of oak sheerstrakes. Both NIAGARA and ISOLDE (the latter boat was shipped to Germany) were praised for their performance and quality of construction, but were severely criticized for their lack of accommodations. Five feet of headroom was no more appropriate for a proper yacht in those days than in our own time.

The 20-Rater
NIAGARA, a fin-keeler,
sailing in England

HMCo #451, 1895
LOA 65'0"
LWL 45'0"
Beam 12'0"
Draft 10'0"

Vigilant was the first Herreshoff defender of the America's Cup and the first to be plated with bronze. Her unusual transomless stern shows clearly, as does the fisherman-type steering wheel.

Vigilant's story is best told by NGH himself; and, as his essay, which follows, makes clear, there were two other big sailing yachts that slid down the Herreshoff Mfg. Co. ways in 1893.

"Just following Mr. Carroll's order, the New York Yacht Club received a challenge for the America's Cup; and an order was given us, by a syndicate headed by Archibald Rodgers, for a defender." [This was COLONIA, bringing Rodgers back to the Herreshoff Mfg. Co. for the second time in as many years. In 1892, his boat had been WASP. Mr. Carroll's order was for the 85-foot LWL sloop NAVAHOE, the Herreshoff Mfg. Co.'s first really big sailing boat.]

"As Mr. Rodgers had been sailing keel yachts of the English cutter type, he wanted this craft to be keel, but limited the draft to 14 feet only, as that was all that was allowable near his home in Hyde Park on the Hudson. This was plainly not enough for an 85-foot-waterline sloop; and it so worked on Commodore E. D. Morgan that she might fail, that he induced some of his friends to build a centerboard yacht, and so we had three big sloops to build that winter and spring.

"NAVAHOE was launched in February and moored in a dredged hole between piers to have her cabins finished, and COLONIA was set up in her place in the South Shop, soon to be followed by VIGILANT being set up in the North Shop. This was a busy winter for me as well as for the working men. I had not time with my force in the drafting room to work out complete detail drawings for each yacht, so both the defenders' rigs

were alike and many of the details were the same as worked out for NAVAHOE.

"NAVAHOE was under sail early in May. I had no experience in sailing large yachts and neither had Charles Barr, her skipper, so we had much to learn.... COLONIA was under sail and tried out by the middle of June. Aside from her mast bending by the thrust of her gaff, there was little to do to her rig.... VIGILANT was under sail the first part of July.... I was under demand by the managers of both syndicates to sail their early races. I compromised by alternating from one to the other. It soon became quite evident that VIGILANT's centerboard was an advantage whenever they came on the wind.

"It was on this first set of trial races that VIGILANT's sailing master, Captain Stone, was not doing well and had got back to third place. [The Boston contender JUBILEE was the third boat racing that day.] I saw Mr. Iselin, the syndicate manager, having a very animated talk with his friends on the after-deck; then he told Captain Stone he wanted me to take the wheel, and asked me to. We succeeded in rounding the first mark abreast of JUBILEE and soon took a good lead, and so ended the race well ahead. I was asked to sail VIGILANT in all the following races." [VIGILANT won three straight races against the British challenger VALKYRIE II.]

"The following year, I was induced by George Gould, who had bought VIGILANT, to go to Great Britain and oversee the sailing of her there. Our shops were very busy at this time, and it behooved me to be back as soon as possible."

VIGILANT in an English drydock, 1894

HMCo #437, 1893
LOA 128'0"
LWL 85'0"
Beam 26'1½"
Draft 13'0"

"As the great sloop [DEFENDER] slowly swung down the ways, a sailorman on the stern flung aloft the Stars and Stripes, and the multitude cheered afresh vociferously."

It was a day of great celebration, considerable national pride, and high expectations —all very much justified by DEFENDER's graceful shape and the now-worldwide reputation of the Herreshoffs. NGH, working this time without interference from the owning syndicate and, at least to some degree, influenced by Watson's designs for VALKYRIE II and BRITANNIA of 1893, had made DEFENDER deeper, narrower, and, because of her shorter keel, more maneuverable than VIGILANT. Also, she'd be carrying a loftier and more aerodynamic rig, along with the new Herreshoff crosscut sails.

New and deeper launching ways had been built but were untried at the time of the launching. Seconds after this photo was taken, DEFENDER came to an abrupt halt, her cradle having fetched up on a lag screw projecting from the ways. There she sat, half in the water and half out, until high tide on the third day when attempts to pull her off by tug were finally successful.

Although, like VIGILANT, DEFENDER was victorious over the British challenger (this time, Lord Dunraven's newest Watson creation, VALKYRIE III), the 1895 races were marred by as much controversy as accompanied the Cup matches of 1988. There were protests from both sides, bad press, and a great deal of ill feeling. Both disputes—nearly a century apart—went to arbitration.

As built, DEFENDER was fitted with living quarters. To match the stripped-out challenger, however, the joinerwork was later removed and its weight compensated for by inside ballast. By far the largest part of DEFENDER's ballast, however, was outside at the bottom of her deep keel— 177,000 pounds of it against a total displacement of 322,200 pounds, giving a ballast ratio of 55 percent. Her steel-framed hull was plated with bronze below the waterline, as was VIGILANT's, but with aluminum above in order to save weight. The aluminum quickly corroded, especially where it was attached to bronze or steel. DEFENDER has been ridiculed because of this; she did, however, last for about five years—long enough to be trial horse to COLUMBIA in the 1899 races. According to NGH, "she had performed the mission, and that was all that she was constructed for. From the start, durability was put aside."

DEFENDER, caught by an amateur photographer as she slides down the ways on June 29, 1895

HMCo #452
LOA 123'3"
LWL 89'0"
Beam 23'1½"
Draft 19'0"

KILDEE, a favorite Herreshoff family knockabout

HMCo #460, 1895
LOA 24'10"
LWL 18'0"
Beam 5'10"
Draft 4'4"

ALTHOUGH FIN-KEELERS were still going strong in 1895, KILDEE is of a different type. She carries a so-called "bulb keel" (one that fairs into and is an integral part of the hull) and has an underwater shape much like that of DEFENDER.

According to NGH's notes, KILDEE was built in the fall of 1895 for his wife's sister, Miss Florence DeWolf, known by the family as "Flossie," who sailed the boat in many races over the next six or eight years, and often won; KILDEE was subsequently used by NGH and his family. KILDEE was fast, and according to Sidney Herreshoff, NGH sailing his sleek new sloop DELIGHT (HMCo #679, 1908) couldn't keep up with L. Francis sailing KILDEE. NGH sold DELIGHT soon after she was built, and KILDEE stayed in the family.

The 21-foot class (LWL) sloop COCK ROBIN also had a hull of the bulb-keel type and in overall shape was much like both KILDEE and DEFENDER. In NGH's later bulb-keel designs, the rounded profile shown here gave way to keels that were straight on the bottom and had some drag so that the boats, when grounded on a sloping beach or railway, would set level without tipping forward.

Designed for Massachusetts Bay racing, COCK ROBIN became well known as "the boat to beat." Besides her large original gaff sloop rig, which she carries here, she was fitted with at least two smaller rigs so as to comply with evolving rules for classification. Fitted with a 500-square-foot rig, boats like this were known as "knockabouts." Another 100 square feet made them "raceabouts" and placed them in a different class. COCK ROBIN, at times, sailed with rigs of each size, and as a knockabout, abandoned her bowsprit altogether and was rigged with a jib tacked to the stemhead.

Although in 1896 fin-keelers were still very fashionable for afternoon 'round-the-buoy racing, it was not long before bulb-keeled boats with hull shapes like COCK ROBIN's showed their superior speed in light airs and surpassed the fin-keelers in popularity. Over the next twenty-five years, NGH would go on to design a great many outside-ballasted day boats based on the COCK ROBIN concept. They would be of about the same size, with deep, comfortable cockpits and small cabins outfitted only with a couple of settees and a couple of storage shelves. The S-Class boats, designed in 1919, for example, stem from this design.

COCK ROBIN
grounded out for
bottom cleaning,
August 6, 1896

HMCo #461, 1896
LOA 32'7"
LWL 21'0"
Beam 7'6"
Draft 5'7"

One of the Newport
30-Class sloops

HMCo #463 class,
1896
LOA 42'0"
LWL 30'0"
Beam 8'4"
Draft 7'2"

Aᴛ ᴛʜᴇ ʜɪɢʜ ᴘᴏɪɴᴛ of the fin-keeler fad came the Newport 30s—twelve boats, all alike, built for wealthy Newport summer folk.

The same half model that NGH used for ɴɪᴀɢᴀʀᴀ (shown earlier in this chapter), with an appropriate reduction in scale, was used for the Newport 30s. Although $2,850 would today seem like a bargain price for one of these boats, in 1896 it was considered expensive, but justifiable because of the Newport 30s' sophisticated construction. These boats had tapered frames of only 1 inch by 1 inch at their heads, double planking of only ⅜ inch total thickness, diagonal strapping in both hull and deck, and stirrups under the mast for additional support against compression.

With the Newport 30s, racing became more of a passion than a pastime. Forty or more races took place in a single season, and it became as much fun for the professional skippers who often competed in an owner's absence (in addition to crewing at other times) as it did for the owners themselves. A number of women even raced regularly with their husbands. The Newport 30s were an active class for over a decade, and with good reason, for they were high-spirited boats. In the words of NGH, "The racing was very keen and sporty. It was a remarkable sight to see them around the starting line, after the owners got used to them. They would get bunched up very closely and weave in and out with seldom a foul. Having short plate keels and balanced rudders that would swing athwartships, they would turn in a very small space." Another reason for the enthusiasm was that the boats were all alike, a new concept in racing which subsequently led to many more one-design fleets from the Herreshoffs as well as from other designers and builders.

WASP, worthy successor to GLORIANA in the 46-foot Class

HMCo #414, 1892
LOA 72'0"
LWL 46'0"
Beam 14'0"
Draft 10'8"

COLUMBIA,
successful America's
Cup defender of
1899 and 1901
(see page 90)

PART TWO

Heydays Before the Great War

HEYDAYS BEFORE THE GREAT WAR

Following the marvelously successful Newport 30s, the Buzzards Bay 15s became NGH's second one-design class—and one that would achieve even greater popularity. The first fleet of eleven 15-footers came out at about the same time as the great Cup defender COLUMBIA, and because there was a family resemblance (in spite of the vast difference in size), the boats were known for a time as "little COLUMBIAS." The prevailing Length-and-Sail-Area rating rule set the style, and resulted in boats with long, flat overhangs and shallow hulls sometimes with deep, almost fin-type keels. This class, however, having been designed for shallow-water anchorages and sailing conditions, was given centerboards and relatively long keels drawing less than 3 feet of water.

The #503 model (so designated from the first boat of the class) resulted in nearly one hundred boats, and included the Newport 15s, which were identical to the Buzzards Bay 15s except for having keels 6 inches deeper, and the fleet of Marconi-rigged Watch Hill 15s (shown in Chapter XI). There were also a couple of full-keeled versions of the #503 model (LITTLE ROBIN, HMCo #559, and FLICKER, HMCo #674), and one (HMCo #556) that was given a larger rig and bowsprit for competing in the Long Island Sound 21-foot Class. A new Marconi sail plan fitted with a "wishboom" mainsail was devised in the 1930s, and this model was quite heavily promoted by the Herreshoff Mfg. Co.—as were a number of its other stockboat offerings. Few orders came in, however, during those years of the Great Depression.

Compared with some of NGH's later work, the 15-footers seem a bit lacking in strength. They have very light scantlings, no covering boards (the fore-and-aft laid decking runs all the way out over the sheerstrakes), and no special reinforcing for their long, overhanging ends or their shallow-bodied hulls. As a hotshot racing class on windy Buzzards Bay, the boats tended to be pushed too hard for their own good. Out-of-shape sheerlines and leaky hulls, therefore, were not uncommon as the boats aged past the half-century mark.

The photo shows this boat's boom fitted with sailtrack, which assures uniform tension along the mainsail's foot. (Here, the new cotton mainsail has not yet been stretched taut.) A neat and lighter-weight lacing is used, however, on the shorter gaff and jib club. Lazyjacks, then common for containing the sail when lowering, also serve here as topping lifts, holding the boom up off the deck when necessary until the boom crotch is in place.

The door of the East Construction Shop at the left of the picture has been slid open on this warm summer day. At the right is another 15-footer also out of her element. On the dock watching, and no doubt wishing, stands a small boy.

Buzzards Bay 15-footer, sails hoisted and skipper aboard for dry-land portrait

HMCo #503 class
1899–1927
LOA 24'6"
LWL 15'0"
Beam 6'9"
Draft (board raised) 2'4"

THE 51-FOOT CLASS sloops of 1900, ALTAIR and her twin sister SHARK (51 being a rating and not indicative of a hull dimension), were shaped much like the larger New York 70-footers shown in Chapter VII. Although Cord Meyer, ALTAIR's original owner, thought well enough of the boat to keep her ten years, neither the 51-footers nor the New York 70s were held in universal high regard. "Leakabouts" were what technical editor (and subsequent big-name designer) C. D. Mower and writer W. P. Stephens called them in contemporary issues of *The Rudder*, accusing the boats of being poorly built and a discredit to Herreshoff's reputation.

While it is true that the New York 70s had to be reinforced after their first season, and both classes may have been driven beyond what their overly light construction could take, Stephens and/or Mower may have been reacting, in part, to the Herreshoffs' rough handling of the yachting press. Perhaps they were offended by the signs like the one on the fence in front of ALTAIR which says, "All persons are strictly prohibited from trespassing on this property...." Perhaps they didn't receive the welcome they felt entitled to. In any event, it certainly appears that one can read a lot between the following lines about the Lawley yard at So. Boston that appeared in the May 1900 issue of *The Rudder*: "One of the best features of the [Lawley] yard for the yachting enthusiast is the perfect freedom which is allowed him to go about and see whatever he pleases without danger of being surrounded by guards and unceremoniously thrust out into the street." The article was entitled, "Work in the Yards," and although it covered the entire northern East Coast, there was not a single mention of the Herreshoff Mfg. Co. or any of the boats being built there.

Beneath ALTAIR's stern ZINGARA, Alexander Forbes's new Buzzards Bay 30-Class sloop, and an as-yet-unnamed sister can be seen. Note that ALTAIR steers with a tiller, an indication of how well balanced she must have been under sail.

Chances are that the girl standing in front of the fence has rowed over in the tender GEM from the main yard with her friend Katherine, JBH's daughter, who took this photograph. (Chapter X contains more about Katherine and GEM.) The two-door shed on the shore served as a bathhouse.

ALTAIR at the Walkers Cove storage yard, probably in the spring of 1902

HMCo #539, 1900
LOA 74'0"
LWL 45'0"
Beam 14'3"
Draft 10'4"

RADIANT, a keel-centerboarder for Buzzards Bay

HMCo #548, 1901
LOA 33'4"
LWL 20'6"
Beam 9'10"
Draft (board raised) 3'8"

HAD THE design of RADIANT resulted in more than one boat, chances are that the class would have been known as the Buzzards Bay 21 Class; there are distinctly similar features that RADIANT has in common with the Buzzards Bay 15s, such as bow and stern watertight compartments for keeping the boat afloat if capsized. As it turned out, only this one boat was built. She was for C. M. Baker, for whom ownership of a Herreshoff-built daysailer was nothing new. The 17-foot-waterline sloop EDITH (HMCo #456, 1895) was his first, followed by a 21-footer of the same name in 1898. The 25-footer BLAZING STAR (#515 of 1899, now at Mystic Seaport) had been his most recent NGH-designed yacht before RADIANT. Miss Edith C. Baker is listed as RADIANT's owner shortly after the boat was built.

Racers like RADIANT were popular as an open class (as opposed to a one-design) along the Massachusetts coast, and, although there were rules governing other characteristics besides a 21-foot waterline length that a boat had to have to measure into the class, there were astonishing differences between the competing boats. To compare, for example, RADIANT with the keelboats ONAGH and ROGUE—all three NGH designs, created one after the other for this same class—we find RADIANT with about 2 feet more beam (her ample beam is apparent here from the shadow cast by her bow) and some 1½ feet less draft. It is a good rule indeed which allows both keelboats and keel/centerboarders to compete on more-or-less even terms.

Trivia and the other racer/cruisers shown on the following pages are typical mid-sized Herreshoff sailing craft of this era. Even today they represent a reasonable combination of performance and accommodation.

The photo shows that TRIVIA's mast has just been stepped (no doubt by the Herreshoff Mfg. Co. scow USEFUL, lying alongside her) and that the standing rigging has yet to be completely secured. There's another mast, or eight-stave glued-up spar of some kind, roughed out and lying on the dock awaiting rounding, finishing, and rigging. At the left is the dockside coal bin with the loading apparatus above it, where steam yachts get their bunkers filled. On the far side of the dock lies a large and elegant, but unidentified, steam yacht with fidded topmasts and her steadying sails snugly bagged under the gaff jaws. Astern of TRIVIA lies one of the Herreshoff-built lapstrake tenders put to use as a yard workboat.

TRIVIA was built for young Harold S. Vanderbilt as the first of several Herreshoff yachts he would own, each larger than the last and culminating in the Cup defenders ENTERPRISE and RAINBOW, in which he was a leading member of the syndicate. TRIVIA's building contract, signed in January 1902 by Vanderbilt and JBH, is quite specific in its details. To quote, in part: "All, or nearly all, ballast to be on the outside, and of lead cast to form. Framing to be of best white oak. All fastening below deck frame to be of bronze and copper. Planking to be of yellow pine, to be double from below the turn of bilge to sheerstrake, the inner thickness to be of cypress. Deck to be of selected white pine, deck seams to be filled with marine glue." The cost would be $6,300, to be paid in four installments as the work progressed. Delivery would be on or before July 1. The Herreshoff Mfg. Co. would provide life jackets, cockpit awning, dishes, mattresses, and pillows, as well as a lapstrake dinghy. Contracts such as this leave the oft-repeated story of the Herreshoffs doing just about as they pleased, customers be damned, as nothing but folklore. Indications are that the Herreshoff Mfg. Co. conducted its business in a business-like way, even if the paperwork was not always as complex as current practice.

TRIVIA was a powerful boat having the wide beam of the keel/centerboarder AZOR (HMCo #578), whose model she was built from, and carrying the same 1,251-square-foot sail plan, but fitted with a full keel. Besides TRIVIA and AZOR, there was NELLIE (HMCo #586), a keelboat like TRIVIA, also using the same model. By adjusting its scale, NGH utilized the same half model for three slightly smaller keel sloops including the 30' LWL BAMBINO (HMCo #616) of 1904. TRIVIA is now on display at the Museum, NELLIE is undergoing restoration, while BAMBINO is in her second century still winning races for the Museum.

Harold Vanderbilt's new cruising sloop TRIVIA being rigged, probably for her first season

HMCo #580, 1902
LOA 45'0"
LWL 33'6"
Beam 12'3"
Draft 7'3"

As each new design saw fruition, NGH made a point of personally putting the completed boat through its paces and carefully noting its handling characteristics. He appears to be at the helm here, and the man with him is no doubt cleating off the windward runner after their just-completed tack.

ELECTRA's cabin has drop-curtain sides (that's the rectangular patch of white) and a steam-bent, curved front of wood. The white-hulled steam yacht alongside the wharf looks like JBH's new 112-foot EUGENIA and beyond that, with masts, stack, and dark hull, may be PARTHENIA, Morton Plant's new 130-foot yacht. Next season, new sheerlegs will be installed, replacing those shown here at the end of the North Wharf; the new ones will be tall enough to handle stepping the 1903 Cup defender RELIANCE's mast with ease.

Two years before, for the Massachusetts Bay 21-Class sloop RADIANT (HMCo #548, shown earlier in this chapter), NGH made the half model that was reused in building ELECTRA. New and larger molds were needed, however, because there was a change in scale, meaning that the offsets (taken from the #548 model and recorded in a notebook) would all be increased by fifteen-twelfths. Because NGH reconfigured ELECTRA's keel profile, making it proportionally longer and less deep, she drew only 3 feet of water—some 8 inches less than the smaller RADIANT. HAPPY PRINCESS (HMCo #644), which came out in 1905, rigged as an open catboat, was built over the same molds as those used for ELECTRA. For HAPPY PRINCESS, a larger rudder and additional bronze hull strapping were called for as compensation against the balance and stress problems inherent in the cat rig. NGH frequently reused half models, even though changes in scale, deck layout, and rig disguised the fact.

ELECTRA skims past the Herreshoff waterfront, presumably on builder's trials in the spring of 1902

HMCo #582, 1902
LOA 42'5"
LWL 27'6"
Beam 12'3"
Draft (board raised) 3'0"

A just-completed
Bar Harbor 31-Class
sloop on her way
to the Walkers Cove
storage yard, in the
early spring of 1903

T HIRTEEN OF these one-design
sloops were built the same winter as
was the Cup defender RELIANCE, for
yachtsmen (mostly from the Boston area)
with summertime connections at Maine's
famous resort town of Bar Harbor.

The horse-drawn low gear carried
each finished boat from the shop where it
had been built (in production-line fashion)
down rough, unpaved Hope Street and
deposited it in an open storage yard awaiting springtime. Double-flanged, cast-iron
wheel assemblies, temporarily attached to

each corner of the boat's cradle, allowed
railroad track sections to be used, making
the rolling on and off a relatively smooth
operation. Once on the low gear, the cradle
was lashed down and its wheels were
chocked against shifting during the move.

HAVING ALL thirteen boats of this new one-design class lined up side by side appears to be the objective here; the remaining boats spanned outward from those that show in the photo. The precious load is being supported by heavy timbers in two long rows, blocked to the height of the low gear, upon which the individual boat cradles rest. More boats will arrive soon, so the man at the left is laying out more supporting timber. At the right, a couple of transfer tracks, still in place, can be seen.

The simple, individual boat cradles give adequate support while in transit, but the boats need the added security of shores that reach to the ground after the move is complete. These rest against the hull, using the same notched scab pieces that were screwed on in the shop and used there for exactly the same purpose. The canvas covers fit like gloves, and on examination it appears that they are made up of several rectangular pieces coarsely sewn together here on the site. The cover framework consists only of a posted ridgepole; rope lashings leading to chainplates, chocks, or other deck fittings out near the rail take the place of rafters.

Four newly finished Bar Harbor 31-footers covered and stored and awaiting spring outfitting, 1903

THE TRICED-UP JIB would suggest that this boat is getting a good scrubbing, and she obviously needs it. The scupper streaks probably result from a layer of ever-present coal dust that washed off the deck and down over the topsides during a rainstorm. Keeping yacht-like standards back when steam yachts and shoreside factories burned coal and spewed dust from their stacks meant having a full-time professional sailor living aboard who would, every day, turn to and wash down thoroughly. This less-than-fastidious owner, however, seems to be depending on the yard at less-frequent intervals. The toolboxes of yard workers on deck may mean that more than a simple cleaning will take place. Painters' rags that have been strung up to dry after washing show at the photo's left.

Bar Harbor 31-footer alongside the South Wharf, workers aboard, probably in the fall of their first season

HMCo #592 class
1903
LOA 49'0"
LWL 30'9"
Beam 10'5"
Draft 7'3"

I T'S INTERESTING to speculate on what conversations must have taken place during the conception of this, the best loved of all NGH's designs. Robert W. Emmons surely participated, for as manager of the Cup defender RESOLUTE syndicate, Bob Emmons had spent much time at the Herreshoff shops in the winter and spring of 1913–1914. A few years before, in 1898 and 1899, he had managed the ordering and delivery of the first Buzzards Bay 15-footers. Now, perhaps, he was after a somewhat less-spirited craft that could be used in teaching young people to sail. Herreshoff Mfg. Co. drawings show "Buzzards Bay Boys Boats" as the initial class name.* There may have been other influences as well; surely the lapstrake daysailer KATOURA JR. (HMCo #742), a davit boat of almost identical dimensions and similar layout built for Robert E. Tod's new schooner, KATOURA, had something to do with this inspired design, perhaps even serving as the prototype. As with most Herreshoff boats, however, the most vital ingredient was NGH himself.

By the fall of 1914, NGH had used his 26-foot sloop ALERION (shown in Chapter IX) in Bermuda for a season, and, being well satisfied with her, he had adapted her half model (by the addition of a full keel and an expansion of scale) to produce the Newport 29-Class racing/cruising sloops. Also in 1914, a larger and sleeker version of ALERION was created in the Buzzards Bay 25-footers. So, later in the year, when NGH modeled these 12½-footers, he had considerable recent experience to draw upon.

The photo shows the mainsail rigged with lazyjacks (which serve also as topping lifts) and a downhaul for the jib. Both seem like good ideas, but both were later given up as being unnecessary on a boat this small. The two-part mainsheet, shown here, was subsequently changed to three parts, to make sail trimming easier. The jib club attachment at the stem was later altered as well. The mainsail is laced to both boom and gaff on this first boat; later booms were fitted with sail track.

On the day of this photo, there must have been some wharf building or repair taking place that required the services of the piledriver shown at the far left. The yard's scow USEFUL is visible beyond the mast-stepping sheerlegs. The open doors in the North Construction Shop probably await ROBIN's return.

*Although early boats were alternately known as "Buzzards Bay Boys Boats" and "Buzzards Bay 12½-footers," or other names such as "Doughdish," "Bullseye," and "Herreshoff 12" have been applied later and in other locales. Throughout the rest of this chapter, the boats will be referred to simply as "12½-footers."

A. Sidney DeWolf Herreshoff (NGH's oldest son) trying out ROBIN (HMCo #744), the first boat of the Buzzards Bay 12½-foot Class, December 1914

There were twenty boats in the first batch of 12½-footers; all were built the winter of 1914–1915, and they sold for $420 each. (These early 12½s were fitted with rowing thwarts, metal tiller sockets, and stretched-out coaming ogees.) The full keels drawing only 2½ feet made the boats suitable for reasonably shallow water, yet easier than centerboard boats to build. The jib-and-mainsail rig, as compared, say, to a single-sail cat rig, made the boats faster for their sail area and provided young sailors with an understanding of the sloop rig that they'd need later on for their adult sailing years.

The big, open cockpits gave the 12½-footers a large-boat feel and enabled several persons besides the skipper to go sailing. With the narrow side decks, swamping under a press of sail was distinctly possible, and therefore a watertight buoyancy compartment was created underneath the forward deck by means of a bulkhead just forward of the mast. (A few 12½-footers were built in 1939 with wider side decks and metal buoyancy tanks under the seats; these were known as Long Island Sound Bullseyes.) The sunken afterdeck served as a seat, perching the helmsman just enough higher than the passengers (who sat on the bench seats) so that he could see over their heads. A small storage locker was formed under the afterdeck as well.

Before 1924, all 12½-footers were gaff rigged; then a Marconi option became available, and in 1935 that rig could be purchased with the new and much-promoted "wishboom rig and sail plan," examples of which appear in Chapters XI and XII.

Sitting in ROBIN's cockpit is young Charlie Sylvester, who had worked on the building of ALERION a couple of years earlier as his first job at the Herreshoff Mfg. Co. Charlie, no doubt, had a hand in the building of this boat as well. Later, he would have charge of and personally build many of the 12½-footers and yacht tenders for the company.

ROBIN, set up inside the North Construction Shop, December 1914

HMCo #744 class
1914–1943
LOA 15'10"
LWL 12'6"
Beam 5'10"
Draft 2'6"

RESOLUTE, built the previous winter as an America's Cup defender, has been hauled into the South Construction Shop for winter storage, after what turned out to be a fruitless summer of tuning up for races that were postponed mid-season because of World War I. Astern of her is JBH's power yacht, DIANTHUS.

The white lapstrake hull at the far right is KATOURA JR. (HMCo #742), mentioned earlier as having many of the same features as the 12½s.

As to the 12½s themselves, notice the two vertical transom stiffeners and margin pieces, necessary in these early boats to reinforce their ⅝-inch-thick transoms (⅞-inch thickness, used subsequently, would make these pieces obsolete).

What a change this scene is from what took place only the previous winter! The shop was humming then, while workers put the finishing touches on the 162-foot schooner-yacht KATOURA.

(Photos of both KATOURA and RESOLUTE under construction in the South and North Construction Shops, respectively, are in the following chapter.)

Completed 12½-footers
clustered around
RESOLUTE's keel,
winter of 1914–1915

Building 12½-footers in the East Construction Shop, about 1938

IN 1939, a quarter-century after their introduction, 12½-footers were still a-building and have become the Herreshoff Mfg. Co.'s most popular product. The hull in the foreground has just been turned right-side up and held level by shores running down to the floor. Her interior is being painted—now, while it can be most easily done. Stretchers have been screwed temporarily to the timbers (this before all the molds were removed) to stiffen the hull until more structure goes in. The two forward stretchers are especially important, as they hold the flaring bow in shape and prevent that part of the hull from pinching together and putting a hump in the sheerline. Soon the sheer clamps will go in, above the stretchers. The tops of the clamps will be even with the sheerline in way of the cockpit, but will dip down forward to support the beams of the foredeck. Although the painters are at work in this picture, there

are boatbuilder's tools conveniently at hand: on the big, wooden tray within the foreground boat, and on the between-the-boat benches. Within easy reach are gooseneck-mounted electrical outlets.

The 12½-footers shown here are an updated model; these were given plywood decks and bulkheads, fixed bench seats, non-opening mast bails, and store-bought (rather than Herreshoff-made) bow chocks.

Over some forty years the Herreshoff Mfg. Co. built about 360 12½-footers, nearly 150 of which were built and sold during the last eight years of production, 1936–1943. After World War II, the Quincy Adams yard was licensed to build them and produced fifty or so boats that were planked with Philippine mahogany instead of cedar. Then the building rights were sold to Cape Cod Shipbuilding Co., of Wareham, Massachusetts, which shifted to fiberglass shortly afterward in the mid-1950s and, at

the same time, with Sidney Herreshoff's design assistance, made some basic changes to the layout. Herreshoff "Bullseyes" were the result, and the Cape Cod Shipbuilding Co. has been producing them ever since. Cape Cod's "H-12" and the "Doughdish," by a rival boatbuilder, are fiberglass-hulled, less-altered versions of the original 12½s that are currently in production. Today it is estimated that 200 of the Herreshoff built 12½s survive, faithfully maintained by proud owners, with quite a number providing the training for which they were designed at schools operated by the Herreshoff Marine Museum and the WoodenBoat School.

THE NEWPORT 29-footers have occasionally been hailed as the best all-around design ever created by NGH or any other designer; certainly it is one of the most beautiful. Their reputation for speed comes largely from the hundreds of races won by DOLPHIN, the first boat of the class, and a boat that seems even today to be unbeatable in any kind of competition; she has proven herself a winner over the many decades she was campaigned by the Lockwood family. Although MISCHIEF, shown here with her original gaff rig, has not sailed as many races, she too has proven to be a formidable competitor. As of this writing, both DOLPHIN and MISCHIEF still sail and have long carried Marconi rigs.

COMET was the third boat of this class that was built for the 1914 sailing season,

and she was stretched out aft about 7 inches for a less abrupt ending at the transom. (COMET was lost in the hurricane of 1938.) The Herreshoff Mfg. Co. built a fourth Newport 29-footer in 1926, PADDY (HMCo #999), also with the added length of COMET; as of this writing, she is still going strong under the name TEASER. TEASER, as well as DOLPHIN and MISCHIEF, have been completely and beautifully restored.

The Newport 29s stand out as cruisers and daysailers as well as racers. They are just big enough for four berths, a galley, and an enclosed toilet room. Under the self-bailing cockpit there is space for an auxiliary engine. The rig is small enough to be easily handled, and the hulls are seakindly and of moderate draft—a far cry indeed from the Herreshoff Mfg. Co. one-designs of 1897 with nearly the same name. Those boats, the Newport 30s shown in Chapter V, were low-sided, high-strung fin-keelers that were strictly for 'round-the-buoy racing.

One might think that NGH worked especially hard to create such an outstanding design as the Newport 29-footers, but that was apparently not the case at all. He simply used the half model he'd made for the building of his own ALERION and changed its scale so the new design would be about a third larger than the old, then added a deeper ballast keel for sufficient lateral plane without a centerboard. (He also worked the minor alterations in bow profile and beam that were incorporated in ALERION's near-sister SADIE, HMCo #732.) One can't help speculating how many more of these magnificent designs NGH would have come up with had he lived into the family racer/cruiser era of the last half-century, and been able to concentrate on that type.

MISCHIEF, one of
the original three
Newport 29s

HMCo #727, 728,
and 737, 1914
LOA 36'0"
LWL 29'0"
Beam 10'4"
Draft 5'0"

A<small>LL FIVE</small> Buzzards Bay 25-footers came out in 1914 as sleeker versions of NGH's personal sloop ALERION. According to his son Sidney, this was NGH's favorite among the many hundreds of models he made. A persistent story of why the class never grew to more boats involves a sudden squall and sinkings the very first season, and indeed this event is confirmed by the 1915 Beverly Yacht Club's yearbook. The fact that these Buzzards Bay 25s cost about twice as much as the Buzzards Bay 15s and four times as much as the 12½-footers might also explain why more were not built. The boats are breathtakingly beautiful, however, and they sail as well as they look. It is a pity that the class didn't blossom.

Four of the five Buzzards Bay 25s still exist. BAGATELLE (HMCo #736) has been faithfully restored for sailing—gaff rig and all; the same is true of VITESSA (HMCo #734) except she's rigged as a Marconi yawl; MINK (HMCo #733), a derelict, awaits restoration; and ARIA (HMCo #738) is now an important central exhibit in the Museum's Hall of Boats.

The appeal of this design endures. Over a dozen have been recently built, in both cold-molded and traditional construction. These boats are particularly admired by all who observe them.

BAGATELLE,
a Buzzards Bay
25-Class sloop,
with her original
gaff rig

HMCo #736, 1914
LOA 32'0"
LWL 25'0"
Beam 8'9"
Draft (board raised) 3'0"

THE YEAR 1916 saw the Herreshoff Mfg. Co. launch a dozen New York 40s for members of the New York Yacht Club. The boats were alike in shape and rig, but owners could select from several interior arrangements. Soon, because of the intensity of their racing, they became known as the "Fighting Forties."

Designed as roomy flush-deckers—some yachting writers criticized them as "sailing houseboats"—the New York 40s lacked the grace of their predecessors, the New York 50-footers (shown in the next chapter), but were less expensive to operate, requiring fewer paid hands and less costly boatyard maintenance. Given their overall dimensions and freeboard, it is doubtful if a designer other than NGH could have created such good-looking hull shapes. The New York 40s have some hollow in their bows, a handsome sheer, and nicely sculpted transoms; they remind one of the Cup defender RESOLUTE, foreshortened to fit within a 59-foot overall length.

Although not planned for ocean racing, one boat of the class, MEMORY, rigged as a Marconi yawl, entered the Bermuda race of 1924—and won! Perhaps because of the publicity accorded MEMORY, two more boats, MARILEE and RUGOSA II, shown under construction in Chapter XI, were ordered shortly afterward. RUGOSA II won the Bermuda race of 1928. In 2001, MARILEE was restored as a sloop; RUGOSA II as a yawl. Both boats competed in the 2001 America's Cup Jubilee in Cowes, England, RUGOSA making the trans-Atlantic voyage (the start of a 24,000 mile four-year cruise) under sail with her most appropriate owner Halsey Herreshoff as skipper. Of 58 vintage yachts racing in the prestigious Jubilee Regatta, RUGOSA finished first and MARILEE second in the fleet. ROWDY, the latest NY-40 to be restored, is sailing again in California waters.

MAISIE, the first of the New York 40s, during her trial sail in the spring of her first season

HMCo #773, 1916
LOA 59'0"
LWL 40'0"
Beam 14'5"
Draft 8'0"

MAISIE's launching
from the ways of the
North Construction
Shop, spring 1916

As INDICATED by the above photo, the first New York 40s had to be put overboard as soon as their hulls were finished in order to make space in the shop for setting up the others of the twelve-boat contract. The North Construction Shop's length allowed three hulls of this size to be worked on simultaneously.

Behind MAISIE in the photo at the left is a second New York 40 lying under the Herreshoff Mfg. Co. sheerlegs, having just had her mast stepped. As a result of this first trial and early sailing experience among the fleet, the boats were given bowsprits in order to eliminate their excessive weather helm.

Using the model he'd made for the 12½-footers two years earlier and changing its scale, NGH developed the offsets and construction drawings for these larger daysailers.

Rather than going to the Buzzards Bay area, the first batch of twenty-two Fish-class boats was delivered to the Seawanhaka Corinthian Yacht Club on Long Island Sound, at a cost of $875 each. All twenty-two were gaff rigged, and all were named after some species of fish. In the years that fol-

lowed, about an equal number of additional Fish-class boats were built for other yacht clubs and owners, many carrying Marconi mainsails in the post–World War I fashion.

Although the separate guardrails shown on the boats in this photo were standard for the Fish class, some later boats were built with the varnished molded sheerstrakes that so enhanced the 12½-footers.

Fish-class sloops racing, about 1916

HMCo #788 class
1916–1939
LOA 20'9"
LWL 16'0"
Beam 7'1"
Draft 3'1"

The schooner
HASWELL on a trial
sail in the spring
of her first season

HMCo #743, 1915
LOA 62'0"
LWL 44'0"
Beam 14'2"
Draft 8'1"

I N CRUISING boats of this size, NGH preferred high topsides as a means of achieving full headroom (as well as an uncluttered deck), thus avoiding the expense and inherent weakness of a trunk cabin. The result was a practical, but not always beautiful, craft. Simplicity seems to have

been especially sought in HASWELL, because she carries pole topmasts (meaning that her topmasts are simply extensions of her lower masts), sails with no battens, and a single headsail rigged to a boom so as to be self-tending.

NGH, as was so often his custom, used one of his existing half models for HASWELL

—the one made for the sloop FLYING CLOUD (HMCo #703) five years earlier. Both boats were of composite construction.

Within a few years of her building, HASWELL was taken to the West Coast and renamed DIABLO.

CHAPTER VII

Years of Glory

The Big Sailing Yachts, 1898–1917

BEFORE 1898, the Herreshoff Mfg. Co. had built only four sailing craft that were over 50 feet on the waterline: NAVAHOE, COLONIA, VIGILANT, and DEFENDER. After 1917, it built just a handful more—and these were chiefly J-boats to outside designs. So the majority of the large Herreshoff sailing yachts came into being in the twenty years between 1897 and JBH's death in 1915, when the Herreshoff brothers were at the height of their fame and influence.

NGH's most celebrated creations of the company's middle period were his last four America's Cup sloops: COLUMBIA, CONSTITUTION, RELIANCE, and RESOLUTE. But no less imposing or less costly to build and sail were the seven great riveted-steel schooner-yachts that the Herreshoff Mfg. Co. produced between 1903 and 1915.

INGOMAR	HMCo #590, 1903	86′ LWL	for Morton F. Plant
QUEEN	HMCo #657, 1906	92′ LWL	for J. Rogers Maxwell
WESTWARD	HMCo #692, 1910	96′ LWL	for Alexander S. Cochran
ELENA	HMCo #706, 1911	96′ LWL	for Morton F. Plant
VAGRANT (II)	HMCo #719, 1913	80′ LWL	for Harold S. Vanderbilt
KATOURA	HMCo #722, 1914	115′ LWL	for Robert E. Tod
MARIETTE	HMCo #772, 1915	80′ LWL	for J. F. Brown

INGOMAR (the first) and KATOURA (the largest of these schooners) figure prominently in the following pages. Two final steel schooners to NGH's design, OHONKARA (HMCo #827, 1920, 80 feet LWL, for Carll Tucker) and WILD-FIRE (HMCo #891, 1923, 68 feet LWL, for C. L. Harding), were built by the Herreshoffs before the company was sold to the Haffenreffer family in 1924.

For sailing yachts not quite as large as these all-metal Cup sloops and big schooners, a combination of wood and metal known as composite construction was specified by NGH. Composite hulls usually had wooden planking and decking (and spars) over steel fames and deckbeams. The 56-foot LWL sloop DORIS (HMCo #625, 1905) was the largest all-wood sailing yacht ever built by Herreshoff.

Including the boats just mentioned and the four composite New York 70-footers and nine all-wood New York 50-footers discussed in this chapter, the Herreshoff Mfg. Co. built about forty sailing yachts of a waterline length of 50 feet or more during the first two decades of the twentieth century. They ranged in price from $162,400 for KATOURA and $174,000 for RELIANCE, to $14,250 for a New York 50. Considering that Herreshoff's price for a new 12½-footer in 1914 was $420 and for a new New York 40, $10,000, it is not difficult to understand why the financial health of the company had come to depend on a steady influx of big-boat commissions—or why the company fell into difficulties after World War I, when such commissions all but evaporated.

ALTHOUGH there is no date on this photograph, the odds are that it as taken between the evening of May 6, when CONSTITUTION was launched, and the following Tuesday, May 11, when her mast was stepped.

The task of rigging the Herreshoff Cup boats of this era, including the stepping of their masts, was farmed out to the Boston firm of Charles Billman and Son, and Billman's riggers appear to have been just getting organized when the picture was taken. CONSTITUTION's mast was of steel, and, like the steel masts of COLUMBIA and DEFENDER before her, it carried a telescoping wooden topmast within it.

Up to this time, NGH had specified wooden decking of white pine for Cup boats. In CONSTITUTION, however, as the photo shows, the deck surface was of a cork-like material in rectangular panels laid over the aluminum deck plating.

CONSTITUTION
dockside at the
Herreshoff Mfg. Co.,
in the spring of 1901

"NOTHING so handsome in naval architecture was ever seen…. To all came the impression that here was the acme of American genius and skill in building for the defense of America's Cup, and that if the SHAMROCK were to win from the COLUMBIA, she would have to be more than a wonder."

With these words, which he wrote for *The Rudder*, W. E. Robinson reflected the general feeling of the hundreds who watched COLUMBIA's launching on the evening of June 10, 1899. Compared to 1895, there was a new spirit in the air. National pride called for another victory, of course; but, after the bitter controversy surrounding the previous Cup match four years before, the entire country hoped for good sportsmanship as well. The United States government had done its part by authorizing, through an 1896 act of Congress, the use of naval vessels in patrolling the race course. (For this 1899 contest, President McKinley dispatched several of the Navy's new torpedo boats to keep the spectator fleet from interfering, as it had in 1895.) Sir Thomas Lipton was the challenger in 1899, as he would be again in the 1901, 1903, 1920, and 1930 matches. In spite of his winning but two races out of the eighteen sailed during his five attempts, Lipton's genial commitment to good racing, above all else, would more than regain the ground that had been lost by his predecessor, Lord Dunraven, in 1895.

COLUMBIA entered the water slowly from the new South Shop railway, and was tried under sail on June 25, two weeks afterward. Charles Barr was skipper; at last, a Herreshoff Cup defender would be in the hands of someone (other than NGH) who could bring out all the potential that had been built into the design. C. Oliver Iselin would be back (he had managed the previous two Cup defenders) as managing owner, with the virtually unlimited financial backing of J. P. Morgan, COLUMBIA's principal owner. And as a symbol to the nation that this was an all-American undertaking,

COLUMBIA was to have a crew from Deer Isle, Maine, instead of the usual Scandinavian professionals. It proved to be a winning combination, justifying the faith that the American people were putting in this sleek, new Herreshoff creation.

As with VIGILANT and DEFENDER, the new boat's bottom was plated with bronze; but steel, rather than the aluminum of DEFENDER, was used on her topsides.

The photographs on the next two pages were taken midway through the 1899 season, when COLUMBIA returned to Bristol to be fitted with a new steel mast and to be hauled out for a bottom cleaning and polishing. This was the first year that steel, rather than wood, was used for a Cup defender's mast. DEFENDER, which was to be COLUMBIA's trial horse, had been fitted with a steel mast early in the season, and now it was COLUMBIA's turn. Her sails— at least, the spinnakers and ballooners, and probably the other headsails as well— were removed during the changeover and stored in the sail loft above the North Construction Shop. In the photo, a headsail can be seen, in stops, on its way up; another headsail, also in stops and hoisted clear of COLUMBIA's deck, will probably be next in line. On the wharf are various spars, dinghies, piles of lumber, people, and clutter of a hard-at-work boatyard. Over COLUMBIA's bow can be seen the short-lived extension to the South Construction Shop, built to accommodate the pair of 175-foot-6-inch LOA torpedo boats DUPONT and PORTER, which, along with the smaller torpedo boats, GWIN, TALBOT, and MORRIS, had been delivered only a year or two before this picture was taken.

COLUMBIA at midseason, her sails being removed in anticipation of a new steel mast

HMCo #499, 1899
LOA 131'0"
LWL 89'8"
Beam 24'0"
Draft 19'9"

IN THE PHOTO to the left, COLUMBIA has been landed on the railway carriage and is being scrubbed by her crew as she clears the water. (Perhaps because the yard had a struggle with DEFENDER's rounded keel profile when she was hauled for work the previous fall, NGH gave COLUMBIA a keel that was straight on the bottom.) Angled posts extending upward above the water from each corner of the carriage serve to hold the hull more or less where it belongs until it can be tied off precisely over the keel blocks. The hard-hat diver (working off the scow, moored nearby) checked that all was well before the sliding poppets were hauled in against each side of the keel to hold the hull upright and in position. Then the carriage was hauled ahead, rising as it moved up the inclined railway and bringing COLUMBIA along with it.

COLUMBIA
being hauled and
scrubbed, 1899

COLUMBIA, her forward stays cast off, has been hauled ahead as far as her mast permits and, most important for the task at hand, fully clear of the water. Those aren't scupper streaks running down over the topsides, but lines holding the starboard sliding poppets in place. The portside poppets, held by similar lines leading to starboard, show just to the left of the rowboat. For additional support in the event of a big wind, preventer tackles have been run out from the masthead to the dock on both sides. Slung under the stern is the beginning of the staging from which COLUMBIA's bronze-plated bottom will be polished before she is relaunched.

Within a week, COLUMBIA will have her new steel mast. In preparation, her mainsail has been stripped off and lies on deck.

COLUMBIA, on the
South Construction
Shop railway, 1899

COLUMBIA's new mast, said to weigh a ton less than the original wooden one, was stepped on July 30, and it was with high hopes that she began tuning up with DEFENDER three days later. NGH's new mast design was an exceptionally neat arrangement featuring a wooden topmast that could be raised and lowered—telescope fashion—within the steel lower mast. Earlier all-wood designs had their topmasts stepped in the traditional and more cluttered manner on the forward side of the lower mast.

On August 2, in her first race (against DEFENDER) with the new mast, COLUMBIA had worked out a good lead, when a spreader collapsed and the mast broke—and she ended up looking like this. It is said that both Mr. Iselin and NGH were near the spot where the masthead landed, but they, along with everyone else, escaped injury. (NGH can be seen in the photo, standing on the after deck.) Because of their scheduled participation in the New York Yacht Club's annual cruise, COLUMBIA's crew very quickly cleared away the wreckage, and she was towed back to the Herreshoff Mfg. Co. Within a few days, she was back sailing—once again with her wooden spar, while the steel one was being repaired.

COLUMBIA's superior speed emerged slowly in 1899, and her victories over DEFENDER were by less-than-hoped-for margins. But as Charlie Barr's crew became more experienced and COLUMBIA got her steel mast repaired and restepped, she came into her own. She was hauled out for a final bottom polishing at the Brooklyn Navy Yard just before the Cup races. She won handily against the Fife-designed, green-painted SHAMROCK.

COLUMBIA's new steel mast went over the side the first time it was used, August 2, 1899

A wagonload of sail, with a Cup defender's crew to help dry it

S AILS OF THIS era were of cotton, and to prevent mildew they were always dried after use. This Cup defender's crew is taking a mainsail for drying on the large and well-manicured lawn of Blithewold, owned by the VanWickles, a Bristol yachting family.

The transportation was slow and careful, with crewmen making sure the sail didn't shift or drag. One crew member can be seen holding a stick to keep the sail from chafing against the wheel of the wagon. It seems that, in spite of the presence of an officer or captain (at left), the sailors are clowning a little for the camera.

The wagon and team belonged to the Herreshoff Mfg. Co. and were maintained by a resident teamster who lived in a cottage just east of the sail loft on Burnside Street.

THE INDOMITABLE Sir Thomas Lipton, in spite of losing on his first try, was back with another challenge two years later in 1901, and CONSTITUTION was built by the Herreshoff Mfg. Co. that year for the defense. Just as COLUMBIA was a refinement of DEFENDER, the new boat was designed to be better and faster than COLUMBIA. For a variety of reasons—but mostly because the two-year-old COLUMBIA was so well sailed as a trial horse by Charlie Barr—CONSTITUTION never could consistently demonstrate her superiority, and after a season of trials, COLUMBIA was selected for a second time to meet the new challenger.

CONSTITUTION's failure to be chosen was a disappointment to NGH as well as to her owning syndicate. Reflecting on her performance in later years, NGH wrote: "In this boat, I spent much thought on the construction of the hull, and worked out a longitudinal plan of framing; the hull was the lightest and strongest yet built, and she might have been quite long-lived, had she not very soon been given to the junk dealer so as to close the syndicate. The longitudinal construction of CONSTITUTION preceded by several years the well-known Isherwood patent in England for longitudinal construction of vessels.

"Commodore E. D. Morgan had taken COLUMBIA to fit out as a trial vessel to CONSTITUTION. He took Charlie Barr for skipper, and [they] got together the best crew they could—men of spirit, disregarding nationality.

"Barr and his crew proved too much for the captain and crew of CONSTITUTION, and would get the best of them every time, until they [were] thoroughly demoralized. So, COLUMBIA was chosen by the committee to defend the Cup, which she did for the second time, but with very little margin, for this second SHAMROCK, designed by Watson, was the fastest yacht that England had yet sent over." Thames Shipyard, in New London, Connecticut, is the setting of this photograph, said to be NGH's favorite of CONSTITUTION. In contrast to the earlier defenders and a number of those to follow, CONSTITUTION's topsides are flush plated, the plates being butted on her full-length longitudinal stringers. Both RELIANCE and RESOLUTE, which followed as the Herreshoff defenders of the 1903 and 1920 races, were similarly built, as their photos later in this chapter indicate.

CONSTITUTION
hauled at Thames
Shipyard, New
London, Connecticut

HMCo #551, 1901
LOA 132'0"
LWL 90'0"
Beam 25'1"
Draft 19'6"

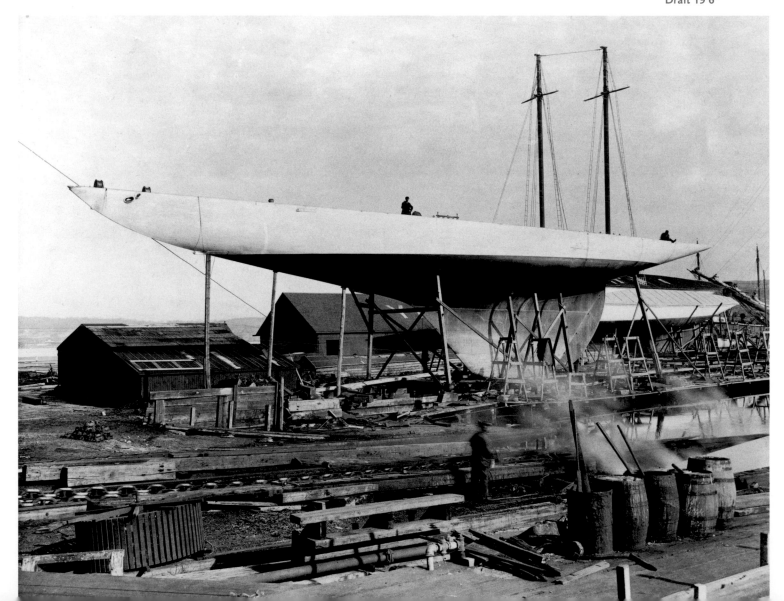

IT WASN'T until her launching on April 11, 1903, that RELIANCE, the longest and sleekest of all the Herreshoff Club defenders, could be viewed by either the press or the public.

Secrecy had long been an issue between journalists such as W. P. Stephens and the Herreshoff Mfg. Co. Each party had his own viewpoint, of course. NGH wrote to Stephens in later years that, in his opinion, "no well-regulated factory of any description should have its doors open to prowlers and loafers, and not even to reporters. In the beginning of building Cup defenders, it was learned that the challenger was building behind closed doors, and our clients instructed us

to close our doors and have a watchman. The reporters did so many things that were dishonorable, [such as] trying to steal information that they knew was not to be published, that they got a bad name with us."

Naturally, W. P. Stephens disagreed, and with good reason. "If this policy is carried to its legitimate conclusion, it means that yachting history must be limited to a bare record of the times of races—all records of experiment and technical advancement being consigned to oblivion."

The matter did get partially resolved, in that NGH wrote Stephens at length about the works of the Herreshoff Mfg. Co.

(This information is contained in Stephens's book *Traditions and Memories of American Yachting*.) However, he did not do so until the mid-1930s. By then, there was already in print considerable speculation and misinformation regarding Herreshoff creations such as RELIANCE.*

The big steamer at the right of the photo is RELIANCE's tender, SUNBEAM.

---

*See the subsequent book, *Their Last Letters 1930–1938*; Nathanael Greene Herreshoff; William Picard Stephens. Annotated by John Streeter. Published by the Herreshoff Marine Museum.

O NLY SUPERLATIVES adequately
describe RELIANCE, until the twenty-
first century, the largest single-masted
vessel ever built. Her topmast sprit towered
199 feet 6 inches above the water; it took
sixty-six men to race her; there was enough
square footage in her sails for eight modern
12-Meter boats; her mainsheet measured
1,000 feet in length (it was rolled up on a
drum below deck); and she carried over
100 tons of lead ballast in her keel.
A marvel of engineering, RELIANCE has
lived on as a most appropriate logo for
the Herreshoff Marine Museum.

RELIANCE was underway two weeks
after launching, being manned during her
early trials by a crew from the Herreshoff
shop, with Charlie Barr as skipper. Unless
there was a reason to do otherwise, her
professional crew laid themselves out along
RELIANCE's windward rail when racing,
acting as live ballast and cutting down on
windage. RELIANCE proved to be a good
performer (she easily won all races against
Lipton's third SHAMROCK) and experienced no serious gear failure. However,
NGH recorded his opinion that she was
too scowlike in form. Her extreme shape
had been requested by syndicate manager
C. Oliver Iselin, an old sandbagger sailor,
whose influence had earlier shown up in
the wide beam of VIGILANT. It is possible
that NGH was influenced as well by the
shape of INDEPENDENCE, an America's Cup
contender designed by B. B. Crowninshield
for 1901, which had the potential for great
speed but not the structural reliability to
show up well against the Herreshoff boats
COLUMBIA and CONSTITUTION.

RELIANCE sailing,
1903

RELIANCE below
deck, looking aft
during construction

HMCo #605, 1903
LOA 143'9"
LWL 89'9"
Beam 25'10"
Draft 19'9"

NGH designed RELIANCE's hull as he had CONSTITUTION's, with bronze plating over a steel framework consisting of widely spaced web frames connected by longitudinal stringers, much as found in an airplane fuselage. Below deck she was open, with over 100 feet of clearly viewable hull structure—"a most striking sight," according to NGH's son Griswold, who was aboard for the Bristol trials. A single stateroom and toilet aft and a canvas-shrouded crew toilet forward were the only accommodations.

RELIANCE was built with two steering wheels on a common shaft so that four persons could lend their strength in keeping the boat on course. According to NGH, however, RELIANCE steered easily and never required more than a single helmsman.

During trials, with no escort vessel at hand, a dinghy was always towed as a lifeboat in case someone fell overboard. (Cup defenders had no lifelines and only a low toerail.) Writing in the Spring 1983 issue of the *Herreshoff Marine Museum Chronicle*, Griswold, himself only a youngster in 1903, described RELIANCE's first sail in a strong 20-to-25-knot easterly. At a speed that reached 20 knots at times, RELIANCE's afternoon trial took her from Bristol to Block Island and back. She shot the last mile to the mooring on momentum alone, after all her sails had been lowered.

RELIANCE's forward overhang, all 28 feet of it, indicates, perhaps as much as her towering rig, how extreme the turn-of-the-century racing yachts had become. Highly stressed in both hull and rig and decidedly an engineering triumph not ever likely to be repeated on such a scale, RELIANCE and her ilk were as impractical as the Cup boats are today in the twenty-first century. In earlier times, rational hull forms carrying reasonable spreads of sail had been built for this contest and had become useful as cruisers and 'round-the-buoy racers after their America's Cup years were over. RELIANCE certainly was not one of them.

Considering that you're looking at hull plating covered only by paint and not filled with the usual fairing compounds, RELIANCE's hull is remarkably free of waviness. Because of its shape, and the great sloop's speed, her bow took an unmerciful pounding as it drove into the seas, and metalworkers were called up two or three times during the season to pound out the dents. The structure behind the plating had to be reinforced as well.

Wire-to-rope splices for sheets and halyards can be seen in this photo. Wire's small diameter and resistance to stretch are an advantage for the portions under load, and the rope tails make the rest of the length easier to handle. Notice that there are two independent bobstays. It has been recorded that a single wire rope of sufficient diameter was not to be found. Notice also the adjustable thrust strap at the heel of the bowsprit by which the bobstays are tightened.

RELIANCE at the Herreshoff Mfg. Co. dock, 1903

THE FOUR BOATS of this, Herreshoff's largest one-design class, went at it tooth and nail in their first season, driving their long-ended hulls way beyond their structural limitations and earning for them the nickname "Leakabouts." MINEOLA, RAINBOW, VIRGINIA, and YANKEE were their names, and the fact that the owners, afterguard, and crews had, for the most part, been groomed aboard the intensely competitive Newport 30-footers established their hard-driving attitude toward sailing these far bigger craft. There was some ethnic rivalry between the professional crews as well; two of the boats were manned entirely by Englishmen, while the other two had Scandinavian crews and American skippers.

Herreshoff's reputation suffered as much as the "Leakabouts" themselves did, with numerous jibes coming from the yachting press and considerable owner dissatisfaction. Internal metal trusses were added during their second season which cut down on the leaking, but these scowlike monsters continued to demonstrate the ills of the prevailing Length-and-Sail-Area rating rule. (The New York 70s also demonstrated that racing craft this big should be plated with metal rather than planked with wood.) Owners and observers alike became convinced that the New York Yacht Club and other leading clubs should consider a new rule that favored less-extreme hull shapes. Within two or three years, NGH's Universal Rule was adopted.

A New York
70-foot Class sloop

HMCo #529 class
1900
LOA 106'0"
LWL 70'0"
Beam 19'4"
Draft 14'0"

INGOMAR
in English waters,
1904

HMCo #590, 1903
LOA 127'0"
LWL 86'1"
Beam 24'2"
Draft 14'0"

Ingomar was the first of the nine great Herreshoff steel-hulled schooner-yachts. She was designed and built the same year as RELIANCE—and sadly, at the time that NGH's wife Clara was dying of cancer.

Before INGOMAR, all the big Herreshoff sailing yachts had been single-stickers, consisting mostly of the America's Cup boats shown previously. By commissioning INGOMAR, Morton F. Plant persuaded NGH that schooners, too, had merit. In his notes, NGH calls INGOMAR a wonderfully good schooner that easily proved the fastest of her type. He wrote that he had sailed on her a few times and was well pleased. Charlie Barr, who had sailed RELIANCE to victory the summer of 1903 when both

yachts made their debut, became INGOMAR's skipper the following season, and he, too, was well pleased. Writing to NGH, after a 1904 trans-Atlantic crossing, he said: "INGOMAR is as good a cruising yacht as you will find anywhere…."

For the 1904 sea voyage, a smaller rig was fitted, and her racing spars were shipped across by steamer. For racing in Europe, the Herreshoffs had fitted INGOMAR with a 2-foot-deeper keel; her centerboard was removed in the process. (In 1906, after her return, the procedure was reversed to restore the yacht's original 14-foot draft. In 1925, records indicate the removal of both the lead keel and centerboard, resulting in a 12-foot draft—this along with the installa-

tion of an auxiliary engine.) INGOMAR brought back seventeen trophies from her single season in European waters. Only the legendary schooner AMERICA had campaigned abroad with more success.

Big yachts, especially metal ones like INGOMAR, were usually built in the South Construction Shop, but because that space had been assigned to RELIANCE in 1903, INGOMAR was set up and built in the North Shop. At the launching (on greased ways, because that shop had no railway) she hit the water at such great speed that she kept going and going until, after turning a full circle, she gently hit the dock stern first.

AT 72 FEET OVERALL, the New York 50s were among the largest Herreshoff sailing hulls to be built upside down and entirely of wood construction. They were built in a kind of production line. While one hull was being planked, the previous one, turned upright, was having its interior and deck installed. This same two-boat cycle was repeated all during the winter and spring of 1912–1913, until the last of the nine New York 50s slid overboard from the North Construction Shop's launching ways.

Like all but the smallest Herreshoff-built wood-hulled racing yachts, the New York 50s were double-planked and diagonally strapped with metal, which gave them unusual strength for their weight. As shown here, the double planking begins several planks out from the keel (about where the tool retainer batten is fastened) and will run to the sheerstrake (which is of single thickness with a rabbeted joining edge). The outer layer planks are bedded in thick shellac, and they center over the inner layer seams. The butt joints of the inner layer land directly on the frames, while those of the outer layer (the thicker of the two) use

New York 50-footers
being built in the North
Construction Shop

HMCo #711 class, 1913
LOA 72'0"
LWL 50'0"
Beam 14'7"
Draft 9'9"

conventional butt blocks located between the frames. Here, the strapping (which, unfortunately in these boats, was of steel rather than bronze and rusted as the boats aged) is being let into the planking. (On some yachts, Herreshoff notched the frames rather than the planking, but in all cases the straps were pre-punched for the round-headed screws that secured them to the hull planking.) Flat-head screws, driven from inside the hull between frames, are used to fasten the two layers of planking together; the cam-type wooden clamps that squeeze the layers tightly against each other for this back-fastening process can be seen lying idle at the right in the photo.

No caulking is used with double-planking, so it is important that the planks, especially the outer ones, fit tightly edge-to-edge. Wooden wedges and timber dogs, the latter driven into the face of the frames, are used for that purpose, and a typical wedging setup can be seen at the lower right, pushing against an inner plank. Wooden blocks, rabbeted so as to clear the inner planking, are used to edge-set the outer layer. (Planks in this part of the hull are narrow enough to be bent sideways. Thus, all double-planked strakes, each one consisting of several planks, butted together end-to-end, could be made exactly alike to a single pattern having the correct taper but no spiled shape; that is to say, one edge could be perfectly straight. These "manufactured" planks could subsequently be edge-set into position as already described, and the usual spiling/custom fitting process completely eliminated.

Facilitating the upside-down hull construction were a pair of overhead traveling cranes which played a key role (see Chapter III) in turning over the hulls and in moving them from one work station to the next. A big advantage of the Herreshoff method, obvious from the photo, is that the staging planks could be arranged to form a working platform all around the boat (even between the frame stations) without the usual braced support posts running down to the shop floor. Support instead comes from athwartship joists (temporarily attached to timber molds) that project a few feet beyond the hull. Fore-and-aft staging planks are then laid on the joists, followed by transverse planks (numbered for location) as the photo shows. Thus, from a standing position, the work falls pretty much at eye level, where it can be clearly seen and comfortably worked on, and the tools are within reach as they rest against a batten fastened temporarily to the completed hull planking. As the planking progresses, the joists are simply lowered to suit until standing directly on the shop floor becomes possible. The planking is faired, smoothed, caulked (single thickness only), and bunged as soon as it is in place so that all the hull-building operations are complete before the staging is moved.

THESE WORKMEN are about to begin beveling the frames so that the planking will lie fair against them. The frames are of oak, and each one has been steamed and bent around its own mold and held there with several forged drawdogs, which can be seen in the photo. As the beveling operation progresses, the drawdogs will be pulled off one at a time, then driven back in place again after that part of the frame has been planed fair.

The molds around which the frames are bent will be reused for the subsequent hulls of this nine-boat one-design class. Shimmed, marked pads under the feet of each mold establish each mold's height and athwartship alignment. The method of diagonally bracing the molds shows at the far left, where a key mold has been braced and squared upright to the somewhat imaginary reference plane on the shop floor known as the construction baseline. Using this mold as a fixed guide, the remaining molds—with frame assemblies bent around them—are then set up and the backbone (keel timbers and stem) installed and fastened to them. Besides the keel, several battens (shown behind the carpenters) hold the molds and frames in position until the planking takes over and makes their presence unnecessary.

Throughout its life, the Herreshoff Mfg. Co. was wedded to this mold-for-every frame, upside-down setup for its wooden-hulled yachts—from 8-foot rowboats and dinghies (where the hull was sometimes planked over every other mold-and-frame) to the 72-foot New York 50s shown here. Almost any method practiced long enough in one boatshop becomes so well understood and so automatic among the workers that it might be called efficient. The Herreshoff method, although time-consuming in the building of the many molds, produced hulls precisely faithful to the design—NGH furnished his mold loftsman with hull

Carpenters pose after installing the keel timber on a New York 50

offsets at every single frame. Only a single set of so-called timber molds was needed for any given design, however, and if, as in the case of the New York 50s, there were to be several identical hulls built, the Herreshoff method became totally consistent as well as efficient by any standard.

Although Herreshoff scantlings and general hull structure have been adopted by many a subsequent designer and builder to the point where square-sectioned frames, screw fastenings, and plank-type floor timbers for every frame have long been the wooden boat standard, it is indeed curious that so few boats by other builders have been set up like the one shown here. Or, to put it another way, it is strange that designers and builders have saddled themselves with the restrictions that the Herreshoff building method imposes. Copper rivets, for example, have proven more durable than bronze screws as plank fastenings, and could be used to advantage on boats where frames are accessible for peening and not dogged down over molds.

In 1928 NGH, upon urging from the New York Yacht Club, compiled some rules for wooden yacht construction based on his many years experience. These have been published, most recently in *Skene's Elements of Yacht Design* by Francis S. Kinney. Much of NGH's presentation, however, was based on his assumption that whoever used the book for sizes would also be using the Herreshoff setup. Unfortunately, NGH didn't go into a detailed description of that process.

Sparmaking, 1913

CHANCES ARE, this spar is for one of the New York 50-Class sloops. At the Herreshoff Mfg. Co., where lightweight structures reigned supreme, spars (except for the very smallest ones) were made hollow —most of them glued up from either carefully tapered staves of Sitka-spruce or Douglas-fir. Here, one half of a spar has been shimmed to be straight along its centerline and is being planed for a fit against the other half, which lies on the bench at right. The special Herreshoff sliding-bar-type spar clamps can be seen hanging from the overhead and will see service when the halves are glued together.

The gluing operation required great speed, great care, and very many clamps, because the glue had to be heated for use and flowed only while hot. The glue was not gap-filling, and the spars, when vanished, were expected to show no gluelines what-soever. Gluing demanded quite a large crew, in addition to the sparmakers. Usually this job took place right after lunch so as not to interrupt the work of other departments. Each man selected for the team was assigned a hot gluepot, a brush, and a certain number of clamps to tend.

The spar bench's overhanging cross-pieces, shimmed level and to a common height, provided a working surface where clamps could be used. From this "bench," glue could drip directly to the floor, and a plank could be placed on it, as shown here, if continuous support were needed. This spar loft was located in the East Construction Shop's overhead, where there was good north light. (The mold loft occupied part of this space as well.) Jim Davison was Herreshoff's head sparmaker for years, and his skill was legendary.

At 162 feet in length on deck and 30 feet in beam, KATOURA filled the shop in all directions and was the largest sailing craft that Herreshoff would ever build. The man standing on her lower deck gives some idea of scale.

The steel bulb angle frames were heated and bent to shape in the blacksmith shop across Hope Street where a suitable facility existed. It appears that assembly took place right here, where the boat is being built under the watchful eye of shop foreman Jack Brechin.

Brechin, and his predecessor Mr. Morgan, enjoyed widespread respect for their riveted metal hulls and especially for their fair plating. Fillers, so necessary with today's welded steel hulls, were never used at Herreshoff's.

It appears that KATOURA has been let down the railway far enough for shipping her bowsprit. At $1,000 per foot of overall length, KATOURA was exceeded in cost only by RELIANCE when it came to Herreshoff-built sailing yachts.

Framing KATOURA in the South Construction Shop

HMCo #722, 1914
LOA 162'0"
LWL 115'0"
Beam 30'0"
Draft 18'0"

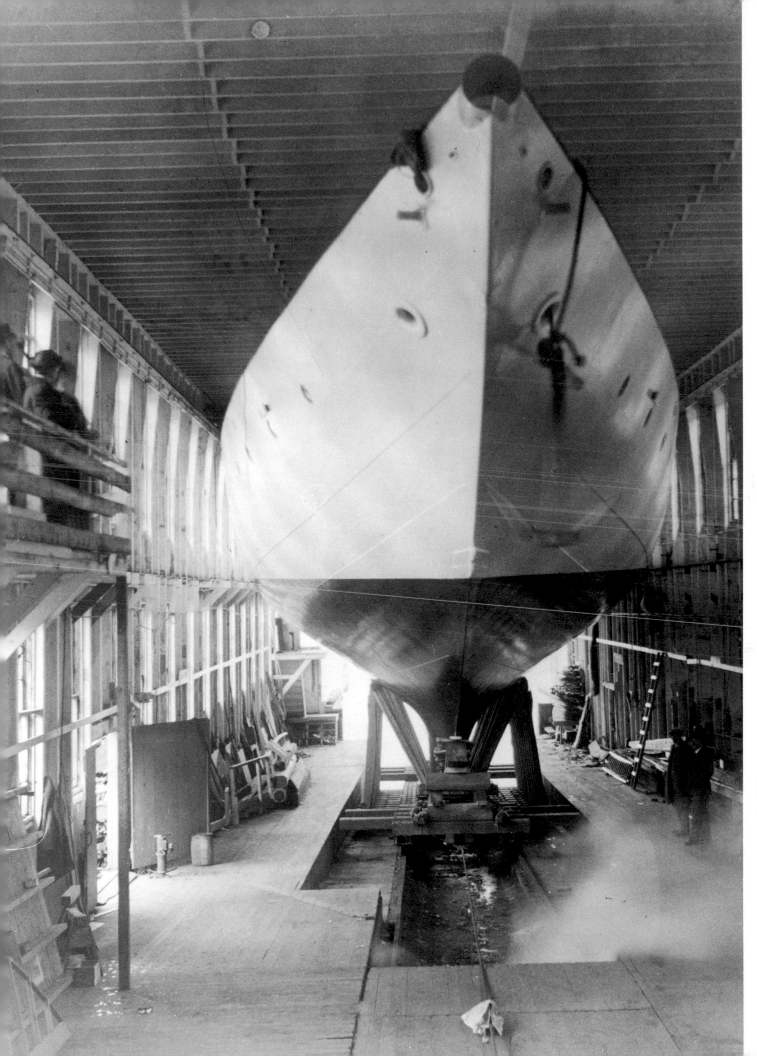

KATOURA,
just before
launching,
April 2, 1914

After several years of negotiation, both the challenger (once again it was Sir Thomas Lipton, this time with his fourth SHAMROCK) and the New York Yacht Club agreed to compete in smaller boats having 75-foot instead of 90-foot waterline lengths and designed to the Universal Rule rather than the previous Length-and-Sail-Area Rule, which had spawned extreme racing machines like RELIANCE. Accordingly, this newest Cup boat was more practical, relatively speaking, as well as being NGH's smallest. Widely spaced web frames with longitudinal stringers—the so-called "longitudinal method of construction"—were used as RESOLUTE's skeletal framework and show clearly in this photo. CONSTITUTION and RELIANCE had also been built this way; it saved weight without sacrificing strength and allowed for more outside ballast. (L. Francis Herreshoff carried his father's idea into his own wooden hull designs, and in his R-boat LIVE YANKEE of 1926 achieved a phenomenal 80-percent ballast ratio. That is to say, the hull amounted to only 20 percent of the boat's waterborne displacement. Longitudinal construction isn't practical for most boats, however, because too much interior space is taken up by the web frames.)

Notice RESOLUTE's lovely stemhead casting, a one-piece unit that has sides rabbeted for the hull plating and a circular opening on centerline for the bowsprit. The two portable, lead-melting furnaces, from which RESOLUTE's ballast keel poured forth in liquid form, rest on the shop floor under the staging and out of the way. Formed steel mast sections with pre-punched rivet holes along their edges lie in the foreground awaiting assembly.

Although big metal yachts were usually built in the South Construction Shop, where they could be eased overboard on a wheeled railway (the North Shop had only greased launching ways), that custom had to be given up for the building of RESOLUTE because the schooner-yacht KATOURA was already well along. Thus RESOLUTE became a product of the North Construction Shop, where wooden hulls were usually built, and was launched April 25—only about six weeks after this photo was taken. Her hull was of bronze plating over steel framing, all riveted together.

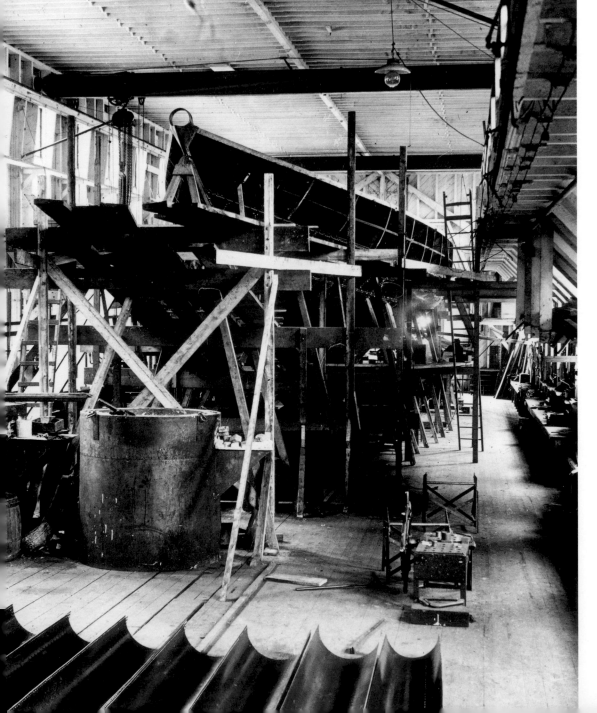

Cup defender
RESOLUTE in the
North Construction
Shop, March 8, 1914

HMCo #725, 1914
LOA 106'3"
LWL 75'0"
Beam 21'2"
Draft 12'11"

WHAT A marvelous sight greets Bristol's early risers this morning as the Cup candidate RESOLUTE (center) and the schooner KATOURA—both brand new —get underway! It has been more than a decade since an America's Cup challenge and, as always, intense curiosity surrounds any contender. This will be RESOLUTE's second builder's trial and KATOURA's first, and NGH will command first the one great yacht and then the other on this proud Sunday. Although the previous day's sail in RESOLUTE was cut short when a peak halyard block parted, this day's trials for both boats will go off without a hitch.

RESOLUTE has only been overboard for eight days, and in less than two weeks, May 12 to be exact, the Herreshoff Mfg. Co. will officially deliver her for the final payment of her $123,000 cost. She is the first of the three 1914 America's Cup candidates to be under sail—DEFIANCE and VANITIE are the others, built elsewhere. The steamer CAPE COD, at right, has been chartered this season by RESOLUTE's syndicate. Messrs. Emmons, Nichols, Adams, and Cormack— the afterguard's principals—along with the others of her afterguard, officers and crew will live aboard CAPE COD for the rest of the summer.

RESOLUTE
gets underway,
May 3, 1914

WITHOUT HEADSAILS raised, RESOLUTE handles like a dinghy; only the running backstays need tending when she tacks. Here, her crewmen tie rotten stops (weak, yarn-like cotton twine always used for the purpose) at regular intervals on one of the jibs so it will remain docile while hoisting, then can be broken out to fill with wind with a quick tug on the sheet. More, yet-to-be-dealt-with headsails show at the base of the mast.

RESOLUTE
after tacking,
May 3, 1914

RESOLUTE has just tacked, and all sails are now set, except for the jib topsail which has been sent up in stops and is about to be broken out. During their first use, these cotton sails always show wrinkles, especially in light weather.

Only three people appear to be aboard CAPE COD; most of the others are on board RESOLUTE.

NGH brings RESOLUTE to her mooring, May 3, 1914

AFTER HER morning trials, NGH, at the wheel, brings RESOLUTE to the mooring while the afterguard look on. A sailor walks aft preparing to unhook the running backstay so it will not interfere with the boom if the mainsheet has to be slacked away.

NGH brings RESOLUTE to her mooring, May 3, 1914

NGH aboard RESOLUTE, May 3, 1914

RESOLUTE's afterguard, although they were wonderful small-boat sailors, were not mechanically inclined, and so NGH (facing the camera in this photo) claimed he could never make them understand his work fully nor talk with them intelligently about it. RESOLUTE's sail has been lowered here, and a crotch (steadied with quarter-tackles) supports her hollow steel boom. RESOLUTE's broad stern and general appearance are reminiscent of 1913's beautiful New York 50-Class sloops.

In later years, NGH would reflect: "1914 was a busy one for me. Between sailing KATOURA and many times in RESOLUTE there were about one-and-a-half dozen smaller boats under 30 feet LWL to be tried out." (In retrospect, after ninety years have elapsed, we would call 1914 just as significant for these small boats as for the big ones. The 12½-footers, the Buzzards Bay 25-footers, and the Newport 29-footers of Chapter VI, for example, first came out in 1914.)

Resolute's crew is posed here at attention, their work of making things shipshape completed. There were twenty-seven in her crew, as compared to sixty-six in the crew of RELIANCE.

RESOLUTE was the last NGH-designed defender, although the Herreshoff Mfg. Co. would continue to build defenders for the America's Cup through 1934.

RESOLUTE at anchor, her crew at attention, May 3, 1914

Owners and guests aboard for KATOURA's trial sail, May 3, 1914

If, earlier in the day, RESOLUTE's after-guard had been curious as to how the great schooner KATOURA would perform compared to their sporty new Cup defender, they have a chance to find out for themselves as they join NGH, and the owners (the Tods), and their party for the trial sail in the afternoon. On board in the photo, left to right, are George Nichols, Charles Francis Adams, Mrs. Robert W. Emmons, Miss Agnes M. Herreshoff, Miss Mary R. DeWolf, J. B. Francis Herreshoff, John Parkinson, Robert E. Tod, NGH, Clarence DeWolf Herreshoff (behind his father) and Mrs. Robert E. Tod.

KATOURA's sailing trial follows RESOLUTE's. Here the afternoon southerly has come in, and KATOURA heels to it as she picks up speed; her boarding ladder is almost touching the water, and she's raising a good-sized quarter wave.

KATOURA's great size sets her off from the eight other big steel schooners from the Herreshoff Mfg. Co., but she can also be identified by the large deckhouse. Her length on deck is 162 feet, compared to RESOLUTE's 106 feet. Her foremast and mainmast are the leftover hollow steel masts of the Cup boats CONSTITUTION and RELIANCE, which, by 1913, had been broken up for scrap.

According to L. Francis Herreshoff, KATOURA was the finest all-around yacht ever built by the Herreshoff Mfg. Co. She was built for speed as well as comfort, but she never raced enough to make a name for herself, as did the famous schooners WESTWARD, ELENA, and INGOMAR, for example. (Records show that she did, however, win the New York Yacht Club-sponsored 264-mile Newport-to-Sandy Hook-and-return race three years in a row, as well as the Cape May Challenge Cup in 1915.) Robert E. Tod sold KATOURA in 1920, and, after six years as R. A. Alger's ELFAY, she was sold abroad and renamed MAGDALENE II.

KATOURA on trial,
May 3, 1914

**Schooners ELENA
and KATOURA**

ELENA
HMCo #706, 1911
LOA 136'6"
LWL 96'0"
Beam 26'8"
Draft 16'11"

KATOURA
HMCo #722, 1914
LOA 162'0"
LWL 115'0"
Beam 30'0"
Draft 18'0"

KATOURA, in the foreground, has been discussed earlier in this chapter. The schooner behind her is believed to be Morton F. Plant's ELENA, built in 1911 as his second big Herreshoff schooner-yacht. (INGOMAR, also shown previously, was the first.)

Both KATOURA and ELENA were very fast, but ELENA made more of a name for herself in the racing circuit. KATOURA was the larger by some 20 feet on the waterline, however, and for that reason had greater possibilities for making record-breaking runs. In speaking of KATOURA, L. Francis Herreshoff laments that Charlie Barr was

never aboard as skipper to squeeze out all of her potential speed. Although it was never proven, L. Francis calls KATOURA the fastest schooner built anywhere at any time.

More than eighty years have passed since the heyday of the big Herreshoff Cup defenders and schooners, and attrition has taken its toll in the face of aging hulls and evolving tastes, technologies, and economics. The 109-foot schooners VAGRANT (the second of that name built for Harold Vanderbilt), and MARIETTE (a sistership, once named CLEOPATRA'S BARGE) appear to be the only survivors. Both now sail in Mediterranean waters.

THE 1914 challenge for the America's Cup, postponed because of the outbreak of World War I, was sailed in the summer of 1920. RESOLUTE was skippered by Charles Francis Adams, probably America's best amateur sailor of that day.

Sidney Herreshoff enjoyed telling the story of how his father, at the age of seventy-two, got to be a member of the RESOLUTE afterguard. After the defender had lost the first two races (three races were needed to win) to SHAMROCK IV, a United States Navy vessel was dispatched to Bristol to transport RESOLUTE's designer to the Sandy Hook race course. With Captain Nat in the afterguard offering the kind of technical advice which only the designer could, RESOLUTE won the next three races, and the Cup remained in the possession of the New York Yacht Club after what, in the beginning, had been a close call. One cannot help but wonder what went through the mind of the old gentleman during the final leg of the third race, because twenty-seven years before, he had steered VIGILANT, his first Cup defender, in an exciting series of races over the same course. In the years between 1893 and 1920, his yachts had defended the America's Cup a total of six times, truly a brilliant achievement.

Historically, the 1920 America's Cup defense is known as a defense of lasts. It was the last to be sailed off Sandy Hook, the last to be sailed with handicaps, and the last to be sailed with gaff-rigged yachts. For N. G. Herreshoff, this defense was the last won by a yacht of his design, and the last which saw his active participation.

NGH under
RESOLUTE, 1920

CHAPTER VIII

The Power Transition

From Steam to Internal Combustion, 1898–1917

Before 1900, the power-driven craft built by the Herreshoff Mfg. Co. had all been steamers. EXPRESS, the 49-foot launch built in 1902 and shown on page 118, was the first Herreshoff boat to use a gasoline engine. The following year, two other gasoline-powered craft of the same model, ADRIENNE and HELVETIA, were produced. The launch 240 and the speedboat X.P.D.N.C. came next in 1904, followed in 1905 by three more boats powered by gasoline; meanwhile, during the time these five were built, the Herreshoff Mfg. Co. produced some fourteen craft equipped with steam plants.

But all across America a trend was being set toward gasoline, especially in the smaller boats. The Herreshoff Mfg. Co. was soon affected, as more and more clients specified gasoline rather than steam. In 1906 not a single one of the seven power-driven craft built that year was a steamer, and by far the majority of those that followed over the next ten years had gasoline engines. Steam made a short comeback during the war years in the larger patrol boats built for military use; but afterwards, with the exception of the 140-foot ALERT (Chapter XI) and the 114-foot commuter NAVETTE (page 123), the Herreshoff Mfg. Co. was out of the steam engine and boiler business for good.

In later life NGH reflected that he and JBH had been wrong in not delving into marine gasoline engines the way they had earlier with steam. Although the Herreshoffs did build an occasional gasoline engine, surely modern power-boating would have benefited from more of NGH's dedication. But by the gasoline engine era, the Herreshoffs had become known for race-winning sailing yachts, and the brisk demand for them pre-empted any attention that NGH might otherwise have focused on motorboats and gasoline engine development.

During the company's second twenty years, its sailboat-building business increased, somewhat at the expense of powerboats. Even though the Herreshoff Mfg. Co.'s powerboat production held at 80 percent of what it had been during the first two decades in terms of numbers of boats, the boats were generally smaller, and only about half exceeded 40 feet in overall length.

EUGENIA, a clipper-bowed steam yacht

HMCo #205, 1899
LOA 96'0"
Beam 14'0"
Draft 5'6"

THIS, THE THIRD of JBH's four EUGENIAS, is typical of the Herreshoff Mfg. Co.'s turn-of-the-century steam yachts. Later she carried the name EMPRESS.

On the day of this photo, EUGENIA's lines have been slacked, taking advantage of an offshore wind, and she has blown sufficiently far from the dock to allow a clear shot with the camera.

With her nearly level sheerline and steeply raked stern, EUGENIA lacks the grace found in the steam yachts of George Lennox Watson, but her appearance is neat and delicate by any measure. The bowed canopy just ahead of the stack protects the open-air steering station when it's not in use.

Looking aft at the
cockpit of EXPRESS,
the Herreshoff Mfg.
Co.'s first gasoline-
powered craft

HMCo #228, 1902
LOA 49'6"
Beam 10'10"
Draft 2'10"

WITH THE twentieth century came
gasoline engines which, although
noisy and smelly compared to steam, were
compact, nearly self-contained, and easy
to operate. Their advantages so outweighed
their disadvantages, especially as power
plants for the smaller launch-type boats,
that designers, builders, and owners shifted
nearly unanimously from steam to gasoline
within only a few years' time. Having enjoyed
astonishing success with steam engines,
NGH made the transition to internal combustion with considerable reluctance. This
may in part have been a consequence of
an accident in which NGH was badly
burned in a gasoline flare up while he and
son Sidney experimented with an early
gasoline engine.

EXPRESS was created to fill an order
from Morton F. Plant, who at about the
same time, commissioned the designing
and building of another first-of-type for
the Herreshoffs; the big steel schooner
INGOMAR, shown in Chapter VII. Other
Herreshoff motorboats were designed and
built as orders were received, but their
gasoline engines were generally purchased
from independent manufacturers, and
not, as had been the custom with steam
plants, manufactured by the Herreshoff
Mfg. Co. to NGH's designs.

Shown here, occupying center stage in
the cockpit of EXPRESS, is her 20-horsepower
Standard engine—completely open to view,
as were the earlier steam engines. There is
ample seating for passengers on tufted
cushions, and by standing on the box forward of the engine, the helmsman can see
over both passengers and cabin. These early
Standard engines were started with compressed air, and, for EXPRESS, compressed
air also operates the whistle.

This boat gets her name partly from her hull number and partly from her expected speed, 2 minutes and 40 seconds having been the record time for a trotting horse to travel a mile. She was built for the purpose of testing one of the few gasoline engines that NGH ever designed.

In 1906, then fitted with a Simplex engine, 240 made the run of over 300 miles from Bristol to Blue Hill, Maine, outside Cape Cod (the canal had yet to be built), cruising at around 14 miles an hour. NGH's son Griswold, then seventeen, his Bristol friend Carl Rockwell, and Rockwell's friend C. P. Thomas, whose family had just purchased 240 and had a summer place in Blue Hill, made the trip in this open boat with only melon-type canvas sprayhoods for shelter. In her later life, but still in Blue Hill, 240 was owned by Dr. Seth Milliken, who, at the time, also owned the big Herreshoff yawl THISTLE, shown in Chapter XI. Today, 240 is in the collection of the Museum, where she can be seen and studied, having been changed but little over the years.

The launch "240" on the Thames River, New London, Connecticut, June 29, 1905

HMCo #240, 1904
LOA 30'4"
LWL 30'0"
Beam 5'0"
Draft 1'5"

X.P.D.N.C., a high-speed gasoline launch, held aloft by hoisting slings

HMCo #245, 1904
LOA 45'0"
Beam 5'4"

Calooda (below) is a slightly smaller sister to the better-known racing launch x.p.d.n.c. ("Expediency," in five letters) but was equipped with a more powerful engine, a 140-horsepower Gnome (x.p.d.n.c.'s engine was 90 horsepower). Frank H. Croker owned x.p.d.n.c.; calooda belonged to Richard Croker, Jr., and Elbridge T. Gerry.

According to L. Francis Herreshoff, both boats were built from a half model that NGH had made nearly 30 years earlier for a proposed torpedo boat. L. Francis observed that this shape is a fast and seaworthy one and that the Navy's destroyers

would be about perfect if their hulls ever evolved to duplicate it.

The photo of calooda shows JBH sitting in the cockpit. Surrounding him are a glass windshield and a canvas canopy on pipe stanchions whose fore-and-aft battens allow it to be rolled up.

The photo of x.p.d.n.c. shows off her long and sleek hull. It also indicates a neat arrangement of hoisting slings that assure even distribution of weight and an always-level boat.

CALOODA, a near-sister to x.p.d.n.c., in Newport

HMCo #254, 1906
LOA 40'0"
Beam 5'4"

The high-speed
pleasure launch
SACHEM, built
originally as FAD

HMCo #292, 1913
LOA 40'0"
Beam 6'11"
Draft 2'3"

IN SACHEM, NGH's aesthetic sense can hardly be faulted, for this boat is striking in her beauty. Her sheer is set off by a varnished sheerstrake of the standard and uniquely handsome Herreshoff Mfg. Co. shape. Her low forward cabin comes to a point, which makes it both sleek to look at and easy to build. Both windshield and day-cabin roof can be removed, if desired; or, the canvas canopy can be rolled up and the windshield folded flat for real wind-in-the-face running.

Because SACHEM's eight-cylinder Sterling engine makes its presence known through vibration, noise, and smell, those on board can never enjoy the peaceful travel that was common to the earlier steamers. However, the enclosed after cabin does give the owner at least some isolation.

This photo was taken in 1928, some years after the boat was built, and motorboat styles are beginning to change, as indicated by the V-bottomed runabout astern of SACHEM.

MAGISTRATE, the
ultimate yacht tender

HMCo #301, 1916
LOA 63'3"
Beam 15'8"
Draft 4'9"

MAGISTRATE's neat, businesslike appearance gives her a special charm; she's halfway between a yacht and tugboat. Her afterdeck has been kept clear for use of the towing bitts. For the best visibility, there is an outside steering station just aft of the pilothouse, as well as the usual one inside.

MAGISTRATE was built for Harold Vanderbilt to serve as a tender/towboat for his 109-foot unpowered Herreshoff-built schooner VAGRANT; she has a gasoline engine—a six-cylinder Speedway, model L. In spite of being a workboat of sorts, it's evident from the photo that MAGISTRATE is maintained to yachting standards; even her bronze foredeck capstan shines from its daily polishing. (Note the unusually large, opening skylight just aft of it.)

Although the records show that MAGISTRATE was constructed during World War I (she was the very next boat after NGH's own HELIANTHUS II), this undated picture was taken later, after Marconi rigs (such as that carried by the 1928 yawl THISTLE, which shows in the background) became common.

LADY GAY, a
World War I–vintage
power cruiser

HMCo #305, 1917
LOA 58'0"
Beam 11'11"
Draft 3'0"

122

If a person could afford its initial cost, the space it took up, and the licensed operating crew, a steam power plant still had some distinct advantages over a gasoline or diesel engine. To J. P. Morgan, who commuted regularly from his Long Island estate to his Wall Street office in NAVETTE, cost came secondary to a quiet and relaxing ride—during which conversation, whether relating to business or pleasure, could be carried on in normal tones as the scenery flashed past. NAVETTE was an anachronism in her day, however, because by 1917 gasoline or diesel were the almost universally accepted power plants. That never bothered Morgan, who owned NAVETTE until 1935, never finding it necessary to replace her original Herreshoff steam engines.

In 1938, NAVETTE was purchased by E. C. Warren, tied up, and used as a floating home—at first near the New York World's Fair grounds, and later in LaBelle, Florida, on the Okeechobee waterway connecting West Palm Beach with Fort Myers, where, as recently as 1982, Warren's two daughters were still living aboard. NAVETTE's triple-expansion, Herreshoff-designed and -built steam engines were removed long ago. Paul Hammond purchased them in 1938, and one has recently found its way— via the Webb Institute of Naval Architecture —to the Herreshoff Marine Museum.

NAVETTE,
J. P. Morgan's
steam-powered
commuter

HMCo #303, 1917
LOA 114'2"
Beam 14'3"
Draft 3'7"

Lovely in her simplicity, LADY GAY shows the raised-deck powerboat hull form that NGH favored during this era and that he had already adopted for his own power cruiser, HELIANTHUS (shown in Chapter IX). Access to the step-down pilothouse is by two sliding companionways, one on each side. You're in this boat, not on it—that's why she enjoys such a low cabin profile. The cabin sole is even lower than that of the pilothouse and carries all the way aft through the small cockpit at the stern.

LADY GAY would end the long tradition of building only from NGH designs. By the time she was built, JBH had been dead for two years; NGH had sold his share of the Herreshoff Mfg. Co.; New York interests were in control; and the next boat, a 112-foot military patrol boat, would be the first in company history built to the plans of another designer. The end, however, was nowhere near. There were some great times ahead for the Herreshoff Mfg. Co., and many more fine boats to be created. The chronology continues with Chapter XI.

CHAPTER IX

Yachts of their Own

Pleasure Boats of the Herreshoff Brothers

J UST AS THERE IS not enough space within these pages to show all the boats that NGH and JBH built for others, space doesn't permit illustrating even all the boats owned by the brothers themselves. In his final years, NGH totaled his lifetime fleet to twenty-nine. JBH owned fewer, and thus far a reliable accounting of his personal boats has not turned up, but we know there were at least seven. This chapter offers a sampling of the brothers' yachts.

Unlike the heads of many business enterprises the size of the Herreshoff Mfg. Co., NGH and JBH were drawn to boatbuilding through their love of the product. As youths in the small waterfront town of Bristol, before there were the amusements that are commonplace today, the Herreshoff brothers took their pleasure from sailing and racing small boats. As grown-ups and successful businessmen, they still took the time to be out on the water in the finely built boats that their company turned out, and they found the thrill undiminished.

Following along in one of his power cruisers, NGH never ceased to enjoy watching his sailing craft, and those of rival designers, race together. And, from the time he was a teenager, he was never without a small, easily handled sailboat. Cruises and daysails with the family often took place as well.

We know less about the use that JBH gave his boats, most of which— at least in later years—were steam yachts. It appears that other interests, such as fine horses, carriages, and automobiles, might have diverted his attention, if not his devotion, from personal watercraft. But he, like his partner and brother NGH, was never without a boat of his own.

T HE STEAM YACHT ROAMER was built for NGH's family in 1902 while NGH's first wife, Clara, was still alive, and while the children were still at an age when cruising together was fun. (Clara died three years later in 1905.) According to L. Francis, one of the five sons, the summertime cruising was extensive, and during the eight or nine years ROAMER was owned by NGH, she was apt to be anywhere between New York City and Bar Harbor, Maine.

That the family enjoyed themselves is well documented in the snapshot albums compiled by Agnes M. Herreshoff, NGH's only daughter. ROAMER would accommodate seventeen, so besides the eight NGH family members, their cook (who was always brought along from home), and

ROAMER's crew of four, there were several berths available for friends.

ROAMER was kept year round alongside the breakwater/pier directly in front of Love Rocks, as the photo shows. When laid up for winter, she was protected by the beautifully fitted canvas cover shown on the following page. A specially designed, space-saving, steeple-type steam engine and a compact boiler, both designed by NGH and built by the Herreshoff Mfg. Co., originally powered ROAMER, and in their day comprised an extremely compact unit. In 1922, after ROAMER had changed hands and after two decades of internal-combustion-engine development, her original steam power plant was considered obsolete and ROAMER was repowered with gasoline.

ROAMER in front of NGH's Love Rocks home in Bristol, where he kept her (and his other personal boats) ready for immediate use

HMCo #215, 1902
LOA 93'9"
LWL 82'0"
Beam 17'6"
Draft 4'10"

A view from
Love Rocks,
February 22, 1912

A WESTERLY WIND pounds the wharf as ROAMER—laid up on the lee side under a fitted canvas cover—strains at her lines. Although Bristol's strategic location between Providence and Newport was good for business, its harbor in front of the Herreshoff Mfg. Co. lacked shelter from this kind of a blow.

The boathouse in the left foreground has been built since the previous photo was taken, and in it are kept COQUINA (Chapters V and X) and a dozen other Herreshoff family small craft.

ALTHOUGH perhaps not the most graceful of the turn-of-the-century clipper-bowed steam yachts, EUGENIA, the fourth and largest steam yacht of that name owned by JBH, was quite a piece of work. From the carved scrollwork at her bow to the curved glass and curtained windows of her deck-house, she was the mark of a successful businessman—and JBH was indeed that.

From his open-air steering station, JBH's personal skipper can move to either the port or starboard bridge wing for better visibility when docking. Yacht tenders abound on board; there are two on the canopy aft of the stack, and a third hanging in davits over the port quarter, where it can quickly be made ready for the crew's use. A saluting cannon is carried on EUGENIA's foredeck. (The turreted building visible at left is the United States Naval Reserve Armory, now the Bristol Harbormaster's office.)

Had there been an income tax back then, it's quite possible that EUGENIA would have been a justifiable write-off. JBH, having only one child, was without the family obligations of his brother Nat, and the guests aboard his yachts were apt to be potential customers. And who among these could fail to marvel at the workmanship, comfort, and other virtues of this well-kept yacht, and promptly order a Herreshoff yacht for himself?

JBH's steam yacht
EUGENIA

HMCo #224, 1902
LOA 112'0"
LWL 91'6"
Beam 18'6"
Draft 5'10"

J. B. Herreshoff and friends aboard steam yacht EUGENIA

AS PRESIDENT and senior partner of the Herreshoff Mfg. Co., JBH was an extremely competent businessman and boatbuilder. During the work week, he looked after the running of the office, traveled on company business, solicited yacht orders, and made all purchases of materials. He familiarized himself with the progress of construction and repair in the shop and earned the respect of the employees. After one of JBH's daily tours of inspection, a worker pronounced, "Mr. John ain't blind, he's only foolin'."

Even though the demands of his business responsibilities were great, JBH found time for recreation and social life aboard his steam yachts. He is pictured here enjoying the companionship of his friends aboard EUGENIA, one of four steam yachts all named after his second wife, Eugenia Tams Tucker (1857–1940), whom he married in 1892.

The fast steam launch SWIFTSURE, running at speed (about 25 m.p.h.) in Newport Harbor in the early 1900s

HMCo #243, 1904
LOA 51'8"
LWL 50'0"
Beam 6'1"
Draft 2'4"

DURING HER four years as a steamer (she was converted to gasoline in 1908), SWIFTSURE raced against the gasoline-powered speedboats VINGT-ET-UN and STANDARD, but without great success. Even if the races themselves were inconclusive, there was no doubt as to which form of propulsion would be the winner in terms of public acceptance. At the time of SWIFTSURE's debut, steam was on its way out; and an avalanche of new gasoline (and soon diesel) engines were coming in.

NGH is at the helm in this photo (dressed in oilskins, in spite of the wave-deflecting nature of SWIFTSURE's lapstrake hull), calling aft for more steam so he can squeak out another knot or two. Because of his background as designer of some of the very fastest steam yachts afloat, NGH

wanted SWIFTSURE to triumph, but VINGT-ET-UN, out of sight to the right, won this race.

L. Francis Herreshoff wrote of a trip he took aboard SWIFTSURE at the age of fourteen: "I remember one run I had in her between Newport and Bristol in a fresh northerly breeze. She may have been going 24 or 25 miles an hour and was running almost noiselessly; it was a run to be remembered."

L. Francis doubtless recalled the boat as well as the run when, some forty years later, he designed the 47-foot fast launch PIQUANT, whose narrow beam and peaked stern were reminiscent of SWIFTSURE. One of the chief virtues of both boats was that they could maintain good speed in rough water. (A sister of PIQUANT, named STILETTO, is in the Museum's boat collection.)

WHILE THIS photo has little relevance to this chapter's theme, it has been included simply for what it conveys. NGH's remarkable independence is obvious as he stands alone, carefully observing some aspect of a design. Chances are the object of his attention is RESOLUTE as she prepares for the 1920 America's Cup contest. The Cup races were given extensive coverage in the newspapers of the day, and the yachtsmen and designers connected with the event were national celebrities. It must have been obvious to NGH as he stood in the aft cockpit of RESOLUTE's tender that he was under the scrutiny of the photographer's lens. Despite this attention, he seems to be concentrating on the practical aspects of his role in preparing his last Cup design for racing.

The double-cockpit launch is believed to be the one that is in Mystic Seaport's watercraft collection, having served for many years at the Seawanhaka Corinthian Yacht Club under the name RESOLUTE. In this photo, for reasons not known, the boat shows a good deal of wear on her guards and topsides. EMERALD, a sister of this launch, is now at the Herreshoff Marine Museum. Both launches have been extensively and beautifully restored.

NGH aboard
RESOLUTE's tender,
1920

RESOLUTE
HMCo #330–334, 1917
LOA 26'2"
LWL 24'1"
Beam 6'6"
Draft 2'1"

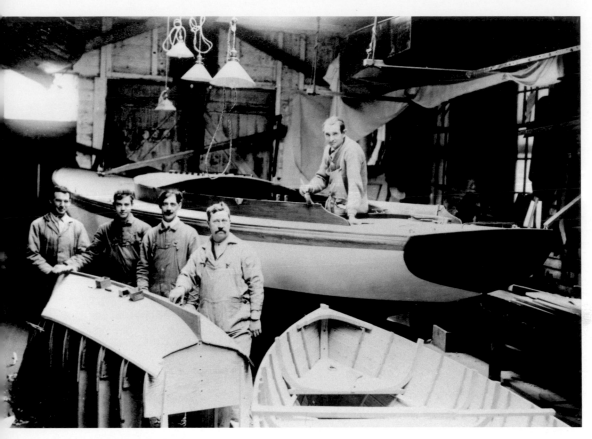

ALERION (the third of that name) and the men who built her: (left to right) Ernest Alder, Charles Sylvester, Henry Vincent, James Clarkson, and Willard Kenny, 1913

ALERION's predecessor, OLEANDER, sailing on Ferry Reach in Bermuda, 1911 or 1912

OLEANDER
HMCo #710, 1911
LOA 23'7"
LWL 20'0"
Beam 6'10"
Draft (board raised) 1'9"

LIKE THE steam yacht STILETTO and the revolutionary racing yacht GLORIANA, this boat, the third of NGH's ALERIONS, was a signal design. Although she was not built for racing and left behind no records of outstanding performance, as did STILETTO and GLORIANA, she was very fast. What made her so admired was her beautiful shape —especially that of her hollow bow, which NGH continued to utilize in her Herreshoff-built successors, the Buzzards Bay 12½-footers, the Newport 29s, and the Buzzards Bay 25s. These boats, shown in Chapter VI, all had short but graceful overhangs, high bows and low sterns with a beautiful sheerline connecting them, and generous beam at the deck. Waterline beam was considerably less. ALERION (the name means "young eagle") has been preserved and can be seen at Mystic Seaport, looking every bit as good now as she did when these photos were taken.

ALERION was built especially for Bermuda, a place that gave NGH a much-needed winter respite. Having a boat was, for him, mandatory, no matter where he was. His 1911 boat OLEANDER (below left) proved to be too small and wet for Bermuda waters, so he had ALERION built for the following season, possibly shaping her after an especially attractive Bermuda sailing dinghy named CONTEST. NGH stayed at Tuckers Town on Castle Harbour, near the east end of the island, where the sailing photo (right) was taken.

ALERION was kept in Bermuda for nearly a decade, stored summers in a rented boathouse, and sailed winters by NGH until he shipped her to New York in 1920. L. Francis sailed the boat from New York to Bristol, and his account of this wild trip home has been published on several occasions, most recently in the book *An L. Francis Herreshoff Reader*. For sailing in Bristol, NGH converted ALERION's gaff rig to a sliding gunter; he continued to use the boat each summer until he sold her to family friend and neighbor Carl Rockwell, about 1928.

A wide-angle view of ALERION off Tuckers Town in Bermuda, about 1914

As to OLEANDER, NGH shipped her back to Bristol after using her only one winter (1911–1912) in Bermuda, and soon sold her to Philip Sawyer. Sawyer, in a sensitive and informative recounting of his subsequent encounters with NGH (*Yachting*, February 1955), tells of racing OLEANDER with NGH at the helm. "He sat erect on the narrow seat, hardly leaning against the straight coaming. He wore, as usual, a gray, nondescript suit, a shirt with a narrow standing collar, a black tie, and one of his formless felt hats. My wife sat just behind him, and Herreshoff, taking a piece of canvas about a foot square out of his pocket, laid it on his windward shoulder to protect him from spray.... The only help that Nat ever asked of me was to get the sheet in so tight that the sail was flat as a board going to windward." (They won the race that day.)

Even more revealing than this photo are the Herreshoff Mfg. Co. drawings of OLEANDER, which indicate her low and narrow bow—two features that NGH set about to correct in her successor, ALERION and even more so in the subsequent SADIE, successor to ALERION

NGH's new sloop ALERION being weighed by steelyard, spring 1913

ALERION
HMCo #718, 1913
LOA 26'0"
LWL 21'9"
Beam 7'7"
Draft (board raised) 2'6"

NGH owned three quite-similar power cruisers in succession after selling the big family steam yacht ROAMER. All were named HELIANTHUS, another name for "sunflower."

This first HELIANTHUS, the prettiest of the three, is shown here with a full-length canvas awning, which, back in the days of steam yachts, had been common in order to shield passengers from smokestack soot. On the gas-powered HELIANTHUS I, it may, at first glance, seem to be an anachronism—at least, until the benefits of shade in hot weather are considered.

HELIANTHUS I was NGH's first personal yacht powered by gasoline, designed while he was in Bermuda the winter of 1911–1912. She was small enough not to require a paid crew, and NGH used her for coastal cruising until World War I, when she was purchased by the Navy and converted for coastal patrol.

However, the noise, smell, vibration, and running cost of gasoline engines, measured against a fondness for and understanding of steam power, as well as a lifetime of experience with it, made the idea of steam still practical in NGH's mind. After a 1918–1919 cruise to Florida in the second HELIANTHUS, a steel-framed 65-footer built during the war years, he pulled out her gasoline engine and replaced it with a steam power plant. There was a suitable unused engine lying around the shop, a new boiler was built to NGH's design, Stanley Steamer controls were fitted and HELIANTHUS II sailed south again during 1919–1920 in what was to be NGH's last use of steam power. HELIANTHUS II was sold in 1920.

NGH reverted again to gasoline in HELIANTHUS III, of 1921, which he took south to Coconut Grove, Florida, winters between 1921 and 1924.

NGH aboard
HELIANTHUS I at
the Harvard–Yale
races, 1916

HELIANTHUS I,
successor to ROAMER,
about 1915

HMCo #288, 1912
LOA 64'0"
LWL 60'9"
Beam 13'6"
Draft 4'0"

ON MORNINGS when Bristol Harbor was calm, Captain Nat tested hull models by using a narrow portable platform suspended at the bow of HELIANTHUS. A bridle mechanism allowed him to test a newly developed hull model against another of known performance. The narrow platform, with the towing models on either side, enabled him to observe his test models carefully, at close range. Hip boots helped keep his legs and feet dry (NGH was rheumatic).

NGH observing towing models, October 15, 1915

Ann Roebuck Herreshoff (1873–1950) at Love Rocks in 1915

THIS FAMILY-ALBUM snapshot pictures the second Mrs. Nathanael G. Herreshoff at about the time of her marriage to Captain Nat; she was then forty-two years of age.

Ann Roebuck, an Englishwoman, came to Bristol to nurse NGH's first wife, Clara, in her final illness in the early years of the twentieth century. Ten years after Clara's death in 1905, Ann and NGH were married, in an informal service on October 8, 1915, in the chantry of St. Michael's Episcopal Church in Bristol. After a brief reception at Love Rocks, the sixty-seven-year-old designer and his bride left on a wedding trip aboard HELIANTHUS I.

Mrs. Herreshoff resided at Love Rocks until her death in 1950. After NGH's death in 1938, she lived with his daughter, Agnes, and a live-in maid. Mrs. Herreshoff was active in a number of Bristol civic organizations, especially the Bristol District Nursing Association. Clarence Herreshoff attributed his father's long life to the fine care given him by Ann Roebuck Herreshoff and Agnes.

Both Herreshoff brothers had new yachts in 1912 (NGH's was HELIANTHUS I, shown on page 132). This would be JBH's last bit of yachting, however, He died three years later at the age of seventy-four.

Here, JBH is on the foredeck of DIANTHUS, in the group's center. The crew must have just finished the morning cleanup: the vanished, paneled cabinsides glisten, and the boarding mats hang over the handrail, drying. Unlike JBH's earlier yachts, DIANTHUS runs on gasoline rather than on steam; thus, there is no need for a smokestack. The burble at the waterline is probably the exhaust from one of her two six-cylinder "Premier" gas engines. How the tender is put overboard with no boat davits is a mystery, but there is the usual davit forward for anchor handling—its tackle protected by a canvas sleeve.

THIS STUDIO portrait of JBH, made at the Koshiba Studio in Providence, Rhode Island, was the last photo taken of the president of the Herreshoff Mfg. Co.

His death, of acute dilation of the heart, on July 20, 1915, was a severe loss to the business. Perhaps the greatest tribute to JBH's ability to manage the yacht-building business came from his brother: "Not having or caring for business ability and not finding anyone that appeared fit and capable to take John's place to manage the business end of the company," wrote NGH in 1934, "I reluctantly consented to sell the Herreshoff Mfg. Co., and 1917 saw the end of what had been a wonderfully successful enterprise."

Although after 1917 the Herreshoff Mfg. Co. may have been less successful in a purely business sense, its boats continued to be innovative and its output high. The story of the Herreshoff Mfg. Co.'s final phase begins with Chapter XI.

John Brown Herreshoff, about 1914

CHAPTER X

Family

The Children of NGH and JBH

Tｈｅｒｅ ｃａｎ ｂｅ little doubt that both Herreshoff brothers derived great satisfaction and pride from the business they had created. Certainly the company occupied most of their waking hours, and about JBH could be said the same as L. Francis Herreshoff wrote about his father, NGH—that "he was altogether too busy to give his family much time." We know, however, that Katie, the only child of the divorced JBH, was very close to her father when she was a girl and frequently accompanied JBH on extended trips, both within the United States and abroad. For his part, L. Francis readily conceded (in *Capt. Nat Herreshoff: The Wizard of Bristol*) that NGH was "very kind to his children and saw that they all had many things to play with. He made model yachts for the older ones, and had a workshop for them with all sorts of good tools, and as they grew up, each child had his boat and bicycle, later to be replaced by motorcycles and automobiles."

Indeed, Katie Herreshoff and her younger first cousins had the good fortune to grow up at a time and in a place that seem, at least in hindsight, almost idyllic. Despite the light industry that the Herreshoff Mfg. Co. helped bring to Bristol, it never altogether lost its small-town, even agrarian character. And the Herreshoffs were not merely economically secure; they occupied a primary position in the social and intellectual life of the region.

For the Herreshoff children, this meant summers at play in some of the loveliest farming country in southern New England, access to first-class schooling and medical attention, opportunity for travel, and acquaintance with the rich and powerful customers who were the source of so much of the Herreshoff Mfg. Co.'s prosperity. It meant close and regular contact with relatives and friends from Providence, Boston, New York. Above all, for this boat-centered family, it meant an all but amphibious upbringing, with Narragansett Bay, Rhode Island Sound, and the broad Atlantic no farther away than the skill and determination of a young Herreshoff to sail there.

That the children of JBH and NGH found much to occupy their imagination and energy, the following photographs delightfully indicate. That JBH and NGH did find the time to sail, picnic, and cruise with them is also clear. It may even have been one of these photographs that led L. Francis Herreshoff to recall (in "Yachting in the 1900s," from *An L. Francis Herreshoff Reader*): "My first command was a 9-foot sailing skiff, which, like most of my clothes, had been handed down to me from an older brother who had outgrown her, but she was a dear little ship and had been designed by the same man who had designed the cup defender COLUMBIA. And if J. P. Morgan was proud to be part owner of COLUMBIA, I am sure I was as proud to be the full owner of that skiff. I remember very well the first day I sailed her alone. It was under the lee of a very small island where the water was shallow, and as I sailed back and forth over the eelgrass, her speed seemed to me to be terrific, and I have never had such a thrill since."

GEM, a finely but sturdily constructed rowing dinghy, was built in 1885 by the Herreshoff Mfg. Co. JBH presented the boat to his daughter, Katie, on her fifteenth birthday. Over the years, Katie took countless photographs of the Herreshoff works from GEM, some of which are reproduced in this book.

GEM has three rowing positions, a stern backrest with name carved in Old English letters, a boathook, oars and oarlocks, and rudder with yoke. Carefully maintained and owned by Katie until her death in 1954, this beautiful example of the Herreshoff Mfg. Co.'s early production has survived in its original condition.

GEM was given to the Museum in 1986 by Katie's daughter, Mrs. Katherine Herreshoff DeWolf Pendlebury. The boat is the oldest dinghy in the Museum's collection.

Katherine Kilton
Herreshoff rowing
GEM, August 22, 1895

LOA 12'0"
Beam 3'9"

Katherine Kilton
Herreshoff
(1871–1954),
JBH's only child,
in 1889

K ATIE WAS a junior at Bristol High
School in 1886–1887, and a surviving
report card from December 17, 1886, gives
her rank as eighth in a class of twenty-six.
(She excelled in deportment with a 98.5
average, and did least well in composition,
in which she averaged 76.7.) The report
card is signed by JBH, suggesting that Katie
was then living with him rather than with
her (separated) mother, Sarah ("Sadie") L.
Herreshoff, who had signed her report card
for 1885.

Although not a Catholic, Katie finished
her formal schooling at the Elmhurst Sacred
Heart Convent in Providence.

In 1889, Katie and JBH traveled to
San Francisco, where JBH investigated the
feasibility of constructing torpedo boats for
the defense of San Francisco in the Samoan
crisis. This portrait was taken in 1889 in
Denver, Colorado, probably on this trip. In
succeeding decades, Katie and her camera
were frequent observers of the Herreshoff
scene. Her photographs display her inti-
mate understanding of the company, its
work force, and the boats it built. They are
a tribute, as well, to her devotion to the
memory of her father, JBH, who, sightless
himself, had helped teach her how to "see."

Katie married and had two daughters,
Katherine Herreshoff DeWolf (Pendlebury)
and Louise Henry DeWolf.

The children of
Clara and Nathanael
G. Herreshoff,
about 1900

THIS TURN-OF-THE-CENTURY
photograph is embossed with the logo
of the Anderstrom Photography Studio,
Church Street, Bristol, Rhode Island.
Left to right, the Herreshoff children are:
Agnes Müller Herreshoff, Clarence DeWolf
Herreshoff, A. Sidney DeWolf Herreshoff,
Nathanael G. Herreshoff, Jr., L. Francis
Herreshoff, and A. Griswold Herreshoff.

Agnes Herreshoff (1884–1965) was a
knowledgeable gardener, a respected student
of local history, and an avid photographer.
She had a lifelong passion for family geneal-
ogy and held memberships in the Society
of Mayflower Descendants, the Daughters
of the American Revolution, and the Rhode
Island and Bristol Historical Societies.
"Miss Agnes" (she never married) enjoyed
guiding and assisting family members and
friends in genealogical research. During the

late 1930s, her knowledge of Bristol's past
was invaluable in organizing the family
records of the Bristol Historical Society.

Sidney Herreshoff (1886–1977) attended
M.I.T. and was employed for most of his
working life at the Herreshoff Mfg. Co.
When the Haffenreffer family purchased
the company in 1924, "Mr. Sid" became the
chief designer and engineer, and was responsible for a number of successful designs,
especially the Fishers Island 31-Class sloops.
After the shop closed in 1946, Sidney
did design work for a number of yacht-
building concerns. In 1971, he and his wife,
Rebecca Chase Herreshoff, founded the
Herreshoff Marine Museum. In 1977,
the Museum was moved to quarters on
Burnside Street, and its large exhibit room
was named in his honor. Sidney and his
wife Becky had two sons, Nathanael G.
Herreshoff III and Halsey C. Herreshoff.

Nathanael G. Herreshoff, Jr. (1888–1926)
was employed at the Herreshoff Mfg. Co.
and worked at a variety of jobs involving
the electrical and mechanical aspects of
yacht building. He had a great interest in
photography, and NGH allowed him to use
a considerable portion of one of the shop
buildings behind Burnside Street as a photography lab, where he processed his own
film. From about 1910 to 1926, he chroni-
cled the work at the shop with his photographs. Nat, Jr., married Helen Warren;
their two daughters were named Clara and
Natalie, carrying on the tradition of family
names. He died of pneumonia in 1926.

(Brief biographies of Clarence,
Griswold, and L. Francis Herreshoff follow
on the next page.)

"THE FARM," an estate of about 150 acres, on Griswold Avenue in Bristol, had been inherited by Clara Herreshoff from her father, Algernon Sidney DeWolf. The farmhouse had been built by Mrs. Herreshoff's great-grandfather, John DeWolf, in 1798. It became a summer retreat for the Herreshoffs, and here the children sailed model boats on the pond and explored the woodlands that stretched to Mount Hope Bay. During their summer sojourns at "The Farm," NGH commuted to the shop on his bicycle.

In this photo, left to right, are Clarence DeWolf Herreshoff, A. Griswold Herreshoff, and L. Francis Herreshoff. All three were to become designers.

Clarence Herreshoff (1895–1983), a marine engineer, lived in Washington, D.C., where he was employed by the U.S. Navy Bureau of Ships. He was married briefly; there were no children. Clarence sailed and rowed for recreation most of his life, and undertook several canoe trips over considerable distances. His chief sports interest was tennis, of which he played a remarkably good game well past his mid-eighties. He was also an avid skater into advanced age.

Griswold Herreshoff (1889–1986) became an innovative automotive designer, and he played an important role in the design and development of the Fifth Avenue bus, the famous Mack "Bulldog," and the 1920 Hermes automobile. He was associated for most of his career with the Chrysler Corporation, where he was a moving force behind the advanced "Air-Flow" models of the mid-1930s. Griswold and his wife, Henrietta, had no children.

L. Francis Herreshoff (1890–1972) was originally designated by NGH to run "The Farm" and was sent to Rhode Island State College (now the University of Rhode Island) to study agriculture. After quitting the farm to take a commission in the U.S. Navy in World War I, however, he set off on his own to learn the fundamentals of yacht construction and design. He worked for W. Starling Burgess between 1919 and 1925, then opened his own yacht design business in Marblehead, Massachusetts, in 1926. In addition to his celebrated design work, he wrote some half-dozen influential and important books about yachting history and design and the Herreshoff tradition, including the definitive biography of his father, Captain Nat. L. Francis never married.

SUMMER FUN included cruising on the family steam yacht as well as playing along the Bristol shoreline. For the family album, Agnes Herreshoff photographed her brother Francis on a Block Island beach wearing a necklace of seaweed. The Herreshoffs had put into Block Island during an extended family cruise aboard ROAMER in the summer of 1904.

Three of NGH's sons on the front lawn of "The Farm" in the late 1890s

L. Francis Herreshoff at Block Island, August 7, 1904

LOVE ROCKS was a wonderful place in winter as well as summer for growing sons to enjoy boating and other sports. The Herreshoff boys were fond of skating and iceboating, and Sidney Herreshoff was, for many years, president of the Bristol Skating Club. As late as the 1950s, "Mr. Sid" would skate on "Fessor's Pond," near the family farm. His younger brother Clarence won a number of medals in figure-skating competition in Washington, D.C., in the 1930s.

This family album snapshot, taken from the back lawn of Love Rocks, offers a partial view of Captain Nat's private dock and boathouse. In the upper left is Walkers Island. (Its trees would be destroyed in the hurricanes of 1938 and 1954.)

Although the Northeastern climate has been warmer since, Bristol Harbor was often frozen over in the bitter winters of the first two decades of the twentieth century. During these hard freezes, many Bristolians skated to Hog and Prudence Islands, and, during the particularly cold winter of 1917–1918, a Revolutionary War barracks was moved over the frozen harbor from Prudence Island to Bristol by a team of oxen.

LIVING IN a waterfront home and having access to the Herreshoff shops and an inventive father, NGH's children surely had some wonderful times together in Bristol.

L. Francis was a teen-ager when he owned this iceboat. Its steam-bent, pointed coaming, jewel-like Herreshoff Mfg. Co. hardware, and fully battened lateen sail plan show the sophistication one would expect in a Herreshoff creation—although which member of the family was responsible for the design and construction has not been recorded.

L. Francis Herreshoff's iceboat GREY GULL at Love Rocks, February 22, 1906

NGH's sons skating on Bristol Harbor, March 3, 1907

THE NOVARA, shown here in a photograph taken at the site of what is now 125 Hope Street, Bristol, on October 21, 1916, was built earlier in the year in the East Construction Shop. Sid Herreshoff had two aims in his design—light weight and exceptional acceleration. By minimizing wind resistance and concentrating on road balance, he expected high speed. The sales brochure guaranteed: "50 miles per hour on second gear and over 70 miles per hour on high gear." At approximately 1,500 pounds on a 110-inch wheelbase, it offered "25 to 32 miles per gallon of gasoline" and "up to 10,000 miles per tire at usual road speeds"—a good claim in those days of notoriously poor casings.

1916 Novara automobile, designed and built by Sidney Herreshoff

Sid Herreshoff formed a partnership with Gorham N. Thurber, who was associated with Isotta Fraschini Motors in New York. The price was set at $2,750 f.o.b. Bristol. A Ford runabout was then selling for about $345 f.o.b. Detroit, so a Novara customer would be paying a good deal for the car's "unexcelled comfort, extraordinary acceleration, and responsiveness."

The Herreshoff boatbuilding skill was evident in the body, which was double-planked with ⁵⁄₃₂-inch cedar as the inner layer and ⁵⁄₃₂-inch mahogany as the outer, fastened to ⅝-inch-square oak ribs. Hardware and fastenings were brass or copper. The body side sills were bolted to a Herreshoff-made nickel-steel frame. The exterior finish was natural mahogany with many coats of the best spar varnish. The engine was a special high-speed, four-cylinder, overhead-valve design by Scripps–Booth. The axles, transmission, and steering gear were also by Scripps–Booth. The electrical system was by Bosch.

The Novara's exceptional road balance was secured by a low center of gravity and a springing system which employed semi-elliptics and a full cantilever design in the rear. Mudguards of hammered steel and a gracefully curved windshield could be fitted in five minutes for road driving. Houk wire wheels were to be standard equipment. The radiator shell and head lamp rims were polished copper, and all the other body parts were painted white. A single door on the passenger side gave access to both driver and passenger.

This single prototype of the Novara was produced as a 1917 model, but the young men for whom the car was intended were heading "over there" in World War I. The car was never put into production, much to the relief of NGH, who had consistently voiced his disapproval of the project. Sidney and others drove this, the only Novara, around town for a few years. It eventually found its way to the dirt-track racing circuit and was wrecked about 1922.

Francis Herreshoff became interested in automobiles as a teenager and owned and drove fine cars throughout his life. He poses here with an unidentified passenger in a small runabout or roadster of 1914 vintage.

A sporty model, this two-seater is equipped with wire wheels, acetylene gas headlamps, and a folding windshield. The top, folded and covered with a boot, rests on the spare tire and wheel. A small door located behind the passenger door covers a compartment used for carrying a golf bag or sporting equipment. A gas cap forward of the windshield locates the cowl-mounted gasoline tank which provided gravity flow to the carburetor.

Light runabouts of this type, relatively low in price, were popular with young drivers in the days just before World War I.

BUILT FOR NGH in 1889 as an easy-to-get-underway daysailer (see Chapter V for her particulars), COQUINA stayed with the Herreshoffs until the 1938 hurricane destroyed her. She is shown here out for a Sunday sail, and it is quite likely that she carries the makings of a picnic lunch for NGH and his lady guests.

COQUINA steers with a rope instead of a tiller; the rope is connected to the rudder blade by means of small tackles from the corners of the transom. A strut keeps the mizzen boom from lifting, which it would tend to do given the inward lead of the sheet.

NGH had her built by Charles Davis, an unusually gifted Herreshoff Mfg. Co. boatbuilder who, according to NGH, "was noted for his fine and strong work and the best workman in our shops at the time." Davis did a beautiful job on COQUINA, holding faithfully to her delicate scantlings: 5⁄16-inch lapstrake cedar planking, 11⁄16-inch square steam-bent frames, a 1⁄8-inch brass centerboard, and a molded mahogany sheerstrake finished bright. Stripped, the hull weighed only 275 pounds.

COQUINA had lifting eyes forward and aft and was kept hoisted on davits in NGH's Love Rocks boathouse, ready for immediate use. NGH claimed she was so easily rigged that he could push off from a lee shore and have her sailing before she drifted back in and touched the bottom again. She had several rig options: two rig sizes (183 square feet or 131 square feet) and three possible mast locations. Under the stern deck was a dry compartment for stowing clothing, food, and gear.

COQUINA was the first boat L. Francis Herreshoff remembered sailing in, at age five. Until about 1901, when NGH designed the so-called Columbia-model tender, all Herreshoff tenders were shaped pretty much like COQUINA, with plumb stems and raking transoms.

THERE ARE numerous snapshots in the Herreshoff family albums of picnics and clambakes on the shores of Narragansett Bay. Captain Nat clearly enjoyed these occasions. Here (seated third from left in the front row) he is smiling and gesturing at the photographer, who evidently clicked the shutter before everyone was ready. Ann R. Herreshoff is seated behind her husband and has been caught arranging her hair. The rather formal attire of the picnickers was fashionable for the period. Seated at the far right is Captain Nat's son Sidney. Sidney's taste in clothing changed little in his lifetime. He always favored snap-brim caps, four-in-hand ties, and fully-buttoned jackets. He gave up high celluloid collars in the late 1920s, but was rarely seen without a tie.

The Herreshoff and Brown families enjoying a Prudence Island picnic, September 14, 1918

PART THREE

Continuing the Legend

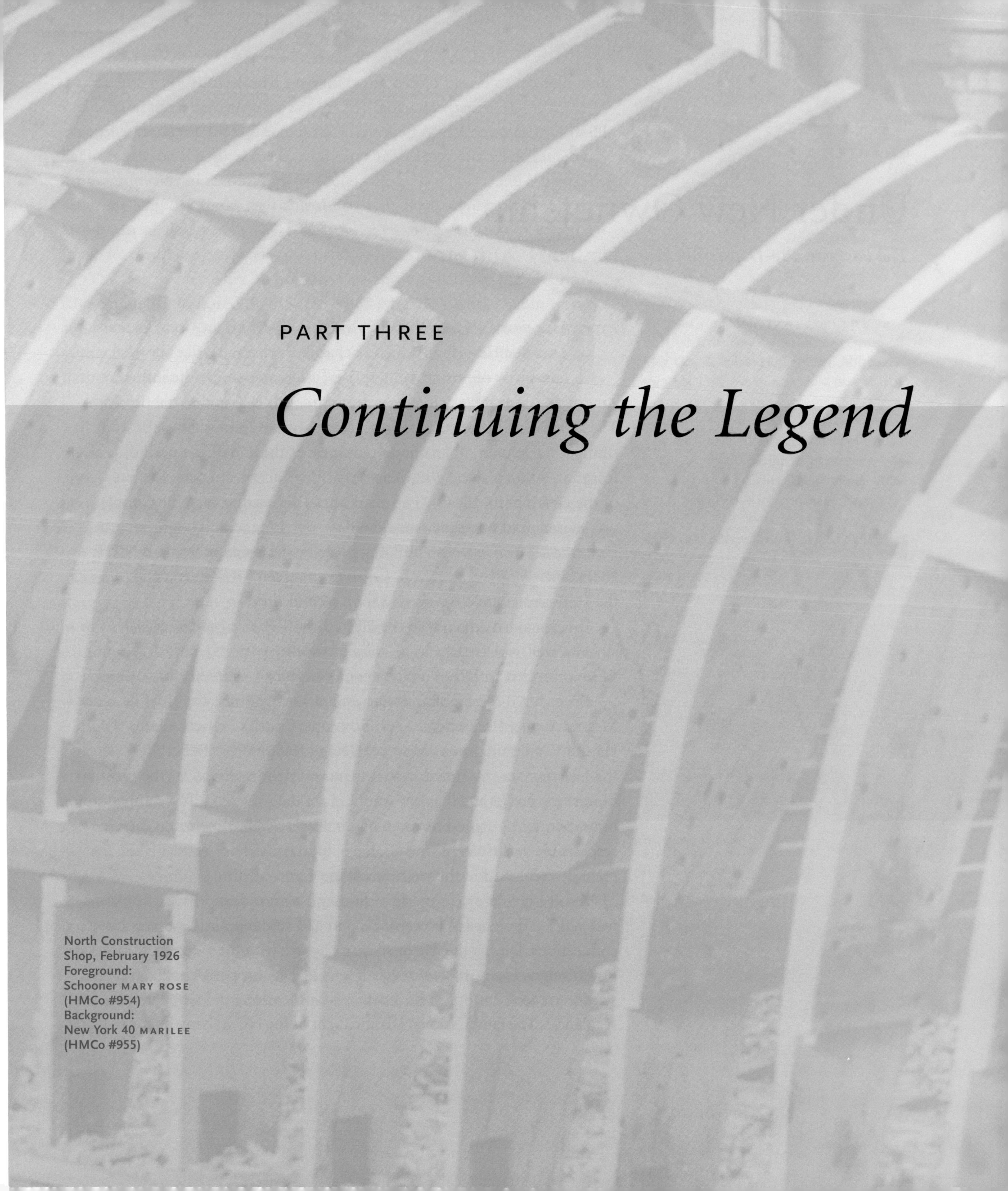

North Construction Shop, February 1926
Foreground:
Schooner MARY ROSE (HMCo #954)
Background:
New York 40 MARILEE (HMCo #955)

in like an angel sent from heaven and, acting through longtime Herreshoff employee Tom Brightman, bid successfully for the key offerings, thus keeping the Herreshoff Mfg. Co. intact. More important, he and his sons, Carl W. Haffenreffer and Rudolf F. Haffenreffer III, rebuilt the work force, improved the facility, and obtained enough work to keep the Herreshoff Mfg. Co. in business for another twenty years. As the boats at the end of this chapter clearly indicate, the Haffenreffers got off to a great start.

A privately funded World War I patrol boat

HMCo #310 class
1917
LOA 62'4"
LWL 61'0"
Beam 11'0"
Draft 3'6"

Nine of these 62-foot patrol boats were built by the Herreshoff Mfg. Co. for the training of World War I Naval Reserve volunteers, having been ordered and paid for as a patriotic gesture by members of the Eastern Yacht Club of Marblehead, Massachusetts. (The EYC clubhouse, having been converted early in the war as a barracks, served as an operational base for these patrol boats.) Their cost was $19,000 each. They were twin-screw vessels, powered by two eight-cylinder Sterling engines. These craft, as the photo shows, each carried a standard, Herreshoff-built Columbia-model tender—a somewhat delicate lifeboat for wartime use.

Since 1902, NGH had lived for weeks at a time aboard his own power cruisers, ROAMER and HELIANTHUS I and II, on extended coastal trips, and by 1919 he had made one or two runs to Florida and back aboard his second HELIANTHUS. So there could be no doubt about his ability, through firsthand experience, to design a thoroughly practical houseboat. SUNFLOWER is such a craft—practical, yet elegant (notice the curved glass in the forward corners of her rounded deckhouse), in true Herreshoff tradition. Power is provided by two six-cylinder Standard gasoline engines. In the background, a New York 50-Class sloop, not yet rigged, lies at her mooring.

The houseboat SUNFLOWER backing away from the dock

HMCo #369, 1919
LOA 72'0"
LWL 70'0"
Beam 17'0"
Draft 4'4"

The first S-boat, in
the North Dock Slip,
March 17, 1920

HMCo #828 class
1919
LOA 27'6"
LWL 20'6"
Beam 7'0"
Draft 4'9"

Marconi rigs made their appearance soon after World War I, and the S-Class was one of the very first one-designs for which the Marconi rig was originally specified. NGH gave the S-boat mast a gentle curve aft, and that had made the sail plan distinctive even to this day. He called for ample sail area and a short keel as well, so the boats are spirited sailers, able to turn on the proverbial dime.

Some two dozen S-boats had been built by 1924, when the Herreshoff Mfg. Co. was auctioned, and the Haffenreffers, as new owners, continued production. In all, during the twenty years S-boats were in production, about eighty-five were built, and as of this writing Narragansett Bay, in Rhode Island, and Sorrento, Maine, still have active fleets in which S-boats regularly race.

Vestigial remains of the Herreshoff Mfg. Co. war effort show here in the background: the low, brick building at the right provided officers' quarters, and the larger one at the left is where pontoons were built.

ALTHOUGH this photograph is from a period later than that covered by this chapter, it serves to show the S-boat's distinctive profile as well as a heavy-weather rig option.

DILEMMA was one of the fourteen so-called #996 class of S-boats built as a group between 1926 and 1928; she was the fifty-sixth S-boat built by the Herreshoff Mfg. Co. She had teak trim, rather than the standard oak and mahogany (teak trim was an option and added an extra $100 to the $4,100 selling price), and she also was ordered with special storm sails.

Rather than risk stretching his cotton racing sails by reefing them, DILEMMA's owner has had her fitted with a storm trysail and a spitfire jib, sewn from heavy canvas and vertically seamed for strength. With their clews lashed to boom and jib club, these sails can be trimmed with the regular sheets. DILEMMA, true to a class known for its light-weather speed, slips along well in spite of these smaller-than-normal, battenless sails.

Heavy-weather sails on the S-boat DILEMMA (HMCo #1022), 1928

THE PRESENCE of yard workers on board ALERT indicates that this is a builder's trial. Whoever is in the boiler room knows his business, because ALERT is showing not even a wisp of smoke.

Built from a design by the talented A. Loring Swasey, who had been connected with the Herreshoff Mfg. Co. as a designer and administrator during the war years, ALERT reflects the style of recent naval craft. She has a steel hull, and each of her two propellers is powered by a Herreshoff triple-expansion steam engine. ALERT was the Herreshoff Mfg. Co.'s last steam-powered vessel. She was built for Charles A. Stone (of the Boston-based engineering firm Stone and Webster) and sold for $139,000. ALERT was a big job for the Herreshoff Mfg. Co. in the lean years following the war. Her building coincided with the Herreshoff Mfg. Co.'s other big job that season, RESOLUTE's recommissioning for the 1920 America's Cup races.

In the foreground is a varnished, lapstrake, Herreshoff-built Columbia-model tender of the type furnished as part of every major yacht's outfit.

The new steam yacht ALERT heading down the bay

HMCo #374, 1920
LOA 140'0"
LWL 138'8"
Beam 17'3"
Draft 6'4"

One of the two boilers for the steam yacht ALERT, in the Boiler Shop, March 31, 1920

ALERT's two boilers are of the three-drum type where the steam rises (as it is produced in the tubes) to the upper drum, while sediment and other impurities settle to one of the so-called "mud drums" at the bottom. A coal fire located in the space between the tube banks furnishes the heat.

The Herreshoff Boiler Shop connected directly with the Machine Shop, thus placing these key and related trades near each other. The Boiler Shop was without a second floor and measured 25 feet to the eaves. It could accommodate boilers of considerable size.

In the foreground, a full-length stave for a very sizable hollow wooden spar (possibly for the Cup defender RESOLUTE or VANITIE) is about to be run through the mill's four-sided planer, where it will be dressed to the correct taper and cross-sectional shape. Herreshoff hollow spars usually required eight of these staves, glued together, edge-to-edge, to form their circular shape. It looks as if one of these big spars is being brought to its finished shape, after gluing, on the wharf in the background.

Above the mill in the same building is the Cabinet Shop, where interior joinerwork and deck structures were pre-fabricated. The attached, low, brick building housed the Herreshoff Mfg. Co. central steam plant in whose fireboxes the mill shavings were consumed, carried there by the blower and the ductwork which shows near the smokestack. A covered overpass connected the Cabinet Shop with the North Construction Shop. According to Herreshoff Mfg. Co. boatbuilder Charlie Sylvester, this overpass, known as the "Bridge Room," was wide enough so that small boats could be built within it when things were busy and space was tight elsewhere.

Looking west, toward Bristol Harbor, from Burnside Street, about 1920

EXCEPT FOR their sail plan, these boats are very much like the Buzzards Bay 15s shown in Chapter VI. The Marconi rig was widely accepted after about 1920 as being more aerodynamically efficient to windward than the gaff rig. It was also somewhat simpler to use, since the mainsail could be hoisted and lowered with only a single halyard. Because there was no gaff and no throat halyard, the building cost for the Watch Hill boats must have been a little less than for the standard 15-footers. In any event, the new boats were given pointed coamings as well as pointed sails, and were delivered to the Watch Hill Yacht Club for the 1923 season. There were eleven boats, all identical, and all using the #503-Class molds of 1899.

A good boat is a good boat no matter how old its design, and the sailors of Watch Hill understood this in 1922. They came to the same realization again in the mid-1960s when they sponsored more new boats of the same hull design, this time in fiberglass, and with even taller and more modern rigs. The class today, now made up mostly of these new boats, is still active. But going strong as well, although no longer a part of the racing fleet, are a number of the original boats. Often, wooden 15-footers have ended up in nearby Noank, Connecticut, a veritable wooden boat mecca.

Back now to the winter of 1922–1923 at Bristol: These weren't good times for the Herreshoff Mfg. Co. The economy was depressed and good orders were scarce, so many of the plant's skilled workers had drifted off to other jobs, and records indicate that some operations, such as the sail loft and upholstery shop, had been shut down altogether. The successful defense of the America's Cup by RESOLUTE was two years past. NGH and the new ownership were at odds. It would be only a few more months before the Herreshoff Mfg. Co. would be offered for sale at public auction.

JOSEPHINE, the first boat of the Watch Hill 15-foot Class, on her trial sail, December 18, 1922

HMCo #880 class, 1922
LOA 24'6"
LWL 15'0"
Beam 6'9"
Draft (board raised) 2'3"

SHEILA was the first sailing yacht built by the Herreshoff Mfg. Co. that had not been designed by NGH or a member of the Herreshoff family. It is fitting, however, that W. Starling Burgess should have been the designer to break the long-standing tradition. Like his father, Edward, W. Starling Burgess was a close family friend, had owned boats designed by Herreshoff, and had spent a good deal of time in Bristol, most recently revamping VANITIE for the 1920 America's Cup trials. Moreover, NGH's thirty-year-old son L. Francis was now working for the Provincetown-based (soon to be Boston-based) Burgess and had drawn many of SHEILA's plans.

Burgess's years as an aircraft designer had put him in the forefront among yacht designers experimenting with the Marconi rig. SHEILA's mast is curved like an S-boat's, but is rigged quite differently, with double spreaders and a long, forward-looking span stay. Her double-cockpit arrangement and short overhangs created considerable comment.

SHEILA was designed and built for Paul Hammond, who later owned the famous schooner NIÑA and was a member of the syndicate that built the 1930 J-boat WHIRLWIND. SHEILA, along with three other boats of the same class by other builders, was shipped to England for the 1921 newly inaugurated international Six-Meter races, where she and the other American boats fared rather poorly. This is not to say, however, that SHEILA went unappreciated in English waters. Indeed, her cruising exploits became the subject of a book, and she remains in active commission in England today.

Behind SHEILA in the photo is the high-speed steam-powered commuter ALERT (shown earlier in this chapter) with her own windowed wooden cover for winter storage afloat.

The Six-Meter sloop SHEILA being tried out after a May launching

HMCo #861, 1921
LOA 27'0"
LWL 23'6"
Beam 7'0"
Draft 5'2"

GEORGE F. BAKER, JR., VENTURA's owner, could, and did, own about any boat that suited his fancy, including the 217-foot steam yacht VIKING. His previous Herreshoff Mfg. Co.-built boats included a New York 50 sloop, also named VENTURA.

The VENTURA pictured was the antithesis of a New York 50, made shallow and roomy—a special-purpose boat—to be a shooting platform and floating lodge for Baker and his guests in the shallow haunts of Southern waterfowl. On the day of this photo, however, the men in VENTURA's cockpit, with suits and ties, are more likely coming from the boat's launching instead of going to a bird shoot. It appears from the bend in the mast as if the rigging has yet to be tuned. The stern davits are beautifully tapered steel forgings, made in the Herreshoff Mfg. Co. shops, and VENTURA can be fitted with a full-headroom cockpit awning of canvas.

VENTURA was built to an NGH half model made for a boat named AU REVOIR (HMCo #681) nearly two decades earlier, and that same model would be used once more when YAWLCAT (HMCo #1226) was built in the middle 1930s. Each time, it was modified by a raised sheerline or scale change. With her shallow draft and a ballast ratio of only 30 percent, VENTURA is far from being a racer, but her chief virtues of comfort and utility were capitalized upon some forty years after she was built when she was converted to a nice-looking, but scarcely recognizable motorsailer. VENTURA continues in service today.

VENTURA,
a shallow-water cruiser

HMCo #867, 1922
LOA 60'7"
LWL 45'0"
Beam 14'0"
Draft (board raised) 4'0"

The diesel yacht ARA
nearing completion

HMCo #377, 1922
LOA 165'0"
LWL 152'0"
Beam 24'0"
Draft 8'6"

THE ERA OF the clipper-bowed steam yacht was coming to a close in the years following World War I. Hulls were less ornate, and diesel power was coming into its own. Plumb-stemmed, yet graceful, and driven by two big six-cylinder Winton diesels, ARA represents a design philosophy born of wartime's functional thinking. ARA is undoubtedly the creation of A. Loring Swasey, who was a pioneer in handsome, yet comparatively plain power vessels, having designed the Navy's sleek 110-foot subchasers.

This steel-hulled beauty was ordered by Alexander Winton to demonstrate the virtues of diesel power—especially those manufactured by his firm. She was sold to Ernest B. Dane (for nearly a quarter of a million dollars, the highest price paid ever for a yacht built by Herreshoff) before completion.

The photo shows ARA with masts stepped, smoke-stack in place, and pilot-house landed. Because of limited overhead clearance in the shop, all these items had to be installed after launching.

WORK FELL off in 1923 when the country's economy slumped, and J. P. Morgan, GRAYLING's first owner of record, may well have been persuaded to sponsor this new boat's design and construction in order to give the shops some much-needed work. (Morgan's son Junius had become a Herreshoff Mfg. Co. stockholder shortly after JBH's death.) GRAYLING was a prototype of a proposed replacement for the venerable Herreshoff New York 30-Class sloops (Chapter VI), and orders for more boats of GRAYLING's design would have been welcomed. There was insufficient interest for a new class, however, and this was the only boat built.

All was not lost, because GRAYLING, while about the same size as the New York 30s, also rated as a Q-boat under the prevailing Universal Rule. She was purchased soon after she was built by J. V. Santry, renamed SPINDRIFT, and joined the spirited Q-boat racing at Marblehead.

The photo shows GRAYLING not yet finished (there are bits and pieces scattered about on deck, and the brass and bronze hardware, including the keel straps, are untarnished); she's being rolled into one of the Walkers Cove storage sheds prior to being sold. The selling price is listed as $9,250.

NGH designed GRAYLING's lead ballast keel to be an integral part of the boat's structural backbone. (It is rabbeted to receive the garboard planks.) Although this building method is considerably more difficult, it has the advantage of there being no wooden keel timber to check or rot. Building such a hull upside down by the Herreshoff Mfg. Co. was still possible, according to Sidney Herreshoff; the garboards were simply left off until the hull was turned right-side up and the rabbeted ballast keel bolted on. This is the same keel construction used in L. Francis Herreshoff's R-Class sloop YANKEE, built two years later in 1925, and in a number of his subsequent designs.

GRAYLING on the Herreshoff Mfg. Co. low gear

HMCo #892, 1923
LOA 46'4"
LWL 30'0"
Beam 9'1"
Draft 6'0"

GAME COCK was designed by NGH and built for George Nichols and Junius Morgan, who asked that she be at her best in heavy weather. Accordingly, NGH modeled GAME COCK with more beam and harder bilges than he would have preferred. The boat was never a winner. Co-owner Nichols must have been especially disappointed, for in 1925, as rear commodore of the New York Yacht Club and a great supporter of the R-Class boats, he had prevailed upon the club to offer its New York Yacht Club Cup to that particular class. NGH must have had some mixed feelings about the outcome as well, because the Cup was won by the visiting Marblehead-based R-boat YANKEE, designed by his son L. Francis.

GAME COCK, one of the first sailboats to be built under Haffenreffer family ownership, was about ten years old at the time of this photo. When GAME COCK was new, her cabin trunk was smaller and was pointed at its forward end, like that of an S-boat. And, of course, her rig was different. Originally, NGH gave her a rig that was nearly as curious, at least for a racing boat, as the one shown in the photograph. It was a conventional Marconi rig, but the tall mast stood without any spreaders whatsoever and had only a single pair of shrouds and a forestay as standing rigging. (There were, of course, the usual running backstays.) The mast was stouter than usual, but was designed to be flexible enough to bend aft automatically under the pull of the mainsheet as it breezed up, thus flattening the mainsail. Having fitted his own smaller cruising boat PLEASURE with such a rig earlier in the year, and in his retirement becoming ever more committed to simplicity, low cost, and reliability, NGH did not fail to promptly try out this concept on a racing craft. But while NGH was working to make mainsails more efficient, other designers—his son a leader among them—were discovering that racing success depended more upon larger headsails than upon finely tuned mainsails.

The "wishboom" rig with which GAME COCK is fitted in the photo came out during the 1930s and is discussed more fully in the next chapter. For now, it is sufficient to note that her mitre-cut sails are setting beautifully, without the usual twist or tension on the sheets.

Note: The word "wishboom" is derived from "wishbone boom," and the rig's advantages are described in the book *Yachts by Herreshoff* and in *Yachting* for June 1935, Vol. 57, No. 6.

The R-Class sloop GAME COCK as fitted with a wishboom rig, 1935

HMCo #932, 1925
LOA 40'0"
LWL 26'0"
Beam 7'8"
Draft 5'9"

North Construction Shop,
November 30, 1925

During the summer of 1925, work picked up. The first orders to come in were for a 65-foot LOA schooner and a new sloop of the same design as the ten-year-old New York 40s. At about the same time, the Herreshoff Mfg. Co. was asked to build eight S-boats for the Bar Harbor fleet.

By November, the time of this photo, the North Construction Shop holds the schooner MARY ROSE and three of the S-boats, shown here nearly finished, and the New York 40 MARILEE, all timbered and nearly ready for planking. (A second New York 40, RUGOSA II, would follow her.) Only a little more than a year has passed since the Haffenreffers acquired the Herreshoff Mfg. Co., and all the shops are filled. Production is on its feet again, and in this single winter of 1925–1926, the Herreshoff Mfg. Co. turned out something like thirty 12½-footers, four 15-footers, seven Fish-class boats, and fourteen S-boats, plus eight larger craft:

65′ LOA NGH-designed cruising schooner MARY ROSE, HMCo #954

59′ LOA NGH-designed sloop-rigged New York 40 MARILEE, HMCo #955

59′ LOA NGH-designed yawl-rigged New York 40 RUGOSA II, HMCo #983

47′ LOA Burgess-designed Q-Class sloop FALCON, HMCo #962

43′ LOA NGH-designed R-Class sloop GRAYLING, HMCo #966

36′ LOA NGH-designed Newport 29-Class sloop PADDY, HMCo #999

34′ LOA NGH-designed centerboard cruising yawl GEE WHIZ, HMCo #1002

31′ LOA NGH-designed launch for the steam yacht CORSAIR, HMCo #381

A FEW MONTHS later, the scene is quite different. MARILEE's hull has been completed and she's been turned right-side up, and planking is well along on RUGOSA II, a second New York 40 ordered this year. Fish-class boats have taken the place of S-boats wherever there's space in this crowded shop. Beyond RUGOSA II and the Fish-boat deadwood, and astern of the partly planked Fish-boat, is the lead-melting furnace with its attached stack. (Because of their weight, the ballast keels for the large sailing yachts like MARY ROSE, MARILEE,

and RUGOSA II were poured in place, as described in Chapter XIII.)

The advantages of the Herreshoff construction method are evident from this photo. There is a separate mold for every frame (or timber, as NGH often called them), which assures that the hull holds its shape while it is being planked. The staging—simply built, using the molds for support—brings the workmen close to their work. A batten nailed partway down on the planking keeps tools and fastenings within reach, and the frames, planking, and backbone are where natural light falls

directly on them and where they can be easily reached and worked on.

RUGOSA's single-thickness longleaf yellow pine planking has been completed, and the first piece of inner-layer, double planking has been laid. The first piece of outer-layer planking will begin at the rabbeted edge of the last strake of single planking. Only the seams of the single planking are caulked (the double planking is laid in heavy shellac), and the caulking and bunging can be seen following along behind the planks that are hung.

North Construction Shop,
February 1926

South Construc-
tion Shop,
February 1926

166

THESE PHOTOS show what was going on about concurrently in the two waterfront construction shops. (Across Hope Street in the East Construction Shop were a number of other boats under construction in an equally crowded area, but, as of this writing, no photos have been found to show them.)

At right is a view of the North Construction Shop with its three big projects (RUGOSA II, MARILEE, and MARY ROSE) and several smaller ones, taken at the same time, but from a different vantage point as the picture on page 165. The photo at left is of the adjacent South Construction Shop, also looking west toward the water end of the building, and shows the Burgess-designed 112-foot 23-Meter sloop KATOURA (HMCo #1050) nearly finished. Surrounding her and still under construction are an S-boat (right foreground), a Buzzards Bay 15-footer (left foreground), and a gasoline-powered 31-foot launch for J. P. Morgan's famous CORSAIR (astern).

This KATOURA, later and better known as the yawl-rigged MANXMAN, followed a dozen years after the even larger 162-foot schooner of the same name shown in Chapter VII. Both were built for Robert E. Tod.

As can be seen from the photo, laying the shiplapped cedar deck of a 15-footer could go quickly, because there were no covering boards on these boats. The decking could simply be run out over the sheer-strakes and trimmed later. And, at the cockpit opening, the decking could be treated the same way, since the steam-bent coaming was not installed until after the deck was all laid and trimmed to shape and covered with canvas. Only at the projecting stem and the not-yet-cut-down transom (and, of course, the chainplates) would the decking have to be carefully fitted before it was fastened.

North Construction Shop, February 1926

The bronze-plated
yawl THISTLE being
decked in the South
Construction Shop

HMCo #1078, 1928
LOA 103'0"
LWL 75'7"
Beam 21'6"
Draft 13'6"

During the boom years of the late
1920s, THISTLE's owner, Robert E. Tod,
ordered a major yacht annually. Having
commissioned the great schooner KATOURA's
construction in 1914, Tod was already an
important customer as well as having been
a stockholder during the 1917–1924 period.
After returning to the Herreshoff Mfg. Co.
in 1926 for his second KATOURA, shown
on the previous pages, he ordered THISTLE
(shown here), and a year later had his
third KATOURA built—this one a 92-foot
power cruiser.

THISTLE was designed by the then-
retired NGH; she carried the same name as
the 150-foot steel schooner Tod had owned
before his first KATOURA.

The photo shows THISTLE's teak deck
nearly laid; it has yet to be caulked and
payed, and that's why the teak hatch coaming, lying loose at lower right, has not yet

been fastened down. THISTLE was framed
in steel and plated with bronze, and her
metal structure is visible under the teak
railcaps and decking. Legend has it that
Herreshoff Mfg. Co. was the kind of place
where a workman didn't have to keep his
tools under lock and key, but could leave
them on the job site. Seven or more toolboxes have been left here on THISTLE's
deck. This photo also shows protective
canvas set over the deck structures further
aft to prevent damage while THISTLE's
deck is being laid.

Dr. Seth Milliken bought THISTLE
shortly after she was built, and owned her
through World War II. He kept her summers in East Blue Hill, Maine, where she
reigned queen of the area's fleet. Afterwards,
she was sold abroad. She ended her days
in the eastern Mediterranean.

While their J-Class America's Cup contender WEETAMOE (Chapter XIII) was under construction, brothers-in-law Junius Morgan and George Nichols had a matched pair of NGH-designed, so-called Development-Class boats built. NGH had been much taken with the newly formulated Development-Class Rule and carried on a lengthy correspondence with his son L. Francis about its potential in creating practical small sailing boats that could compete against one another and demonstrate the speed-giving qualities of various hulls and rigs.

The boat shown and her sister could be rigged with one, two, or three masts, and, although larger than the usual rowing craft, they were fitted with oarlocks for rowing when there was no wind.

One boat was trimmed in teak, the other in butternut; both had lifting eyes for hoisting on davits. This was the dawn of the Herreshoff Mfg. Co. wishboom era, and the sails are so fitted. One of the middle thwarts (designated as a slip-thwart on the Herreshoff Mfg. Co. construction drawing) can be removed to make space for sleeping on the floorboards. Gear can be kept dry under the afterdeck storage compartment, and steering is by tackle rather than tiller.

NGH designed these boats while in Florida and they were built and launched before his return; thus it was the Herreshoff Mfg. Co. official Charles Nystrom rather than NGH who was at the helm here during builders trials. NGH's Love Rocks home shows in the left background.

These intriguing boats must have been a relaxing alternative to the intensity of the J-boat racing that was soon to follow.

A Development-Class boat on trial, winter 1929–1930

The power cruiser STROLLER underway

HMCo #388, 1929
LOA 46'9"
LWL 46'0"
Beam 10'5"
Draft 2'9"

WITH twin propellers driven by two six-cylinder Sterling gasoline engines, a forward cockpit with its own curved windshield, and the usual elegant Herreshoff detailing (note, for example, the cabin trim molding), STROLLER reflects—albeit conservatively—the style of the Roaring Twenties. She was designed by A. Sidney DeWolf Herreshoff and delivered to C. D. Rafferty Jr. of New York for $24,500.

V ARA, designed by Purdy Boat Co., of Port Washington, New York, was ordered from the Herreshoff Mfg. Co. by Harold Vanderbilt as a cost-plus-fixed-fee, building-only contract. Vanderbilt obviously recognized Purdy's specialty as a leading designer of this type of craft. (Both of VARA's launches, however, were thoroughbred Herreshoff craft.) The twin-screw VARA had a steel hull, and two 750-horsepower Trieber diesels.

Like the other big yachts of this longtime Herreshoff client, this boat was given a name beginning with the letter V. The stern view, taken just before VARA was launched, shows an S-boat being completed and VARA's launching cradle tied up under her hull. As VARA took shape here, the South Construction Shop gave birth to the NGH-designed 103-foot yawl THISTLE, shown earlier, followed by the 87-foot-double-ended M-boat ISTALENA, designed by NGH's son, L. Francis. Here in the North Construction Shop VARA was followed by Robert E. Tod's 92-foot power cruiser KATOURA.

I N THE bottom photo, the newly launched VARA is being warped alongside the dock where she'll receive her pilothouse (on the wharf under canvas). Shop overhead clearance prevented the pre-launch installation of the pilothouse, as well as the smokestack and other tophamper.

Steel trusses, which will soon become the Herreshoff Mfg. Co.'s new dockfront sheerlegs, can be seen at the lower left of this photo.

VARA, ready for launching from the North Construction Shop, March 22, 1929

VARA at the outfitting pier, March 25, 1929

One of VARA's Herreshoff launches shows clearly in this underway photo, as does the glass-enclosed cabin in front of the pilothouse. It would appear from the belching smoke that VARA's diesel engines have yet to be tuned for an ideal air/fuel mixture; in fact, one might assume VARA to be steam-powered.

Besides furnishing elegant high-speed transportation, VARA would see service as a tender for the three Vanderbilt J-boats, ENTERPRISE, RAINBOW, and RANGER, as well as the M-Class sloop PRESTIGE. She was one of the all-time-great tenders.

VARA on trials
HMCo #385, 1929
LOA 158'0"
LWL 149'0"
Beam 24'0"
Draft 8'0"

KELPIE, a newly
built Fishers Island
31-foot Class sloop
leaving the East
Construction Shop

HMCo #1157, 1930
LOA 44'0"
LWL 31'0"
Beam 10'7"
Draft 6'1"

KELPIE was built for Henry L. Maxwell in 1930. She was trimmed in teak and painted red. Records show that KELPIE was delivered in August.

Just inside the shop door, leaning against the wall, are the paneled bulkheads for another boat, probably LAST STRAW (HMCo #1166), which was the final 31-footer built that year.

The design started out in 1912 as the model for NGH's centerboard daysailer ALERION (Chapter IX), and that model, with its offsets suitably expanded through a change in scale, a full keel added, and its ends extended on the mold loft floor, is what Sidney Herreshoff used in creating these wonderful boats. It was the work of great ingenuity, and there have been few all-around better designs ever produced. The boats are beautiful to look at, contain reasonable accommodations, and are out-

standing sailers. One of the class, PATAPSCO II (HMCo #1156), voyaged around the world in the mid-1960s.

Most of the twelve-boat fleet went initially to summer residents of Fishers Island, New York; Ed Maxwell, whose father had KELPIE built, remembered her arriving there, fully outfitted, and ready to step aboard for a sail. Within only a short time, however, the Great Depression downscaled the sailing there to smaller boats (among them the Herreshoff-built Fishers Island 23s, Chapter XII), and many of the 31-footers were sold and converted to family cruising.

KELPIE was later owned by Alan Bemis for nearly fifty years as CIRRUS. She still sails, still looks beautiful, and still has a red-painted hull. The restored TORCH (ex-SAVAGE) is the lead attraction at the Herreshoff Marine Museum (see pages 238, 239).

THE HERRESHOFFS had owned SPRITE for some seventy years when a transfer of title was arranged through James B. Herreshoff of New York, who was her owner at the time. In this photo, SPRITE appears to be headed for the railroad station to be loaded on a flatcar, where she'll be more evenly supported during the long trip west. Subsequently, for a half-century, SPRITE, refurbished in appearance, was exhibited at the Ford Museum's Deerfield Village, Michigan, site. She returned to Bristol in 1979 and can now be seen in the Herreshoff Marine Museum.

As SPRITE is by far the oldest extant Herreshoff-built boat, her history is worth recording. In the fall of 1859 the Herreshoffs started SPRITE as a family project. She was modeled by JBH and his father, Charles, with the full-sized frame patterns laid out from the half model by NGH, who was eleven-and-a-half years old. JBH and NGH scouted out and brought back the wood from which SPRITE was to be built themselves, sailing to various Narragansett Bay mills and even towing some of it home

behind JBH's 12-foot catboat METEOR. "Material was of the best, and the work was carefully done," NGH remembered in his later years, "and SPRITE was launched the following June—rigged and tried out the same day." In her, a month or so later, the Herreshoff boys—in company with their father in his own catboat JULIA—set out for New York to see Brunel's awesome steamship GREAT EASTERN.

NGH and JBH were together in SPRITE for the next three or four seasons, sailing nearly every day between May and November with young NGH at the helm, racing often and with ever-increasing success. SPRITE was rigged with a single mast way forward and a single gaff sail of 450 square feet. By rigging a temporary bowsprit, a light-weather jib could be set. Although there is some outside ballast showing on the keel in this photograph, SPRITE originally carried her ballast (1,000–1,200 pounds of it) as cast-iron weights under the floorboards, with another 400–500 pounds divided among sandbags that could be placed along the windward rail. Although NGH claims

she was a brute to steer with her long boom and wide rudder, he also reports that SPRITE proved to be the fastest boat of her size on all of Narragansett Bay.

In retrospect, it is a pity that SPRITE couldn't have been preserved exactly as shown here, since there is so much to be learned from examining a pedigreed craft of this early age. The photo is a tease, showing a natural-crook stem with a transverse pin at its head, indicating that SPRITE was probably moored by a spliced eye that could be slipped over the stem and under the pin. The delicately capped coaming appears to be of steam-bent, high-grade ash. Her sheerstrake looks like oak. What appear to be stopwaters or wooden dowels show all along her topside plank seams, but their purpose remains a mystery.

The 1860 catboat
SPRITE departing for
the Ford Museum,
April 26, 1930

LOA 20'3"
Beam 8'0"
Draft (board raised) 2'9"

A. Sidney DeWolf
Herreshoff,
1886–1977

S IDNEY HERRESHOFF's skill, knowledge, and expertise were invaluable to the Haffenreffer reorganization of the Herreshoff Mfg. Co. As chief designer and engineer from 1924 through 1946, not only did "Mr. Sid" maintain the high standards of design and construction which in his father's day had made the yard internationally famous, but his own design work is testimony to his visionary creativity. Not content to keep pace with advancements that were being made elsewhere in the 1930s in materials and methods of construction, he carried on his own experiments and research to great advantage. Sidney Herreshoff's brilliance is evident in many of the Herreshoff Mfg. Co. designs of the 1930s.

An extremely reticent gentleman, he was responsible for the Fishers Island 23 and 31, the Amphi-Craft, various frostbite dinghies, power craft, the Silver Heels class, the 30-foot catamaran SEA SPIDER, and others. He conceived and perfected the concept of the wishboom rig and sail plan, consisting of a loose-footed sail, the clew of which was supported by either a triangular boom for small cat-rigged dinghies (Amphi-Craft and Frostbite class) or a curved boom for yachts with headsails.

After the closing of the Herreshoff Mfg. Co. in 1946, Mr. Herreshoff continued work as a self-employed naval architect. He served as a designer and consultant for several firms, most notably the Cape Cod Shipbuilding Co. of Wareham, Massachusetts, which continues to build a number of Herreshoff designs in fiberglass.

ARIEL II was built in the East Construction Shop and brought here to the Walkers Cove railway on the yard's low gear. With little fanfare and apparently no invited guests, the owners, Mr. and Mrs. W. E. Woodward, attend to the bottle smashing and picture taking themselves. As with many of the Herreshoff Mfg. Co.–built yachts of the 1930s, ARIEL II was designed by NGH's son Sidney and built from the same model as STROLLER (HMCo #388) shown in Chapter XI.

Recently, under Ben Baker's ownership, ARIEL II was totally restored by Ballentine's Boat Shop and is again in commission.

The christening of ARIEL II

HMCo #393, 1931
LOA 46'9"
LWL 46'0"
Beam 10'6"
Draft 3'1"

EXCEPT FOR very small craft like dinghies, every Herreshoff Mfg. Co.–built boat was equipped with a Herreshoff anchor. These anchors, along with other hardware items, were offered separately as well during the 1930s; shown here is part of the Herreshoff Mfg. Co.'s anchor inventory during this time.

The genuine Herreshoff anchor is a truly wonderful creation, and has yet to be improved upon for all-around use. These anchors can be relied upon to hold in weeds, sand, mud or rocky bottoms. They were made in two-piece and three-piece configurations in sizes ranging from 8.6 to 1,260 pounds, and every anchor was proof-tested before it left the shop. (The little 8.6-pounder had to withstand a 540-pound pull, and the largest anchor was tested to 41,700 pounds.) Both two- and three-piece anchors are shown here, and some of the larger ones are fitted with lifting straps at their balance points, which makes hoisting them over the rail of a boat easier. In the three-piece configuration, a big, unwieldy storm anchor could be carried below deck, broken down

into its easily stowed, individual pieces: the flukes, the shank, and the stock.

Cast steel was the primary material, although some anchors were forged rather than cast. All were galvanized, except the few that were made of cast bronze for small boats like dinghies and 12½-footers; these lovely little anchors came in either 5-pound or 7½-pound weights.

Herreshoff anchors evolved from the traditional fisherman-type stock anchor. While fisherman anchors had heart-shaped palms so they could be hooked over a vessel's rail for stowage, that feature was not necessary in yachts, where anchors are generally unstocked and stowed flat on deck

inboard of the rail. Charles F. Herreshoff, Sr., is said to have been the first to alter the palm design from the heart to the diamond shape shown in the photo, feeling that the anchor rode wouldn't be as apt to foul it. NGH subsequently perfected the anchor's proportions by a series of oxen-drawn beach tests whereby the anchor could be observed as it dug itself in.

Copies have been made of the Herreshoff anchor, and these are generally known as "yachtsman" anchors. But many are inferior in that their palms are either too blunt or their basic proportions—which are critical to performance—are off.

Herreshoff Mfg. Co. anchors

SILVER HEELS was the forerunner of the Fishers Island 23 shown on the facing page. In 1933, the same concept was used again in designing the Northeast Harbor 30s.

These long, narrow, easily driven hulls combined with small, efficient rigs were a European concept, introduced to this country by NGH's son L. Francis. The idea was to obtain the fastest possible boat for a given sail area. The boats designed to the Baltic-originated Scharenkreuzer Rule were strikingly handsome and comparatively inexpensive, and by the late 1920s German- and Swedish-built 22- and 30-Square-Meter sloops began showing up in New England harbors, with organized fleets in Northeast Harbor, Maine, and Marblehead, Massachusetts. L. Francis, in his enthusiasm for the Scharenkreuzers, went on to design others himself and to promote the type through magazine articles and correspondence. With 225 square feet of sail area, SILVER HEELS is of the 22-Square-Meter genre.

SILVER HEELS was a Herreshoff "company boat" and used for demonstration and development, especially in connection with the wishboom rig and sail plan with which she was rigged in 1935. The sails of her original rig, shown here, leave a bit to be desired. In this light air, the mainsail's leech, held flat by its battens, creates a big wrinkle. Too much roach may be the cause, and recutting the sail might be the only cure. SILVER HEELS is fitted with running backstays, but because they're led aft only a few feet, the leeward one need not be slacked for closehauled sail trim.

SILVER HEELS
under sail

HMCo #1204, 1931
LOA 32'0"
LWL 20'0"
Beam 5'6"
Draft 4'0"

SIDNEY HERRESHOFF designed the Fishers Island 23-foot Class in 1931 based somewhat upon the design of SILVER HEELS. The underwater shape is somewhat reminiscent of an S-boat. The design was first advertised (*Yachting*, January 1932) simply as a 23-foot LWL sloop, but after the first boat (HMCo #1212) was built and sailed and accepted as a class at Fishers Island, New York, the boats were called Fishers Island 23s. As such, they gradually became Depression-era replacements for the Fishers Island 31s shown in the previous chapter.

This photograph shows five of 1932's eight-boat fleet being checked out before delivery. The boats have been launched and their masts stepped by the yard's ever-present scow USEFUL, under whose boom one of the boats still lies.

As time went on, additional boats were built for use in other areas; in all, there were thirteen with the original full-keeled configuration. A fourteenth was fitted with a centerboard to draw only 3 feet of water. Ultimately, the class name for both versions of the Fishers Island 23 was shortened to H-23, the sail insignias shown in this photo.

Brand new Fishers Island 23s being readied for delivery, May 14, 1932

HMCo #1212–1219
LOA 34'0"
LWL 23'0"
Beam 7'0"
Draft 4'6"

**Timber molds
for the Northeast
Harbor 30-class
sloop TSANA,
November 19, 1932**

HMCo #1227, 1933
LOA 47'2"
LWL 30'0"
Beam 7'10"
Draft 5'6"

Following on the heels of the H-23s was a bigger version with cruising accommodations, full headroom, and auxiliary power. Originally advertised (*Yachting*, February 1933) as 40-Square-Meter sloops, the boats were subsequently known as Northeast Harbor 30s. Only three boats were ever built, although the concept—a hull that could be driven fast with a small sail area—was, and still is, a good one. But in those Depression years, many sound ideas went begging.

This East Construction Shop photo shows the setup just before the first hull was started. It is typically Herreshoff, with a timber mold for each frame. The molds have been beveled, so that the square-section frames will lie fair with the planking, and are held in alignment by the longitudinal battens temporarily nailed to them. Now

that the beveling is complete (note the shavings still on the floor), the molds will be taken down to facilitate bending the frames and installing the floor timbers, then set up once again for planking.

For each Herreshoff Mfg. Co. design, a construction baseline (or base plane, actually) was established that was roughly coincident with the shop floor. Individual molds, constructed from half-model offsets, were located with reference to this baseline. The designer (NGH in times past; Sidney Herreshoff and Nick Potter for this boat) selected a construction baseline that would place the upside-down hull at a convenient height for the planking operation. Thus, Herreshoff-built boats sometimes had frames and interior joinerwork which, although square with the construction baseline, were not exactly plumb when the boat is waterborne.

Three weeks after the molds were beveled, the hull is all framed and planked and is being turned upright for completion. Note that every fourth mold stays with the hull, to help it retain its shape while it is lifted and turned over; as extra reinforcement adjacent to the lifting slings, all the molds in these areas have been left in place. As shown here, the turning-over process involves a pair of continuous loops running through blocks hanging from overhead chain hoists that, in turn, hang from the shop's two traveling cranes.

Tsana and her sister Northeast Harbor 30s, as well as the H-23s, departed from long-standing Herreshoff tradition in having single-thickness planking of hard mahogany instead of the double planking that NGH had usually specified for his corresponding designs. After a few seasons, the normal shrinking and swelling cycles of this nearly incompressible planking so stressed the frames that they frequently broke. To make matters worse (and, ironically, to make the appearance better), no caulking was used; the planking was beautifully fitted, wood to wood, at the seams. Thus, even resiliency at the seams was sacrificed. As might be expected, frame breakage plagued these boats and the H-23s throughout their lives. Tightly fitted single planking was common in boats of Northern

Harry Town (front) and Charles Sylvester (back) turn over TSANA's hull, December 8, 1932

European waters, where the Northeast Harbor 30 design concept originated and where, because the climate is more stable than New England's, the boats so built survive better. The Herreshoff Mfg. Co.'s adoption of this European method perhaps saved some time in building, but, in retrospect, was clearly a mistake.

To help hold its shape and keep it from wracking, TSANA's hull has been diagonally strapped internally with bronze, as can be seen in the above photo.

The photo at left, taken only minutes after the one above, shows that TSANA's hull had been smoothed and made nearly ready for painting before it was turned over. The waterline and boottop have yet to be scribed. Softwood pads protect the planking from the rope slings. The teak sheerstrakes will be varnished, setting off their molded shape and accenting the boat's subtle sheerline.

From here, the hull will be carried sideways and lowered onto its lead ballast keel, and another hull will be set up on the same carefully shimmed pads which represent the construction base plane.

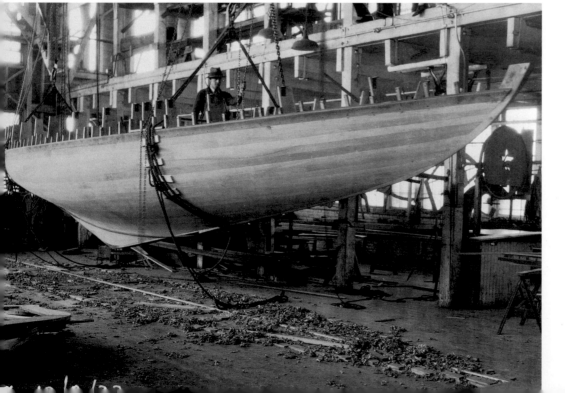

TSANA upright, still in the lifting slings, December 8, 1932

TSANA's teak deck has been laid and a caulker is at work making it watertight, while other workers paint out the interior before the trunk cabin is lowered into place. The heads of the chainplate fastenings still show, and the upper topsides are still in the process of being faired. A staging will soon be set up for these and the other deck-level operations. In addition to the usual ballast keel bolts, TSANA has been fitted with external bronze straps connecting ballast keel to hull (and let in to be flush with both); these straps, according to NGH, were vital elements in holding body and soul together.

The wheeled dolly upon which the boat rests rides on tracks leading out the East Construction Shop's door. Although this and the other Herreshoff Mfg. Co. shops were well lit by natural light coming through their many windows, the entire plant had long been electrified and there were light-bulb units at hand. These hung from struts as shown, and allowed a worker to light his work artificially and position the bulb exactly where it would be most effective. Showing under the bow of TSANA against the wall are the stacked-up molds for a powerboat, indicating how compactly a Herreshoff boat's tooling could be stored.

Crew at work
finishing TSANA,
December 27, 1932

THE VENERABLE Herreshoff Mfg. Co. "low gear," an iron-wheeled carriage built low to the ground, was the means by which yachts built in this shop reached the water. With flanged iron wheels and railroad track, it was an easy matter to make the transfer from the shop floor, out the door, and onto the low gear.

Although evocatively sleek, these 47-foot LOA Northeast Harbor 30s made surprisingly sensible cruisers, having four berths, a 'midship galley, and sails small enough to be easily handled by one person —the mainsail's area being less than 400 square feet. There was full standing headroom under the trunk cabin, and the all-up displacement was well under six tons. Had the mid-1930s not been such incredibly hard times economically, the Northeast Harbor 30s might well have caught on.

TSANA, ready
for launching,
February 1, 1933

SNOW ON the deck didn't interfere with the Herreshoff Mfg. Co.'s customary trial of a new design. As a result of this trial and the Northeast Harbor 30s' first season of use, the design's initial sail area of 430 square feel (40 square meters) was increased to 560 square feet.

William Strawbridge, who summered in Northeast Harbor, Maine, bought TSANA. In a couple of years, Strawbridge would return to have the Herreshoff Mfg. Co. build his beautiful, double-ended, L. Francis Herreshoff–designed 12-Meter sloop MITENA (page 187).

The second boat, BETSY, owned by J. A. Harris III, entered the 1933 Gibson Island Race, an outside run of some 350 miles from New London, Connecticut, to the entrance of the Chesapeake Bay, then another 125 miles up the Bay to Gibson Island. Placed in Class D with three much larger 10-Meter sloops and plagued by light weather along the way, BETSY finished last in her class.

Of the three boats built to this design, TSANA and BETSY sold at the $8,000 asking price; the third, named LONE STAR, remained with the company until 1937, and was sold for only $5,500.

TSANA on winter trial,
February 5, 1933

THE FEBRUARY TRIAL sail shown on the previous page lasted only long enough to put the boat through its paces. Having spent the balance of the winter in storage, the graceful TSANA is again put overboard for a second time to begin her 1933 sailing season. In this photo she is being hoisted over the edge of the wharf by sheer-legs, whose primary purpose was to step the masts of the big America's Cup sloops. Since hoisting was a common way to launch boats of TSANA's size at Herreshoff's, the boats built there were generally fitted with lifting eyes at the upper ends of the keelbolts, to which lifting straps could be shackled.

The dark vertical lines showing on TSANA's underbody are the external straps of bronze shown and discussed in an earlier photo, which help hold the ballast keel onto the hull. They are let in flush with the planking, and, because marine growth is less attracted to bronze than to wood, they, like the sheet-copper sheathing along the sternpost, have been left unpainted.

Since the early days, when NGH and JBH were being helped by their chemist brother James, the Herreshoff Mfg. Co. had mixed its own antifouling bottom paints, usually green in color. TSANA's unusual white bottom paint is no doubt a Herreshoff Mfg. Co. concoction as well, and, set off by a contrasting boottop, shows off her hull shape to advantage.

TSANA's second launching on April 10, 1933

THIS PHOTO, taken at the entrance to Northeast Harbor, Maine, shows a Northeast Harbor 30 fitted with a wish-boom mainsail.

The new catamaran
AMARYLLIS II
under sail,
September 12, 1933

HMCo #1232, 1933
LOA 33'0"
LWL 30'0"
Beam 27" (each hull)
Draft (board raised) 9"

THE CATAMARAN AMARYLLIS II was sponsored by a Lake Michigan syndicate (headed by K. T. Keller of Chrysler Motors) to be a near-replica of the first boat of that name, designed and built by NGH back in 1876, when, as described in Chapter I, he briefly headed his own catamaran-building business. The new boat, however, carried a sliding gunter rather than a gaff mainsail, and the sail was cross-cut instead of having its panels parallel with the leech. It was hoped that this new boat would be the first of many twin-hulled sisters, priced within reach of the average yachtsman. Whether a profit on building additional boats was out of the question at the $4,000 price, or whether there turned out to be no market at any price, is unclear. But no more were ever built.

Like her predecessor, AMARYLLIS II proved her speed by setting what was then (in 1933) claimed to be a new record of 19.8 m.p.h. She is now in the collection of the Herreshoff Marine Museum, having been many years on display at the Henry Ford Museum.

ONCE A shop's methods become established, they tend to be adapted, even to projects that are out of the ordinary, as in the upside-down, base-plane-on-the-floor setup for AMARYLLIS II shown here. Other builders would, no doubt, have different ways of setting up the frames and backbones of these simple, narrow hulls—perhaps some kind of ladder-like foundation. But what is shown does have its advantages: it brings the work of planking to a convenient height and leaves the floor around the hulls clear of braces and posts.

AMARYLLIS II hulls
set up in the North
Construction Shop,
August 1, 1933

The 12-Meter MITENA
on a trial sail

HMCo #1275, 1935
LOA 72'0"
LWL 44'0"
Beam 11'2"
Draft 8'8"

NGH's SON L. Francis designed MITENA. By the time of her building, the forty-four year-old L. Francis was at the peak of his career as a gifted designer of yachts, with his own office in Marblehead and one or two draftsmen in his employ. For a decade, fast and very beautiful boats had come from his drawing board, and, although he was not in any way connected with the Herreshoff Mfg. Co., the company had built at least one large yacht of his design—the M-Class sloop ISTALENA of 1928—before MITENA. L. Francis was independent of spirit, and he valued beauty in his designs every bit as much as performance—a result, at least in part, of his apprenticeship with W. Starling Burgess, who was clearly a bohemian soul mate.

L. Francis disliked the International Rule to which 12-Meter sloops were designed, feeling that the rule encouraged boats with unreasonably high freeboard and didn't allow the beautiful reverse curves he had grown to admire and to utilize in the hulls of his other designs. And he had no patience at all with the Lloyd's of London construction rules that had been invoked for the class. "They result," he wrote, "in complicated and expensive construction.... They are stupid, arbitrary, and a great detriment...."

Nevertheless, L. Francis did what he could to make MITENA both beautiful and fast. He was far more successful with the former, for MITENA's racing career was a disappointment—and this despite the speed and balance (no one is at the tiller!) demonstrated by this picture. MITENA was the last big double-ended racing yacht from L. Francis's drawing board, following the J-Class sloop WHIRLWIND of 1930 and the M-Class sloop ISTALENA mentioned earlier. Doubtless it had been William Strawbridge's success with ISTALENA when he owned her in 1934 that led him to have L. Francis design this 12-Meter for the following season.

Much to L. Francis's disgust, 12-Meters were becoming popular in the United States, just as the Six-Meters had a few years earlier. Already there was a one-design fleet of German-built, Burgess-designed 12-Meters active on Long Island Sound, and this year (1935) Clinton Crane was designing a new 12-Meter to be built in this country and named SEVEN SEAS.

The MITENA experience was not a happy one for L. Francis. Besides not liking the rules he had to design by, he had differences with the Lloyd's inspectors in interpreting the construction requirements. The Herreshoff Mfg. Co., in his opinion, had become a less-than-satisfactory builder, and, to cap it off, the boat performed poorly. The whole episode was short-lived, however. L. Francis received the design commission in January, 1935, MITENA was launched in June, and, as far as he was concerned, the boat's racing career was finished by September of the same year.

IN THIS, his last design, prepared in the fall of 1934 when he was eighty-seven, NGH created a thoroughly practical cruising boat, giving her his favorite yawl rig and fitting her with a centerboard so she could venture into one-fathom waters without grounding. Most distinctive at first glance are the concave stem profile and the hollow forward deckline, which take the place of a bowsprit and give BELISARIUS's bow somewhat the same appearance as the bows of GLORIANA, PELICAN, and GANNET of the 1890s (described in Chapters III and V). With BELISARIUS, NGH ended seventy-five years of designing.

The cruising yawl BELISARIUS under construction, December 18, 1934

HMCo #1266, 1935
LOA 56'2"
LWL 40'11"
Beam 14'0"
Draft (board raised) 5'7"

Because she was to spend winters in warm, worm-infested southern waters, BELISARIUS—named by owner Carl Rockwell for a swift-sailing, early American ship—was given a riveted-bronze backbone and centerboard trunk along with bonze floors from mast step to sternpost. Her topsides were double-planked in the Herreshoff Mfg. Co. custom, and the hull was diagonally strapped between the planking and frames with galvanized steel. Her hull was further stiffened by two pairs of steam-bent belt frames—one at the mainmast and the other amidships—installed after the ceiling was in place. Although structural bulkheads were becoming commonplace in sailing yachts built elsewhere, NGH stayed with the long-standing Herreshoff Mfg. Co. practice of having full-length, uninterrupted ceiling (inner planking) and light, joiner bulkheads and partitions that landed on it. Decks were of laid teak, and to compensate for the long trunk cabin and the lack of a bridge deck, BELISARIUS was given a 12-inch-wide oak structural shelf under the side decks.

BELISARIUS was rapidly built, compared to what we're used to today, and the building schedule was typical of the Herreshoff Mfg. Co. Launching took place a month after this photo was taken, and on January 25, BELISARIUS set out for a mid-winter shakedown cruise to Nassau. Her first race was early the following summer, when she took first place in the overnight Whalers Race out of New Bedford. In the Bermuda Race of 1936, in spite of being deepened aft and rigged with large headsails for better balance, she didn't fare quite as well, finishing middle-of-the-fleet in Class A.

Carl Rockwell, the Bristol neighbor to whom NGH had sold his green-painted ALERION III a few years before, adopted the same color scheme for his new boat: "Nathanael green" topsides, black boottop, and white bottom. BELISARIUS is now exhibited in the Museum's Hall of Boats, a gift of previous owner Charlie Read. She still wears her green-painted topsides.

Inside a Walkers
Cove storage shed
in the mid-1930s.
The boats are mostly
Fishers Island 23s.

W*HEN WINTER COMES* was the title
given the attractive 1937, twelve-page
brochure describing the new Herreshoff
Mfg. Co.'s Walkers Cove yacht-storage facility. Although the mid-1930s were lean years
for the construction of sizable new yachts,
there were existing yachts to be stored
whose owners would appreciate a clean
and secure undercover facility. It was with
this thought that the Haffenreffers constructed two fine sheds between Hope Street
and the Walkers Cove waterfront, south
of the main yard and not far beyond NGH's
Love Rocks home. These sheds, the largest
measuring 102 feet by 450 feet, show in
the aerial photograph in Chapter XV. Two
sets of tracks, one of which shows in the
lower photo, ran the entire length of this
so-called "Yacht-Drome." The other shed,
a corner of which shows in the top photo,
contained less area (about 18,000 square
feet vs. 45,000 square feet) but boasted a
24-foot overhead clearance.

It was with considerable pride that
Carl Haffenreffer included E. D. Wright's
report to the insurance underwriters in
his new brochure. It said, in part, "I found
the Herreshoff yard in perfect order, in
fact, the best-kept and cleanest plant I have
ever had the pleasure of inspecting..., For
winter yacht storage, I consider it one of
the best risks we have."

Inside the new
"Yacht-Drome"
at Walkers Cove,
about 1937

Although the Amphi-Craft hulls were built upside down, as was the Herreshoff custom, the shop's method, used for the larger craft, of bending the frames directly over the molds gave way in these and certain other small craft to what shows here: a jig-type setup in which the boat's frames are bent over the ribbands sprung around and fastened to widely spaced molds. This system requires less lofting and allows the intact jig to be left undisturbed, boat after boat; it has long been a favored method among other builders.

Except at the bow, this boat's frames run continuously side to side across the keel and are held at each end by turnbuttons at the sheer. The keel has been clamped in place, although not yet bolted, and the rabbet has been cut where the keel and stem join.

The Amphi-Craft was to be an all-purpose boat having wider appeal and a more affordable-price than most Herreshoff Mfg. Co. boats. Although the design was aggressively advertised (in fact, this very photo was run in the hardcover brochure *Yachts by Herreshoff*), only fifteen boats were built. They were elegant and, for what they were, rather expensive.

Two of the boats are known to have been preserved (#1276 at the Museum and another at Mystic Seaport), and they show some features worth knowing about. For example, the mast is in two pieces so that it will store inside the boat, the wishboom rig holds the sail in its most efficient shape, and the rudder is pivoted to kick up in shallow water.

Amphi-Craft #1276 rigged in the East Construction Shop, April 5, 1935

HMCo #1276 LOA 13'1" Beam 4'9"

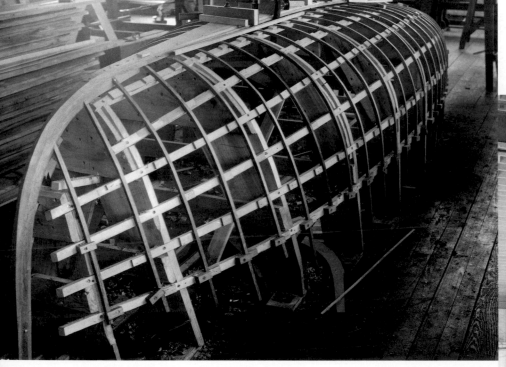

The first Amphi-Craft hull (#1276) ready for planking, March 4, 1935

Sidney Herreshoff designed not only the Amphi-Craft but also a special trailer to go with it. The Herreshoff Mfg. Co. built the trailer as well as the boat, using running gear purchased from the Indian Motorcycle Co. and a steam-bent, varnished oak frame complete with the Herreshoff Mfg. Co. logo hand-lettered in red paint.

The fitted canvas cover over the boat keeps out sun, rain, and dirt, and helps protect the lapstrake hull from drying out during periods ashore.

The 1935 Ford convertible belonged to Herreshoff Mfg. Co. superintendent Tom Brightman, who took this photo.

As part of its promotional campaign, the Herreshoff Mfg. Co. posed Amphi-Craft #1276 as a rowboat, an outboard boat, and a sailboat to demonstrate its versatility.

In the far right photo, the man second from left is Herreshoff Mfg. Co. general manager Carl Haffenreffer. At the helm is Sidney Herreshoff, who had on board his sons Nat and Halsey. The Amphi-Craft could be ordered complete with outboard motor at prices ranging from $400 to $560, depending on the extras.

Carrying capacity as well as rigging details are demonstrated in the bottom photograph. Because the wishboom keeps the sail from twisting, the sheet only has to pull the sail in and out and therefore has far less tension.

The Amphi-Craft as a trailerable boat, April 14, 1935

The Amphi-Craft as a rowboat, April 6, 1935

The Amphi-Craft as an outboard motor boat, April 12, 1935

The Amphi-Craft as a sailboat, April 12, 1935

ALTHOUGH Sidney Herreshoff designed and built VELITA in 1935 for his own family's use (his heirs still own her, in fact), the Herreshoff Mfg. Co. later offered this as a stock design, calling it at various times either the "Sailfish" or the "Lake George" class. No others appear to have been built, however.

VELITA is obviously a handsome and useful boat, with some novel features such as: (1) sliding gunter rig whose short spars can be stowed inside the boat or easily carried; (2) a wishboom mainsail for aerodynamic efficiency and easy trimming of the sails; (3) a balance-type jib which eliminates the need for a forestay and snaphooks; (4) tackle steering, with a continuous hauling part that can be reached from anywhere in the cockpit; (5) shrouds comprised of halyards for economy and convenience. VELITA was not assigned an HMCo hull number. VELITA is on display at the Museum with a subsequent rig fashioned by Sid and his son Halsey.

Sid Herreshoff's W Class centerboard sloop VELITA, March 21, 1935

LOA 16'1"
LWL 15'0"
Beam 5'8"
Draft (board raised) 7½"

VELITA'S
steering tackle

IT'S A SIZABLE yacht that requires this big a launch and is equipped to hoist it out on davits, but the 272-foot T. D. Wells–designed VIKING (built by Newport News Shipbuilding & Drydock in 1929) was indeed a major yacht. She—and, of course, this launch as well—were owned by George F. Baker, who had, in years past, come to the Herreshoffs for other boats. He owned two named VENTURA—one a New York 50-Class sloop, and the other a big, unique shallow-draft sailboat, used for shooting waterfowl, that was shown in the last chapter.

Because the launch will generally be out of the water, there is no need for antifouling bottom paint, and the entire hull can be a single color.

A launch for the steam yacht VIKING

HMCo #395, 1935
LOA 33'6"
Beam 7'4"

HERRESHOFF MFG. CO. records show that forty of these intercollegiate sailing dinghies were built for a flat fee of $10,000, a unit cost of only $250, or only about half what the similar-sized Amphi-Craft shown earlier sold for. Such are the possibilities of an efficient production line and large-dollar contracts. (Subsequently, five more were built at prices ranging to $325.)

M.I.T. professor George Owen was responsible for the "Tech" dinghy design, and if the boats appear to be pure Herreshoff creations, there's good reason. Owen was one of NGH's draftsmen in earlier times, before joining the M.I.T. staff and before becoming a well-known designer himself. Rather more elegant than practical, the structural design reflects Owen's background and the Herreshoff Mfg. Co.'s standards. For example, the steam-bent wraparound caps on the centerboard trunks are a distinctive, but elaborate, feature.

Here in the East Construction Shop, where there was heat (the steam pipes run along the rear wall) and a reasonably dust-free environment, the newly finished dinghies were handed over to the painters for varnishing. Two forms, probably for steam-bending the stems of the 12½-footers

that were constructed in this shop from time to time, are visible on the iron post in the background. A steambox, connected to the central steam-heating system, can be seen as well, with a hood above it for catching and carrying away the escaping steam.

M.I.T. "Tech" dinghies

HMCo #1319–1363
1936
LOA 12'6"
Beam 5'0"

Planking the fast and narrow Alden-designed yawl BRENDA, November 5, 1935

HMCo #1315, 1936
LOA 44'6"
LWL 30'0"
Beam 8'0"
Draft 6'0"

THE HERRESHOFF MFG. CO. held to its upside-down method of hull construction even in building the boats of other designers whose plans didn't especially lend themselves to it. There were still economies to be realized through long-established habits and convenient down-hand positions, though the structure of boats such as BRENDA was more complex than what had been devised and perfected by NGH. For example, most NGH-designed boats of BRENDA's size would have had a shallower-bodied hull and a steam-bent, plank-type keel timber, and there would have been a solid fairing of deadwood between it and the ballast keel. The boat's overall shape might have been similar, but NGH's structural design would have been especially tailored to the Herreshoff Mfg. Co.'s unique building method.

Instead of having a mold for every frame, as did, for example, the New York 40s and 50s (Chapters VI and VII) and the Northeast Harbor 30s (shown earlier in this chapter), BRENDA has been framed out using molds for every other frame, with the alternate frames bent against heavy ribbands from the inside. Note the temporary stiffeners on the transom, used to hold its curved shape until the hull is planked.

AVANTI, built for Walter Rothschild, was a Sparkman & Stephens–designed yawl, with which her owner won second place (Class A) in the 1938 Bermuda Race. Shown below, partly built, is her trunk cabin, which will leave this shop as complete as practicable before being installed.

Off-the-boat fabrication of such items as this and the nearly completed skylight next to it is part of the reason the Herreshoff Mfg. Co. could construct a boat so rapidly. Besides deck structures, the yard also built as separate items raised-panel bulkheads and partitions, cabinets, drawers and doors, shelves, ladders, berths, iceboxes, and galley cupboards. This meant that a boat's interior joinerwork and deck structures could be started as soon as the lofting was done, and be ready for installation just as soon as the hull was far enough along to receive them.

Building these pieces was fussy work that required the special skills and machinery that were conveniently available in the well-staffed and well-equipped Joiner Shop (or "Cabinet Shop," as it was sometimes called). The beautifully fitted dovetails shown here in the cabinside corners and cabintop beams are examples of the exquisite work produced in this shop.

The Alden-designed yawl EVENING STAR in the North Construction Shop

HMCo #1386, 1937
LOA 54'0"
LWL 39'9"
Beam 14'0"
Draft 7'4"

AVANTI's trunk cabin and skylight under construction

HMCo #1384, 1937
LOA 55'8"
LWL 40'0"
Beam 12'7"
Draft 7'8"

EVENING STAR's raised-panel joinerwork has been installed and can be seen through the yet-to-be-planked cabintop. The splined vertical staving forming the cockpit sides is also being fitted. (Note that the edges of each piece have been sealed with varnish against moisture absorption and subsequent staining.) Since the bulwarks are not yet in place to hide them, the beautiful hook-type scarfs in the covering boards can be clearly seen.

Much of the work taking place here requires the special skills of the joiners, as the finish carpenters that work on boats are called, and a ramp providing direct access to the Joiner Shop has been installed; it shows at the lefthand side of the photo.

A study of construction plans produced by the Herreshoff Mfg. Co. indicates that subassembly was very much in the mind of NGH as he prepared each new design. Self-bailing cockpits, for example, were planned so they could be built in their entirety right in the Joiner Shop. But not all designers thought that way, and here, for example, EVENING STAR's cockpit and cabin, because of the way they were designed, had to be built in place—obviously a slower and more difficult process.

Against the shop's far wall are the giant masts of the J-Class sloops. The masts were kept there throughout the mid- and late-1930s while the boats that went with them were hauled out for storage. There are masts here of steel, aluminum (then also called "duralumin"), and wood.

A Marlin-class sloop launching

HMCo #1420, 1937
LOA 20'9"
LWL 16'0"
Beam 7'1"
Draft 3'1"

THE MARLIN is the 1916 NGH-designed Fish-class sloop modified for cruising by a stretched-out cabin, a toilet, two berths, and an inboard engine. In spite of considerable promotion and the Fish-class's popularity, the Marlin never met with success. In fact, only about three Marlins appear to have been built. The design did become popular in later years, however, after the Herreshoff Mfg. Co. closed its doors and the Cape Cod Shipbuilding Co. started building the Marlin in fiberglass, that version lengthened with a counter stern and fitted with a masthead rig.

In the late 1930s, American builders began producing a flood of four-berth, "family-type" auxiliary cruisers, mostly built as production boats to keep the price low. The Herreshoff Mfg. Co. entered the fray with its Seafarer design, but unlike the Alden-designed "Coastwide Cruisers," the Lawley "Weekenders," and Palmer Scott's "Overnighters," the smaller, but nearly as expensive Herreshoff "Seafarers" never caught on. Only two were built.

Herreshoff Mfg. Co. general manager Carl Haffenreffer deserves credit for the Seafarer idea, while NGH's oldest son Sidney Herreshoff actually designed the boats.

The Seafarer is really a pocket cruiser, and in a different league from most four-berth auxiliaries because of its small size. It can be far more easily and economically cared for (with less than 8 feet beam, it's even trailerable), yet it has the big-boat features of standing headroom, a comfortable main cabin to sit, eat, and sleep in, an enclosed head, an inboard engine, and a forward stateroom with V-berths. The design has proven fast and seaworthy under sail. The cruising public missed out on an exceptional boat here, and one of the most practical ever produced by the Herreshoff Mfg. Co.

Seafarer-class sloop
CYGNET
HMCo #1474, 1938
LOA 25'0"
LWL 21'6"
Beam 7'9"
Draft 4'0"

of ENTERPRISE: "She is of conventional shape.... It was not my place to strike out on the many paths of experiment in hull form...a mistake in hull form was a mistake past correcting...so I built a conservative hull and trusted to painstaking engineering and inventive resources above decks to turn the trick." What Burgess was alluding to above decks was chiefly the duralumin (aluminum) mast, designed by his brother Charles and fitted midway through the season. Building a 165-foot mast of any material for the Marconi-rigged J-boats was a challenge; the tapered masts of glued-up spruce with which all four of the 1930 Cup

boats were fitted were among the longest sticks ever stepped and weighed some 6,000 pounds each. Charles Burgess's spindly new riveted mast was a marvel of its time, saving 1,200 pounds aloft and giving ENTERPRISE the stability to outperform WEETAMOE, YANKEE, WHIRLWIND, and, ultimately, the challenger SHAMROCK V, no matter how hard it blew. It was but one example of aircraft technology applied to the rigs of sailing craft, and at the leading edge was the name Burgess. As designer not only of ENTERPRISE, but of the 1934 defender RAINBOW and a co-designer of RANGER in 1937, W. Starling Burgess was proving a creditable successor to NGH, at least in the defense of the America's Cup.

THE PHOTO BELOW and the launching view on the preceding page show how ENTERPRISE's plate edges have been offset and lapped past each other in order to save the weight of backing bars and still allow the plates to bear fully on the transverse framing. The relatively narrow strakes of plating give ENTERPRISE's hull a very distinctive appearance, and make her easy to identify in photos. Rivets hold everything together; the shiny spots visible in the photograph show where the rivets have been ground flush with the hull plating.

ENTERPRISE's deck is of white pine laid in strips sprung parallel to the deck edge. Along the centerline, the strips nib into a kingplank.

Notice that this shop has been equipped with a sprinkler system; sprinkler heads show clearly in the upper part of the photo.

ENTERPRISE
nearing completion
in the South
Construction Shop,
February 23, 1930

ENTERPRISE got a jump on the 1930 season by being the first of the four new J-Class sloops launched and the first under sail. To test her speed, she raced against the Cup boats of the last series, RESOLUTE and VANITIE, both of which now carried triple-headsail Marconi rigs like ENTERPRISE's shown here. ENTERPRISE proved the faster boat, especially when sailing close-hauled. (WEETAMOE was to give her some tough competition later on, however.)

In this photo, ENTERPRISE is out for a trial sail. She is carrying her original mast and a conventional boom, both of which would be replaced by lighter and more aerodynamic spars as the season wore on. Vanderbilt as skipper and Burgess as designer were relentless in their drive to have ENTERPRISE chosen as the defender, and, for them, the season involved many experiments and alterations. Her sail inventory, for example, is said to have reached fifty by the time she raced the challenger, SHAMROCK V, in September.

ENTERPRISE
under sail, 1930

THIS SHOWS WEETAMOE about a month after the bandsawing of the keel. The ballast keel has been jacked up to its proper orientation, and solidly blocked and shored; the bronze keel plate has been attached; and six frames have been erected.

By mutual agreement between the New York Yacht Club and Sir Thomas Lipton (who, in 1930, was challenging for the fifth and final time), Lloyd's scantling rules were used in constructing the British challenger and all four American J-boats. Lloyd's rules called for conventional framing, as shown here, rather than NGH's method of framing a hull with longitudinal stringers over widely spaced web frames— as was done in CONSTITUTION, RELIANCE, and RESOLUTE. This meant, among other things, a heavier hull structure, but one with more usable interior space.

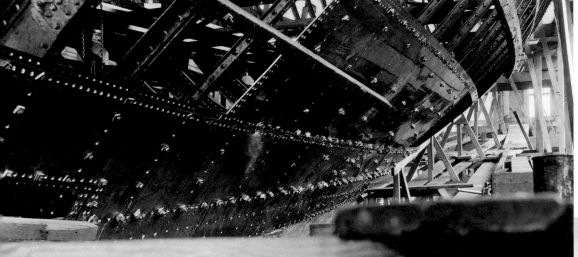

Stepping
WEETAMOE's mast,
May 18, 1930

As with ENTERPRISE, WEETAMOE's steel frames and deckbeams were made up in the Herreshoff Mfg. Co. Blacksmith Shop across the street, then delivered to the Construction Shop for assembly. Her bronze hull plating, shown here on March 1, 1930, was cut out and rolled to shape, then punched for rivets, using the metal-forming machinery located in the covered area between the North and South Construction Shops. As shown in the photo, wooden ribbands are used to hold the frames in alignment until the plating is complete.

Boats with smooth bottoms sail faster, and for this reason WEETAMOE's bottom is being flush plated. Under this system, plates butt together over internal backing bars instead of lapping past each other, as shown in the earlier photo of ENTERPRISE's topsides. Temporary bolts are used to draw the plates into position and hold them there while they're being riveted together. Since riveting doesn't heat up the plates and distort them, and because of the skill of the Herreshoff Mfg. Co. metalworkers in rolling and fitting the plates, there is no need here for fillers and fairing compounds. The bronze bottom plating of Cup defenders such as WEETAMOE was, in fact, polished rather than painted.

WEETAMOE had been overboard about a week when her 165-foot mast was stepped at the end of the Herreshoff Mfg. Co. dock on May 18, 1930. ENTERPRISE had been sailing a month and had had several gratifying skirmishes with the venerable Cup boats of the last (1920) series, RESOLUTE and VANITIE—proving, it seemed, that at least one of the new J-boats was decidedly swifter than her predecessors.

Spare masts were required of all Cup boats in 1930. There had been schedule delays when masts broke in years past, and the risk was greater now. Those gaff-rigged masts had been shorter and, presumably, more dependable than were the new tall and tapered Marconi masts. The New York Yacht Club Selection Committee also ruled that the boats should be prepared to race no matter how hard it blew; so, even though WEETAMOE's backup mast weighed less than the one shown here, prudence ruled against using it. The mast shown, according to Clinton Crane, "was heavy enough to stand in all kinds of weather"—and, indeed, it proved to be reliable throughout the season.

Sheerlegs had long been a familiar sight at the end of the Herreshoff Mfg. Co. dock, but the earlier wooden ones had been less tall and stately. The trussed metal sheers shown here were nearly new when this photo was taken, and are an indication of the business boom of the late 1920s and the fact that the 1930 America's Cup racing would take place in nearby waters.

Designer Clinton Crane stands on WEETAMOE's afterdeck. No doubt George Nichols and Junius Morgan, who head up the WEETAMOE owner/manager syndicate, are also aboard in this early trial sail.

Designer and owners alike had high hopes that, among the four J-boats built in 1930, WEETAMOE—named, by the syndicate, for the Indian "Queen Weetamoe" of Pocasset (now Tiverton), Rhode Island would be chosen to defend the America's Cup in September. As things turned out, she almost made it, showing herself at first to be faster than ENTERPRISE, WHIRLWIND, or YANKEE. Then, in mid-season, when

ENTERPRISE was fitted with her revolutionary new lightweight duralumin mast, it was all over for WEETAMOE, as well as YANKEE and WHIRLWIND.

The year 1930 brought many other important J-Class developments: Marconi rigs made their appearance; parachute spinnakers were introduced; and the three-headsail rig was abandoned in favor of the double head rig, at least on some of the boats. This photo shows WEETAMOE carrying a single-luff spinnaker and very long upper spreaders. She soon gave up both, reflecting the very rapid development of J-boat rigging technology.

WEETAMOE participated in the 1934 Cup trials (for which she was altered in

shape), but she never again showed up as well as she had in her 1930 debut, when this picture was taken.

Clinton Crane was delighted to have had WEETAMOE built at the Herreshoff Mfg. Co., and reported in his memoirs: "It seemed we would get a better boat built here.... There would also be available to us all the wonderful mechanical gear which NGH had invented for use on the RELIANCE and RESOLUTE.... It was a treat to talk with NGH; at over eighty, his mind was as clear as a bell.... I came to know many of the foremen who had trained under NGH, and no one in the world was capable of doing more beautiful work."

WEETAMOE running
before the wind

HMCo #1147, 1930
LOA 125'7"
LWL 83'0"
Beam 20'3"
Draft 15'0"

After the races of 1930, ENTERPRISE was hauled out on the Herreshoff Mfg. Co.'s new North End railway and sidehauled on the rails that show in the foreground. She was considered obsolete at the end of her first season and, unlike WEETAMOE, never sailed again.

In spite of her America's Cup victory, ENTERPRISE's career ended the year she was built

THE HERRESHOFF MFG. CO. had long specialized in producing hollow wooden spars, and many were built in the Spar Loft (shown in Chapter VII). When the America's Cup boats shifted to Marconi rigs and, for a short time, to wooden masts, the Herreshoff Mfg. Co. built them on the ground floor of the Woodworking Mill, north of the North Construction Shop.

This 1932 photo shows work about to begin on shaping VANITIE's mast for her new W. Starling Burgess–designed double-headsail Marconi rig. Chainfalls overhead will lift and rotate the big stick as the adzing and planing progresses, after which it can be rolled out the back door and onto the dock for stepping.

North light is desirable for any naturally lit operation, and the man at the far right is taking full advantage of it as he files a saw.

Shaping a new mast for VANITIE, 1932

RAINBOW's deck
framing, looking aft
(west) in the South
Construction Shop,
March 23, 1934

HMCo #1233
LOA 126'7"
LWL 82'0"
Beam 21'0"
Draft 14'7"

Fʀᴏᴍ ᴋᴇᴇʟ laying to launching on
May 15, the job of building ʀᴀɪɴʙᴏᴡ
took just one hundred days. Three days
after she took to the water, ʀᴀɪɴʙᴏᴡ began
sailing. Owned by the Vanderbilt syndicate
and designed by W. Starling Burgess—key
members of the ᴇɴᴛᴇʀᴘʀɪsᴇ team of 1930
—ʀᴀɪɴʙᴏᴡ was the only American J-boat
built in America for the 1934 challenge.

The J-boats of 1934 had to comply
with new requirements for mast weight
and accommodations (earlier J-boats had
no accommodations). ʀᴀɪɴʙᴏᴡ, therefore,
was designed with below-deck living quarters that had skylights on the deck above,

the openings for which can be seen in the
photo. ʀᴀɪɴʙᴏᴡ's yet-to-be-planked deck
framing has been drawn into alignment
by means of longitudinal wooden ribbands
temporarily bolted to the deckbeams. The
diagonal metal deck strapping shows as
well; it helped prevent the hull from wracking under a press of sail. Here ʀᴀɪɴʙᴏᴡ
is nearly ready for her white-pine deck and
mahogany trim.

ʀᴀɪɴʙᴏᴡ would end the era of
Herreshoff-built America's Cup defenders,
a tradition unbroken since ᴠɪɢɪʟᴀɴᴛ
of 1893.

RAINBOW's hull plating is partly installed, and the diagonal hull and deck strapping, as well as the deck-support stanchions, show clearly. The deckbeam flanges have been punched for the bolts that will secure the wooden deck. (The spacing of those holes has been carefully laid out to accommodate the finished width of the white-pine deck planks.) Staging is still in place for working on the sheerstrakes and waterways. RAINBOW and her English rival, ENDEAVOUR, will each have below-deck accommodations for two dozen crew members.

Although well built and unusually handsome, RAINBOW nearly forfeited the America's Cup.

Looking forward inside RAINBOW during her construction, March 23, 1934

The Cup boats
ENTERPRISE,
WEETAMOE, and
RAINBOW, 1935

Tʜɪs ᴀʀᴇᴀ of Hope Street, just north of Burnside Street, called "Peacock Alley" by Bristol residents, was the only place where all three Herreshoff-built J-boats were ever together. It was there that, for the single winter following the 1934 races, ᴇɴᴛᴇʀᴘʀɪsᴇ (left), ᴡᴇᴇᴛᴀᴍᴏᴇ (middle), and ʀᴀɪɴʙᴏᴡ (right) were stored side by side. ᴡᴇᴇᴛᴀᴍᴏᴇ had had the questionable good fortune to have sailed against both the others, beaten out both times in her quest to be the defender.

Lɪᴛᴛʟᴇ remained of ᴇɴᴛᴇʀᴘʀɪsᴇ when this picture was taken on September 6, 1935. After one year afloat and five years stored here, she was sold for scrap and dismantled. The reported price paid was $5,000.

ᴇɴᴛᴇʀᴘʀɪsᴇ's famous duralumin mast outlasted her by good measure. In December of 1938, possibly as part of a general post-hurricane cleanup, the mast was pulled out of its North Construction Shop storage racks, loaded aboard the scow ᴜsᴇꜰᴜʟ, and taken across Narragansett Bay to Wickford, then, by land, to nearby Scituate, Rhode Island, where it was to serve many years as the state police barracks radio antenna.

ᴇɴᴛᴇʀᴘʀɪsᴇ being
dismantled, 1935

W EETAMOE sailed for the last time in 1936. Her dismantling began in the spring of 1938 and is shown here in April of that year alongside the super J-boat RANGER, champion of the 1937 America's Cup contest. Because RANGER's hull was plated with steel instead of bronze, she survived on Peacock Alley until 1941, when America was on the verge of declaring war and even steel had become worth recycling.

WEETAMOE'S
demise came in 1938

CHAPTER XIV

Pleasure and Sunset

NGH in Retirement, 1924–1938

NGH OFFICIALLY went into retirement after the Haffenreffer purchase of the Herreshoff Mfg. Co. in 1924, but he remained available to the company as a consultant and designer on various projects and functioned in an advisory capacity. His lifelong habits of designing and overseeing the building of yachts would not permit his retirement years to be spent in idleness. At Love Rocks, close by the Herreshoff shops, he continued his work, cutting models and designing in the third-floor room where he had worked since 1883. His wife Ann and his daughter Agnes provided him with the utmost support and encouragement.

During the 1920s, Nat and Ann avoided the harsh New England winters and cruised to Florida and Bermuda. Here the elderly designer enjoyed some fine sailing in the company of old friends. His warmest friendship was with Commodore Ralph M. Munroe, at whose cottage at Coconut Grove, Florida, the Herreshoffs passed the winters. Here NGH built superb model yachts which sailed, and he enjoyed sailing them with his host.

In the 1930s, Captain Nat spent more of his time at Love Rocks, carrying on considerable technical and historical yachting correspondence with the likes of W. P. Stephens, Henry C. White, C. H. W. Foster, and his son L. Francis. His four grandchildren were nearby, and their "old Grandpa," as he called himself, took considerable pleasure in their activities. In the summer of 1933, Ann urged him to write his reminiscences in a notebook. He worked at this into 1934, and these penciled notes provide remarkable insight into NGH's work and contributions to the development of yachting.*

Working in the model room was still a source of enjoyment for Captain Nat well into 1936. When Rod Stephens (of Sparkman & Stephens, co-designers of the J-boat RANGER) visited at Love Rocks after the Cup races of 1937, NGH delighted all with his succinct comments during the showing of a film that Stephens had brought with him. NGH's ninetieth birthday on March 18, 1938, brought honors from the Town of Bristol and visits from family and friends. He died at Love Rocks on June 2, 1938.

*Recollections and Other Writings by Nathanael G. Herreshoff; Herreshoff Marine Museum 1998

THIS VIEW of NGH's home, "Love Rocks," was photographed by his son Griswold from the end of the wharf that jutted out into the Walkers Cove section of Bristol Harbor. At left can be seen the rocks from which the house took its name. According to Bristol history and legend, this site had once been occupied by a windmill used for grinding corn for Bristol families. Also, courting couples often walked to this site; hence its name. When NGH designed the house and had it built in 1883, it was logical to use the local name for the property.

Originally painted dark red, the house, by 1937, was its now-familiar light gray, with white trim. On the lower floor of the main house were a living room and a dining room to the left of the porch. The kitchen was in the attached wing at right, with the cook's quarters above it on the second floor. On the second floor of the main house were the bedrooms, with Captain Nat's on the south-facing side. On the third floor, at left, are the south windows of the model room where, for over fifty years, NGH's half models were made. An ample attic was on the fourth floor. On the basement level were a playroom and workshop for the children. The flagpole at the left of the house is probably the former mast of the 1878 steam yacht LEILA.

The property at Love Rocks was ideally suited for NGH's family. Not only was the house spacious, but the site afforded the children every opportunity to swim, sail, skate, go iceboating, and play lawn games.

The boathouse at the right of the picture was, in the early years of the century, located near the dock (as shown in Chapter IX), at about the position of the covered dinghy house shown here. During the 1920s, the boathouse was moved to its new location, leaving more room at the dock for both Sidney's and NGH's small sailing craft. The boathouse would be swept away during the hurricane of 1938, and thirteen small craft destroyed.

This photo shows the proximity of Love Rocks to the Herreshoff Mfg. Co. shops (seen in the background, at left) where, during this America's Cup summer, the J-boat ENDEAVOR II, T. O. M. Sopwith's British challenger, is being worked on at the South Construction Shop. The mast of another J-boat can be seen at the right of the flagpole, probably that of RANGER, which was at that time also being serviced by the Herreshoff Mfg. Co. A mirror had been arranged at Love Rocks in order that NGH, from his bed, might see the yard work in progress.

Love Rocks,
midsummer 1937

WATER LILY at
Coconut Grove, Florida,
about 1930

HMCo #982, 1925
LOA 20'6"
LWL 18'0"
Beam 6'5"
Draft (board raised) 1'6"

WATER LILY was NGH's last boat, brought to Florida for the 1927–1928 season as a replacement for PLEASURE.

According to his son Sidney, NGH designed WATER LILY as a sample boat for a rating rule he had devised in the mid-1920s. Although she was round-bottomed and fitted with a pendant-type inboard rudder, WATER LILY bore a strong resemblance to the Biscayne Bay 14-foot Class of sailing skiffs shown on the preceding page.

For some reason, the so-called "17-foot Limited Class" didn't take, and WATER LILY was still at the Herreshoff Mfg. Co., unsold, in the fall of 1927. NGH purchased her for use in Florida, but before she was shipped south, he had some singlehanding-for-the-elderly modifications made. A reduced-area, sliding gunter rig was substituted for the Marconi one, allowing the shorter spars to be stored within the boat's hull for shipping. For comfort, the cockpit was widened so that bench seating could be installed (the original idea was to sit on the floorboards in light air, and on the side deck as live ballast when it was windy). Lazyjacks were rigged to keep the mainsail and its sprit under control when being raised and lowered, and the mast was moved 8 inches aft and a filler piece added ahead of the shallow lead ballast keel; the latter alterations were made, perhaps, so that a reasonable weather helm could be maintained with the shorter rig.

Soon, even WATER LILY became too much for NGH, and in the early 1930s he turned the boat over to Commodore Munroe's daughter, Patty, and gave up traveling south in the wintertime. As he put it, he had become "awkward in all facilities," and, with obvious sadness, he "ended a sailing hobby after about seventy-three years at it."

DURING HIS numerous visits to Bermuda (he and his wife sometimes returned home from Florida on a passenger steamer by way of Bermuda), NGH had made friends among Bermuda's boating crowd, a number of whom, it seems, were amateur boatbuilders, and in this friendly vacation environment, free from business overtones, he is said to have made available a few of his designs for local building. The 14-foot catboat THRUSH, shown below, is an example built for a Mr. E. Outerbridge.

The boat at the right is HALCYON, now on loan to the Herreshoff Marine Museum from the Bermuda Maritime Museum. About 1925, NGH supplied plans of the Herreshoff 12½ and gave permission to Mr. Graham Boyle to build her in Bermuda.

The photo of HALCYON shows a light strut holding the jib club from lifting when its sheet is slacked as in reaching or running. NGH had used a permanent strut on the overhanging mizzens of his earlier cat-

yawls, CONSUELO and CLARA, and this appears to be a quickly lashed-on version of it. Photos show that he rigged such a strut on PLEASURE's jib as well. These simple struts are most likely the seeds that started the Herreshoff Mfg. Co. on its "wishboom" campaign of the 1930s, as described in Chapter XII.

"NGH in Bermuda," as was written in NGH's hand on the back of this photograph, taken about 1926

NGH (right) and Mr. McCallan (left) aboard THRUSH in Bermuda, about 1926

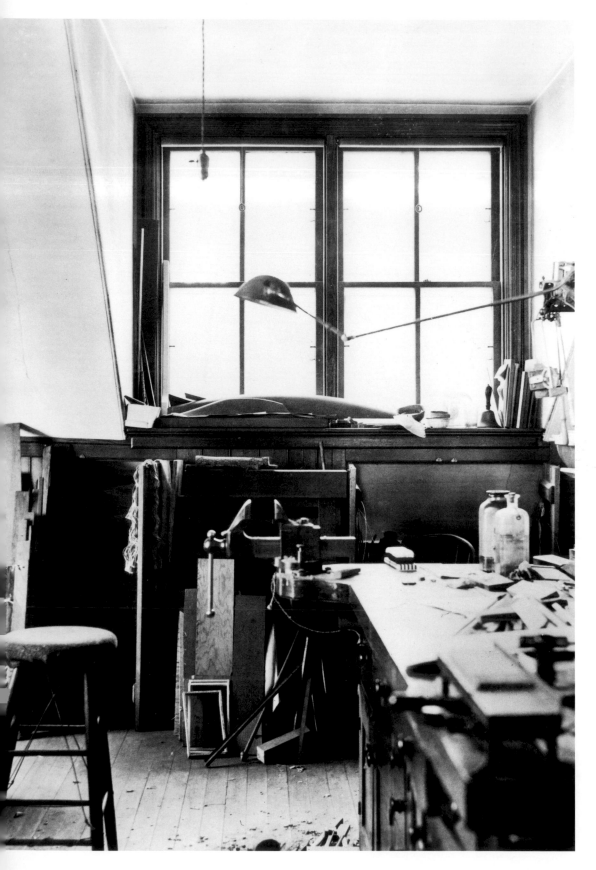

THESE PICTURES of the third-floor model room were taken by L. Francis Herreshoff shortly after his father's death. The work area of the model room, shown in this photo, is where Captain Nat actually made his models. Throughout his life, NGH regularly worked here from about 6:30 to 8:00 a.m. and from about 7:30 to 10:00 p.m.

The patternmaker's vise (on the left corner of the right-hand bench) was used to hold the half model, mounted on a special block screwed to the model's back side, so that the half model could be held in three different positions while it was being shaped. The adjustable lamp above the vise gave sufficient light for this precise, painstaking work. The stool shown here, identical to those used in the drafting rooms at the Herreshoff shops, was padded for the designer's comfort.

After NGH died, his workbench and design tools continued to be used by two more generations of Herreshoffs. The method of designing in three dimensions by half model survives as well, passed on first to son Sidney and currently utilized by grandson Halsey.

The model room and adjacent work-room have been replicated at the Herreshoff Marine Museum where visitors may appreciate the approximately 500 half models.

The model room
at Love Rocks, 1938

THIS PHOTO shows a section of the west wall of the model room. The shellacked half models, secured to battens fastened to the plaster walls, could be removed for study. About 300 models from which yachts were built, along with an almost equal number of study models, were made by NGH. Drawings that related to the making of half models were stored in the drawers of the cabinet, atop which a number of technical reference books were readily available. (The drawings from which yachts, engines, boilers, and fittings were actually built—over 12,000 in number—were kept in the vault of the Burnside Street drafting office.)

As the western windows faced Bristol Harbor, NGH kept binoculars handy to view boating activity. When his children were young, he watched their sailing tactics from these windows. One summer evening, his son Clarence, showing off in a small sailboat for friends watching from the Love Rocks lawn, was brought down to size when he heard the model room window squeal open, followed by his father's words through a megaphone: "*Trim your jib!*"

Another view of NGH's model room, 1938

The two Nats—
NGH and his grand-
son and namesake,
Nathanael Greene
Herreshoff III,
November 11, 1934

NGH HAD a strong affection for his four grandchildren. As the Love Rocks property abutted that of Sidney's home at 125 Hope Street, Captain Nat had the frequent opportunity to visit his two grandsons, Nathanael III (born in 1931) and Halsey C. Herreshoff (born in 1933), and took an active interest in their growth and development. The photo below was taken in the yard at Love Rocks on Armistice Day, 1934; NGH was then eighty-six.

NGH later bequeathed to Nathanael III a very fine, old English jackknife that had been one of this most treasured possessions, given to him in 1853 (when he was five-and-a-half years old) by Dr. Nathanael Greene, the son of Revolutionary War general Nathanael Greene, for whom he had been named.* In his written bequest to his namesake, Captain Nat stated that the knife was the style "made for New England whalers," given with "a wish from his old Grandpa that he try to keep it and honor and cherish it as long as he did."

NGH's granddaughters, Clara and Natalie, were the children of Nat Jr. Clara (1921–1982) was a professional artist. Natalie (1923–2002) was Secretary at St. Michael's Episcopal Church. Both were active in Bristol's civic affairs.

---

* Many visitors to the Herreshoff family plot at the historic Juniper Hill Cemetery in Bristol are mystified by the two different spellings of NGH's first name. The 1905 gravestone of Clara Herreshoff is engraved "Mrs. Nathaniel G. Herreshoff," while NGH's 1938 gravestone reads, "Nathanael G. Herreshoff." As if to compound the mystery, Captain Nat often abbreviated his name in his legal signature as "N.G. Herreshoff" or Natl. G. Herreshoff." In fact, there is no mystery. NGH spelled his name "Nathaniel" until sometime between 1910 and 1915, when he visited the birthplace of General Nathanael Greene in Anthony, Rhode Island, and discovered that the General had gone by "Nathanael." From then on, NGH decided to spell his name as the General had, and from 1915, when he signed the marriage registry of St. Michael's Episcopal church in Bristol as "Nathanael G. Herreshoff," he consistently used this spelling when he signed his full name.

Feeding the gulls
at Love Rocks,
February 2, 1936

THIS PHOTOGRAPH, taken by his daughter, Agnes, shows NGH engaged in his daily ritual of feeding the seagulls at Love Rocks. The pleasure he found in this activity as an old man is indicative of Captain's Nat's kindly side.

In his declining years, NGH busied himself with a variety of interesting pastimes. He paid more attention to his family, his home, and his friends than he did during his active years at the shop. But his love of his life's work never dimmed, and in 1936 he still could be found in his model room working on projects related to yachting. His sons, Sidney and L. Francis, received drafting tools made by the old gentleman at this time.

On his ninetieth birthday, March 18, 1938, Captain Nat received a resolution (a framed document) from the Bristol Town Council that pleased him a great deal. It stated, in part: "By his sterling character and integrity, by his interest in Bristol both as a just and fair employer and as a worthy citizen, extending over an unusual period of years, he has endeared himself to our people and brought renown upon his native town, placing our citizens under lasting obligations to him."

Nathanael G. Herreshoff died at Love Rocks on June 2, 1938. The funeral service was conducted at Love Rocks by Canon Anthony R. Parshley, Rector of St. Michael's Episcopal Church. Burial was at Juniper Hill Cemetery. Six old Herreshoff Mfg. Co. employees served as bearers: Thomas P. Brightman, Harry Munro, Thomas Ashton, Henry Luther, James Wood, and Fred Hodgdon.

The morning after

I N THIS PHOTO, taken on September 22, more than half of the South Construction Shop has been blown over, and the lumber and paint sheds have been obliterated. Miraculously, the wharf-mounted, steel-truss sheerlegs are still standing, and the boom and A-frame mast at the left indicate that the venerable yard scow USEFUL survived intact. Hauled out inside the South

Construction Shop is the 110-foot Lawley-built power cruiser AIDE DE CAMP. Had it not been for her, that part of the shop would have been totally flattened.

Undaunted by the devastation and partially covered by insurance, the Haffenreffers would soon rebuild, and the Herreshoff Mfg. Co. would go through the war years with the South Construction Shop intact.

T HE HIGH TIDE knocked even the larger yachts off their blocking, and the sea tossed them around. Here, the 77-foot Herreshoff-built schooner QUEEN MAB (originally named VAGRANT, HMCo #698, and in 1938 flagship of the New York Yacht Club) rests on her port bilge with visible damage to her transom. In the background, lying on her starboard side, is CHARMIAN, a 59-foot Bath Iron Works–built Seawanhaka-class schooner.

Inside Walkers Cove
Storage Shed No. 1

Of the irreplaceable yachts wrecked by the 1938 hurricane, many had been built by the Herreshoff Mfg. Co. One of these was COMFORT, shown here. Her owner, George P. P. Bonnell, had anchored for the storm behind the Stonington, Connecticut breakwater, a place which at normal times afforded good protection from southeast winds. When the water rose over the breakwater, however, and the lee vanished, the heavy seas that came roaring in tore COMFORT's anchor windlass loose and it went overboard, taking a good bit of the boat's bow with it. COMFORT blew ashore near the head of the harbor, along with a number of other craft. She was damaged beyond repair, but both of her tenders survived and are now in the collection of Mystic Seaport Museum.

COMFORT was built in 1909 as the steam yacht ENAJ III, "Enaj" being "Jane" spelled backwards. L. Francis Herreshoff was her skipper during his Navy days in World War I,

COMFORT, ashore in Stonington, Connecticut

HMCo #267, 1909
LOA 89'4"
LWL 78'9"
Beam 17'8"
Draft 4'10"

and family photos show that he and the boat made a stopover at the Herreshoff yard in Bristol. By 1936, when Bonnell acquired her, the steam engine had been replaced by a six-cylinder gasoline engine.

The boats stored here are in chaos as well. Luckily for her subsequent owners, including Maynard and Anne Bray, the centerboard cruising yawl AÏDA (ex-GEE WHIZ, HMCo #1002, lower right) suffered only superficial damage.

Outside, in the Walkers Cove yard

CARL W. HAFFENREFFER, vice president and general manager of the Herreshoff Mfg. Co., took his job seriously, and, from the time he arrived fresh out of college (Dartmouth) in the early 1930s, his contributions were many. Haffenreffer was coached in the beginning by Charles Nystrom and Tom Brightman; he soon made his influence felt in every shop operation, from advertising to construction.

After increasing the number of one-design sailboats turned out by the yard, he stepped up the merchandising of yacht gear and accessories in an attempt to promote standardization. During the World War II years, when one hundred vessels were built for the U.S. government, his responsibilities and duties increased. He very often supervised construction projects personally and helped to ensure a fine record of uninterrupted production during that four-year period. He frequently served as helmsman in delivering PT boats to New York.

Haffenreffer's management, coupled with the teamwork of the Herreshoff workmen, was a real contribution to the winning of the war. Because of a four-year safety record, the Herreshoff Mfg. Co. was awarded a gold cup and certificate by the insurance underwriters.

Carl W. Haffenreffer
receiving Insurance
Underwriters
Safety Award,
April 10, 1944

EARLY WAR WORK consisted of building these coastal transport vessels known as APcs. In marked contrast to the Herreshoff Mfg. Co.'s longtime practice of setting up all new construction inside one of its shops, the APcs were built outdoors in the Walkers Cove yard.

In the background, beyond the Lobster Pot restaurant, is Love Rocks, neighbored by Sidney's home.

APc 3, APc 4,
and APc 5 set up
outdoors in the
Walkers Cove yard,
August 19, 1942

APc 86 (HMCo #501)
on trials, May 5, 1943

HMCo #425–511
1942–1943
LOA 103'0"
Beam 21'0"
Draft 8'4"

Twenty-two of these "jacks of all trades" were built between October 1942 and July 1943—with an average of nearly one of these 103-footers each week. Each cost $145,750, and they appear to have been contracted for in two batches, with the lead ship of the class (APc 1) included in the first batch of ten; APc 85 through APc 96 constituted the second batch. It was an impressive rate of production, especially so because the APcs were built concurrently with eight 71-foot British Vosper torpedo boats, which were built in the South Construction Shop.

THIRTY-SIX of these boats (about two per week) came out of the big shed at Walkers Cove from the fall of 1944 into 1945; several are shown here as they progress toward completion on the same ground where APcs were built early in the war. The so-called "Yacht-Drome" (the 450-foot-long, arc-roofed yacht-storage building shown in Chapter XII) had been turned into a factory, complete with production lines, for the war effort. But it all ended early in 1945. As the last of several World War II government contracts, these boats spelled the end of serious boatbuilding by the Herreshoff Mfg. Co.

One hundred vessels, of which these Air-Sea Rescue boats were the smallest, had been built in the short span of only about three years. Specifically, there were: two 130-foot YMSs, eight 71-foot Vosper PT boats, four 97-foot AMcs, twenty-two 103-foot APcs, twenty 71-foot U.S. Navy PT boats, eight 85-foot Army Rescue vessels, and thirty-six 63-foot Army/Navy Rescue boats. Before the Herreshoff Mfg. Co. closed for good, the company published a booklet in recognition of its wartime achievements. A copy of *100 Fighting Ships* was given to each employee.

A production line
of Air-Sea Rescue
boats, 1944–1945

HMCo #900–935
1944–1945
LOA 63'0"
Beam 15'0"
Draft 3'0"

A 63-foot Air-Sea Rescue boat on sea trials

T HE FUNCTION of these high-speed craft (also known as "crash boats") was to pick up fliers who had been forced to parachute from their damaged aircraft. The boats were destined for the Pacific, where the war was being waged in the fall of 1944. Two 630-horsepower Hall–Scott gasoline engines provided power.

The Herreshoff Mfg.
Co. from the air,
looking northeast,
November 1944

O N   T H E   E V E of its closing and in the
final days of the war, the Herreshoff
Mfg. Co. looks little different from what
it had earlier. Some obvious changes are
that the South Construction Shop has been
rebuilt after the 1938 hurricane, wharves
have been added to, buildings now cover
part of Peacock Alley, and recently completed Air-Sea Rescue boats lie at the docks
once used by yachts.

THE WALKERS COVE facility, built in the mid-1930s for undercover storage of yachts and known during the war as "the Lower Yard," is at the right in the photo below. An interesting element is the immense tripod hoist over the construction ways. Utilizing available large yacht masts, Sidney Herreshoff devised this simple means for hoisting heavy engines onto boats built during the war.

The Walkers Cove landscape seen here is quite different from that in the photo taken eighty years earlier and shown at the beginning of Chapter I. And today, after the passing of sixty years, it has again changed dramatically, now filled with private homes.

The Herreshoff Mfg. Co. from the air, looking north, November 1944. The square white building was there before the mid-1930's. The long aircraft hanger-type building was greatly expanded in the mid-1930s. Both were destroyed in a sensational fire on Election Day 1948.

A HURRICANE, A WAR, A CLOSING

233

"BECAUSE MANPOWER, materials, and price restrictions prevent Herreshoff from entering civilian production for some time to come, it is with regret [that] we find it necessary to disband our efficient and loyal organization and to dispose of our facilities at Bristol…."
—Carl Haffenreffer,
  General Manager, Herreshoff Mfg. Co.,
  November 28, 1944

"This yard is all I know. I never worked anywhere else. I never thought of working anywhere else from the time I walked in here back in 1899 and picked up a paint-brush and started painting boats. I think of the salt air in my face and the wind and the sun and the way everything smelled good when I'd walk down Burnside Street in the morning and join the other boys to work on this boat or that. I live up the street where I can see the yard from my front steps. When we look down the street toward the yards and see nothing but beach and water, then we'll know there is part of us missing. And it will be just as definite as if we'd lost an arm or a leg—only more so, because there will be something missing inside."
—Thomas Ashton, Paint Foreman,
  Herreshoff Mfg. Co.,
  interviewed November 28, 1944

A handful of pre-war 12½-footers bear witness while, on the heels of the Herreshoff Mfg. Co.'s World War II building boom, the shoreside shops are razed following World War II

★ One Hundred Fighting Ships ★

Rescue Boats for the Army Air Forces

(PTs) Motor Torpedo Boats for the Navy

APc Coastal Transports for the Navy

AMc Minesweepers for the Navy

YMS Minesweepers for the Navy

A TRIBUTE TO OUR CRAFTSMEN FOR A JOB WELL DONE!

MOTOR TORPEDO BOATS (PTs), Aircraft Rescue Boats, Minesweepers and Coastal Transports . . . 100 Fighting Ships, built here in Bristol during the last four years . . . a record of which all may be justly proud.

No shipyard, large or small, here or abroad, can point to a finer record of uninterrupted production . . . production unhampered by petty grievances or disputes . . . an outstanding accomplishment in harmonious teamwork by Herreshoff craftsmen and management . . . and a real contribution to the winning of the War.

Because of our four-year Safety Record, Herreshoff has been awarded a Gold Cup and Certificate by the Insurance Underwriters . . . this record is the envy of the industry the country over . . . here again, Herreshoff craftsmen have speeded up the War Program.

Believing that Herreshoff craftsmanship in all its 80 years has never served a finer purpose, we wish to pay tribute to our craftsmen for a job well done . . . in "shipshape and Bristol fashion."

We salute, therefore, each of these 2,000 Herreshoff craftsmen whose individual effort and harmonious teamwork have helped to build a part of the World's greatest Army and Navy.

R. F. HAFFENREFFER, *President*

R. F. HAFFENREFFER, III, *Treas.*   C. W. HAFFENREFFER, *V. P. & Gen. Mgr.*

Herreshoff
SHIPYARD
BRISTOL, RHODE ISLAND

JUNIOR EXECUTIVES:
A. S. De Wolf Herreshoff   T. P. Brightman   John H. Garrity   H. F. Newman   William A. O'Connor
John J. Conway, Jr.   Leo W. Grenier   Richard Borden   Victor A. Moretti

SUPERVISORS: John H. Millar   Arthur J. Cote   Harry Town

FOREMEN: Thomas Ashton   William Simmons   John Fanara   Leo V. Hayes   George Hibberts
Rocco Migliori   Charles Martin   George Uprichard   Norman W. Hanson   William Cook
Charles Peterson   Ralph Law   Philip C. Lenz   Gene Girard   Joseph Sousa
George Montle

"OLD TIMERS"

Tom Ashton	William Darling	Fred Hodgdon	Leonard Sanford
Otis M. Bailey, Sr.	Charles Davis	Walter Silher	William Simmons
John Barry	Herman Gablinski	Manuel King	Lowell Smith
Knute Berg, Sr.	J. H. Garrity	Christie Lewis	Joe Sousa
Charles Bickford	Gene Girard	Walter Munroe	Harry Starkey
Thomas Brightman	Harold Green	Herbert Newman	Arthur Tuttle
Manuel Cardoza	Walter Handy	Napple Patenaude	Harry Town
Everett P. Church	Lou Hayes	Charlie Peterson	George Upichard
George Coggeshall	Sid Herreshoff	Rocco Migliori	Charles Wall
William Cook	George Hibberts	John Millar	Lowell Wright
		David Rogers	
		Fred Moore	
		Evans Moore	

Herreshoff Marine Museum/America's Cup Hall of Fame

BY HALSEY C. HERRESHOFF

I T SHOULD BE a satisfaction to the reader that, in the twenty-first century, the Herreshoff Marine Museum carries on the tradition of the Herreshoff Manufacturing Company (HMCo). Founded in 1971 by Sid and Becky Herreshoff, and located at the original site of HMCo, the Museum collects, restores and exhibits more than sixty Herreshoff yachts ranging in size from small dinghies to a 72-foot New York 50. There are also steam machinery, anchors, fittings, instruments, models and memorabilia, all augmented by photos and documents to inform and inspire visitors from all parts of the world. Particularly important are the Nathanael Greene Herreshoff Model Room and the Rebecca Chase Herreshoff Library.

The America's Cup Hall of Fame is an important component founded in 1992. Plaques honor more than fifty members, selected for their dominant roles in the America's Cup races. Permanent and temporary exhibits convey all facets of the fascinating history of competition for the oldest and most distinguished of international trophies in sport. Annually, the induction ceremonies have attracted in excess of 300 people to Rhode Island, England, New Zealand, New York City or the current venue for America's Cup Races.

The "New Storehouse," (constructed 1917) as it appears today. (Compare this photo with a similar view on page 34.) Formerly home to the Herreshoff Marine Museum, this building now houses the Museum's America's Cup Hall of Fame.

Active days continue at the Herreshoff site. Twelve-meter America's Cup yachts are moored at the Museum pier on the occasion of a "Herreshoff Rendezvous" regatta.

FOUNDING

The founding of the museum was curious and perhaps unique. Sidney Herreshoff, witnessing the 1970 America's Cup Races, pointed out to his wife Becky and son Halsey the spectator yacht, THANIA, a handsome 60-foot cabin launch built at HMCo in 1905. Sid stated his wish to purchase her, as he was then in the unusual position for a Herreshoff of not owning a cruising yacht.

Nothing further was done until some three months later when a probate lawyer contacted the family and informed them that THANIA's owner, Mr. Daniel Newhall of Philadelphia, had unexpectedly died and that he had bequeathed the yacht plus a modest stipend for her upkeep to the Herreshoff Marine Museum. Advised by the family that no such organization existed, the lawyer offered two options: (a) decline the bequest or (b) form a museum and name it as conveyed in Mr. Newhall's will: "Herreshoff Marine Museum." Thus the Museum was formed. THANIA exists today, proudly restored in the "Hall of Boats," the first of some five dozen watercraft acquisitions.

Bristol's legendary Independence Day Parade marches south on Hope Street between the main Museum building and the "Herreshoff Waterfront," July 4, 2002.

Museum President Halsey C. Herreshoff, Captain Nat's grandson, stands aboard TORCH in the Museum's "Hall of Boats." Prominent behind him are DILEMMA, the first fin keeler (on loan from The Mariners' Museum), BELISARIUS, and INDIAN, a Bar Harbor 31.

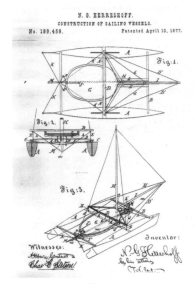

N. G. Herreshoff's 1877 catamaran patent application.

FACILITIES

Progressing from its modest founding, the Herreshoff Marine Museum/America's Cup Hall of Fame acquired in 1985 the waterfront and remaining buildings of the former HMCo. Then, in 1990, Norman Herreshoff bequeathed the adjacent original Herreshoff homestead. Two other buildings of the complex are owned by Captain Nat's grandsons, Nat III and Halsey; it is anticipated they, too, will be conveyed to the Museum.

The largest building on the site is a 150 by 90 foot, two-story steel and masonry structure constructed by Pearson Yachts in 1960. This building is ideally suited to the display of large yachts. Future planned additions to this structure will both facilitate the mission of the Museum and improve its appearance.

The other structures of "The Herreshoff Marine Campus" provide workshops and storage for the Museum plus space for about fifteen small businesses whose rent is an important factor in the Museum's operating budget.

Substantial donations for shorefront improvements are transforming the site of former construction shops into a brilliant waterfront park, providing for Museum

events and entertainments. Vital to this transformation are "The McGraw Pier" and the recent purchase of "Bay House." At this writing, sea walls have been restored, most surfaces have been faced and a substantial string of floating piers extend into Bristol Harbor. Pending is restoration of the marine railway formerly used to launch the first U.S. Navy torpedo boats and most of the giant yachts that successfully defended the America's Cup eight consecutive times.

THE YACHT COLLECTION

With few exceptions the yachts on display have been donated to the Museum. Their acquisition is a combination of exceptionally skillful solicitations by co-founder Rebecca C. Herreshoff and subsequent considerable generosity with a measure of good luck. Most were built by HMCo, along with a few by Sidney or Halsey Herreshoff. A favorite is TORCH, a brilliantly restored Fishers Island 31-footer donated by Toby and Ben Baker. The Museum is gratified to host visitors to the interior of this yacht which looks just as she did when delivered more than 70 years ago. THANIA, the well-restored 60-foot cabin launch described above, is located astern of TORCH. Across the Hall is BELISARIUS,

Looking northwest in the "Hall of Boats." Prominent in the center is TORCH, a Fishers Island 31-footer, restored and donated by Ben and Toby Baker. To the right is THANIA, a 60-foot cabin launch and the first acquisition of the Museum. In the foreground, left to right, are STREAKER, Halsey Herreshoff's modern construction of a 1912 Sid Herreshoff design, a vintage 12½-footer, and COQUINA, a modern reproduction of a classic Herreshoff family cat-yawl.

The Nathanael Greene Herreshoff Model Room. N.G. Herreshoff's portrait over the mantle piece is surrounded by half models, mostly of boats owned by Captain Nat himself.

The Museum's authentic half size America's Cup replica photographed in front of Captain Nat's half models of COLUMBIA, CONSTITUTION, and RELIANCE.

Captain Nat's last design, a handsome clipper bowed racing/cruising yawl launched in 1935. Diagonally opposite is the 1859 catboat SPRITE for which Captain Nat, at eleven-and-one-half years, laid out the full sized patterns from the design. Acquired from the Henry Ford Museum of Dearborn, Michigan, SPRITE is not only the oldest remaining catboat in America, but holds particular significance as described on page 173. Other yachts on display include important examples of the great one-design classes dating from 1898 to the advent of World War II. Aloft, affixed to the ceiling of the "Hall of Boats" is AMARYLLIS II, described heretofore (page 186) as the only true replica of Captain Nat's pioneering catamaran of 1875.

THE MODEL ROOM

Perhaps the most significant, and for many the most interesting, element of the Museum is the Nathanael Greene Herreshoff Model Room. The innovations and design decisions that earned Captain Nat worldwide fame originated in his third floor enclave of the family residence "Love Rocks," which enjoyed the inspiration of a stunning view of Narragansett Bay.

Captain Nat and successor Herreshoffs set to fact the proportion and shape of their designs by constructing half models of the hulls to be built. Following the deaths of the senior Herreshoffs, Captain Nat's eldest son Sidney moved the collection of 500 models to a nearby addition to his own house. Some forty years later, grandson Halsey C. Herreshoff planned the eventual conveyance of the unique collection to the Museum. With the talented participation of the Museum's late esteemed curator (and co-author of this book), Carlton Pinheiro, and of Fred Dick, Jr., Halsey moved the models, instruments, tools and documents to rooms constructed in the Museum to mirror the original "Love Rocks" setting. Today these remain under the care of curator John Palmieri.

N.G. Herreshoff's tool chest with some of his model-making tools.

Architect Friedrich St. Florian's design of the proposed "Reliance Pavilion" to be built along the south face of the existing Herreshoff Marine Museum building.

An artist's rendering of Friedrich St. Florian's proposed substantial additions to the Herreshoff Marine Museum/America's Cup Hall of Fame as viewed from Bristol Harbor.

HERRESHOFF MARINE MUSEUM LIST OF YACHTS

YEAR	HMCo #	NAME	LOA/LWL	TYPE	DESIGNER*	DONOR
1889	405	ALICE	29-6/26-6	Cruising Cat-Yawl	NGH	Frank A. Posluszny
1933	1232	AMARYLLIS II	33-0/30-0	Catamaran	NGH	Henry Ford Museum (purchase)
1905	647	ANEMONE	43-6/30-0	New York 30-Class Sloop	NGH	Emil Gargano
1934	1258	ANNA	11-6/	Frostbite Dinghy	Nick Potter	E. L. Goodwin of Cape Cod Shipbuilding
1914	738	ARIA	32-0/25-0	Buzzards Bay 25-Class Sloop	NGH	Paul Bates
1944		AITU	14-1/	Kayak	ASDeWH	Nathanael Greene Herreshoff III (on loan)
1907	673	AWAHNEE	24-6/15-0	Buzzards Bay 15-Class Sloop	NGH	Daniel & David Cheever
1928	1081	B.H.'s EMPRESS	15-10/12-6	Buzzards Bay 12½-footer	NGH	Mrs. Susan Hurd Greenup
1904	616	BAMBINO	41-9/30-0	Racing/Cruising Sloop	NGH	Louis B. Off
1903		BAT	10-2/	Rowing Dinghy	NGH	Peter Waterman
1935	1266	BELISARIUS	56-2/40-11	Keel/Centerboard Cruising Yawl	NGH	Charles O. Read & Ruth R. Palmer
1920		BILLOW II	11-9/	Columbia Type Lifeboat Dinghy	NGH	Mrs. Rhonda Low Seone
1916	788	BLUE FISH	20-9/16-0	Fish Class Sloop	NGH	Milton Merle
1914	761	BONITA	15-10/12-6	Buzzards Bay 12½-Footer	NGH	Everitt Fullerton, Jr.
1925	991	BULLDOG	15-10/12-6	Buzzards Bay 12½-Footer	NGH	William J. Strawbridge
1909	268	CANVASBACK	59-11/53-3	Cabin Launch	NGH	Independence Seaport Museum, Phila. (trade)
1887	402	CLARA	35-0/29-6	Cruising Cat-Yawl	NGH	Mr. & Mrs. Kerry Geraghty
1926	965	COQUINA	27-6/20-6	S-Class Sloop	NGH	Briggs S. Cunningham
1996		COQUINA	16-8/15-9	Cat-Yawl (Reproduction of HMCo #404)	NGH	Bill Kaiser
1920		CUB	11-0/	Yacht Tender	NGH	Haywood Manice
1931	1203	CYGNET	17-0/	Utility Class Cat-Yawl	NGH	Paul Hammond
1992		DEFIANT	75-0/	International America's Cup Class	A3 Design Team	William Koch
1916		DOLPHIN	20-9/16-0	Fish Class Sloop	NGH	Candace L. Heald
1917	330-Class	EMERALD	26-2/24-1	Motor Launch	NGH	Seawanhaka Corinthian Yacht Club
1922	880	FIREFLY	24-6/15-0	Watch Hill 15-Class Sloop	NGH/ ASDeWH	Charlton & Charles Muenchinger in memory of Herman Muenchinger
1885		GEM	12-0/	Rowing Dinghy	NGH	Katherine H. DeWolf Pendlebury
1925		HALCYON	15-10/12-6	Buzzards Bay 12½-Footer (Bermuda Built)	NGH	Bermuda Maritime Museum (on loan)
1899	513	HOPE	24-6/15-0	Newport 15-Class Sloop	NGH	Dean Wood
1931	1219	HORNET	34-0/23-0	Fishers Island 23-Class Sloop	ASDeWH	John W. Wendler
1903	599	INDIAN	49-0/30-6	Bar Harbor 31-Class Sloop	ASDeWH	George E. Lockwood

* Designers: NGH – Nathanael G. Herreshoff; ASDeWH – Sidney Herreshoff; LFH – L. Francis Herreshoff; CFH/JBH – Charles F. Herreshoff, John Brown Herreshoff

YEAR	HMCo #	NAME	LOA/LWL	TYPE	DESIGNER*	DONOR
1913		JACK	12-7/	Rowing Dinghy	NGH	Louise Henry DeWolf
1898	493	JILT	30-9/21-0	One Rater Fin Keel Sloop	NGH	R. Daniel Prentiss
1938	1420	MARLIN	20-9/16-0	Marlin Class Sloop	NGH/ ASDeWH	John R. Bumstead
1959		MELANTHO	39-9/	Motor Launch (LFH Design #103)	LFH	Richard Kurts
1892	428	MERRY THOUGHT	33-0/25-0	Catboat	NGH	Edward Haack & Wilma Haack-Fowler in memory of Dr. William Haack
1938	1376	MINX	15-10/12-6	Buzzards Bay 12½-footer	NGH	Owen E. Brooks
1931	1164	MIST II	24-0/18-0	18-24 Class Sloop	NGH	William L. Taggert
1936			12-6/	MIT "Tech" Sailing Dinghy	Geo. Owen	Massachusetts Institute of Technology
1927		NATHANAEL	8-2/	Yacht Tender	NGH	Waldo Howland
1919		PANDA	27-6/20-6	S-Class Sloop	NGH	David R. Pierce
1930	1173	PAPOOSE	15-10/12-6	Buzzards Bay 12½-footer	NGH	Mrs. Robert Rulon-Miller
1930		PLACIDA	14-3/	Yacht Tender	NGH	Jackie Astor
1924	907	PLEASURE	30-0/24-6	Keel/Centerboard Cruising Yawl	NGH	Robert & Susan Yaro and William Yaro; Restoration funded by Tom Stark Family
1928	1095	POOKA	15-10/12-6	Buzzards Bay 12½-footer	NGH	Geoff Davis
1935	1276	PRIM	13-1/	Amphicraft Sailing Dinghy	ASDeWH	Rosalie Crocker
1935			NA	PRIM's Amphicraft Trailer	ASDeWH	R. F. Haffenreffer IV in memory of R. F. Haffenreffer III
1914	732	SADIE	26-6/21-9	Sloop	NGH	Chesapeake Maritime Museum (purchase)
1924		SANTEE	11-7/	Sailing Dinghy (LFH design)	LFH	Gordon D. Swaffield
1950			11/	Rowing Skiff	ASDeWH	Halsey C. Herreshoff
1912	712	SPARTAN	72-0/50-0	New York 50-Class Sloop	NGH	Allen Pease (on loan)
1925	913	SPRAY	27-6/20-6	S-Class Sloop	NGH	Sandie Campbell
1859		SPRITE	20-3/20-0	Catboat	CFH/JBH	Henry Ford Museum (purchase)
1978		STILETTO	48-0/	Motor Launch (LFH Design #92)	LFH	J. Brian O'Neill
1926		TENDER	8-6/	WATER LILY's Tender	NGH	Halsey Chase Herreshoff II
1905	248	THANIA	59-8/53-6	Cabin Launch	NGH/ASDeWH	Daniel A. Newhall
1929	1153	TORCH	44-0/31-0	Fishers Island 31-Class Sloop	ASDeWH	Ben & Toby Baker
1902	580	TRIVIA	45-0/33-6	Cruising Cutter	NGH	Dr. Edward S. Fleming
1905	240	TWO FORTY	30-4/30-0	Motor Launch	NGH	Gordon M. MacPherson
1925		URCHIN	15-10/12-6	Buzzards Bay 12½-footer	NGH	Michael Dogali
1934		VELITA	16-1/15-0	W-Class Sloop	ASDeWH	Halsey Chase Herreshoff (on loan)
1892	425	WEE WIN	23-10/16-3	Half Rater Fin Keel Sloop	NGH	Jonathan Janson
1919	834	WIDGEON	27-6/20-6	S-Class Sloop	NGH	Henry W. Breyer
1930	2643-1		8-3/	Pram	NGH	Museum purchase
1915			13-2/	Rowing Dinghy	NGH	John Ferry

Bibliography and Sources

(used in preparation of *Herreshoff of Bristol*)

BOOKS

Adams, C. P. Hamilton. *The Racing Schooner Westward.* New York: Van Nostrand Reinhold Co., 1977.

Anthony, Henry S. & Co., Auctioneers. *Brochure describing the Voluntary Liquidation Sale of the Herreshoff Manufacturing Company, Inc., August 21 and 22, 1924.* Original copy held by Mystic Seaport Museum.

Blanchard, Fessenden S. *The Sailboat Classes of North America.* Garden City, NY: Doubleday & Co., Inc. 1963.

Bray, Maynard. *Mystic Seaport Museum Watercraft.* Mystic, CT: Mystic Seaport Museum, Inc., 1979.

Bunting, W. H. *Steamers, Schooners, Cutters & Sloops.* Boston: Houghton Mifflin Co., 1974.

Burnett, Constance Buel. *Let the Best Boat Win.* Boston: Houghton Mifflin Co., 1957.

Carter, Samuel III. *The Boatbuilders of Bristol.* New York: Doubleday & Co., Inc., 1970.

Crane, Clinton H. *Clinton Crane's Yachting Memories.* New York: D. Van Nostrand, Inc., 1952.

Dear, Ian. *Enterprise to Endeavour, the J-Class Yachts.* New York: Dodd, Mead & Co., 1977.

Dickie, George W. "Torpedo-Boat Destroyers." *Transactions, Vol. 6.* New York: Society of Naval Architects and Marine Engineers, 1898.

Esterly, Diana. *Early One-Design Sailboats.* New York: Charles Scribner's Sons, 1979.

Foster, C. H. W. *The Eastern Yacht Club Ditty Box.* Norwood, MA: Privately printed, 1932.

Fostle, D. W. *Speedboat.* Mystic, CT: Mystic Seaport Museum Stores, 1988.

Gillmor, Horatio G. "Torpedo-Boat Design." *Transactions, Vol. 5.* New York: Society of Naval Architects and Marine Engineers, 1897.

Herreshoff, Jeanette Brown. *The Early Founding and Development of the Herreshoff Manufacturing Company.* Tampa: Privately printed, 1949.

Herreshoff, Lewis F. *The Badminton Library: Yachting.* London: Longmans, Green & Co., 1901.

Herreshoff, L. Francis. *Nathanael Greene Herreshoff, 1948–1938.* Hartford, CT: Wadsworth Athenaeum, 1944.

_____. *Capt. Nat Herreshoff, The Wizard of Bristol.* New York: Sheridan House, 1953.

_____. *An L. Francis Herreshoff Reader.* Camden, ME: International Marine Publishing Co., 1978.

_____. *An Introduction to Yachting.* New York: Sheridan House, 1963.

_____. *The Common Sense of Yacht Design.* New York: The Rudder Publishing Co., 1946 and 1948.

Herreshoff Mfg. Co. *Yachts by Herreshoff.* Bristol, RI: Privately printed, 1937.

_____. *Herreshoff Yachts.* Bristol, RI: Privately printed, about 1930.

_____. *100 Fighting Ships.* Bristol, RI: Privately printed, 1945.

Herreshoff, Nathanael G. *Recollections and Other Writings.* Edited by Carlton J. Pinheiro. Bristol, RI: Herreshoff Marine Museum, 1988. (Contains NGH reminiscences used as source material for this book.)

Hofman, Erik. *The Steam Yachts.* Tuckahoe, NY: John De Graff, Inc., 1970.

Isherwood, B. F., Theo. Zeller, and Geo. W. Magee. *Report of a Board of United States Naval Engineers on the Herreshoff System of Motive Machinery as Applied to the Steam Yacht Leila, and on the Performance of that Vessel made to the Bureau of Steam Engineering, Navy Department, June 3, 1881.* Washington: Government Printing Office, 1881.

Kinney, Francis S. *Skene's Elements of Yacht Design* (eighth edition). New York: Dodd, Mead & Co., 1981.

Lloyd's Register of Shipping. *Lloyd's Register of American Yachts.* New York: various volumes from 1905.

Manning A. J. *Manning's Yacht Register.* New York: A. J. Manning, various volumes from 1873.

Mitchell, Richard M. *The Steam Launch.* Camden, ME: International Marine Publishing Co., 1982.

Morgan, Edwin Denison. *Recollections for My Family.* New York: Charles Scribner's Sons, 1938.

Peabody, Henry. *Representative American Yachts.* Boston: Henry G. Peabody, 1891.

Ringwald, Donald C. *The Mary Powell.* Berkeley, CA: Howell–Norton Books, 1972.

Robinson, Bill (William Wheeler). *The Great American Yacht Designers.* New York: Alfred A. Knopf, 1974.

Rousmaniere, John. *The Golden Pastime.* New York: W. W. Norton & Co., 1986.

Schoettle, Edwin J. (editor). *Sailing Craft.* New York: The Macmillan Co., 1928.

Stephens, W. P. *Traditions and Memories of American Yachting.* Camden, ME: International Marine Publishing Co., 1981.

Stone, Herbert L. and William H. Taylor. *The America's Cup Races.* New York: D. Van Nostrand Co., Inc., 1958.

Streeter, John W. *Nathanael Greene Herreshoff, William Picard Stephens: Their Last Letters 1930–1938.* Bristol, RI: Herreshoff Marine Museum, 1998. (Annotated publication of the N. G. Herreshoff correspondence with W. P. Stephens: Originals held by the New York Yacht Club.)

Taylor, Roger C. *More Good Boats.* Camden, ME: International Marine Publishing Co., Inc., 1979.

_____. *Still More Good Boats.* Camden, ME: International Marine Publishing Co., Inc., 1981.

Thomas, Barry. *Building the Herreshoff Dinghy.* Mystic, CT: Mystic Seaport Inc., 1977.

Time–Life Books, Editors of. *The Classic Boat.* Alexandria, VA: Time–Life Books, 1977.

Vanderbilt, Harold S. *Enterprise.* New York: Charles Scribner's Sons, 1931.

_____. *On the Wind's Highway.* New York: Charles Scribner's Sons, 1939.

PERIODICALS AND OTHER SOURCES

Bemis, Alan. "Cirrus, a Treasure from Herreshoff." *WoodenBoat* No. 34, May/June 1980.

Bray, Maynard. "Herreshoff Legacies." Essex, CT: *Nautical Quarterly* No. 37, Spring 1987.

_____. "The Genius of N. G. Herreshoff." Brooklin, ME: *WoodenBoat* No. 33, March/April 1980.

_____. "Heydays at Herreshoffs" Brooklin, ME: *WoodenBoat* No. 84, September/October 1988.

_____. "Two Views of the Herreshoff Bar Harbor 31s." Brooklin, ME: *WoodenBoat* No. 45, March/April 1982.

Bristol Phoenix (newspaper). Bristol, RI: Various dates.

Forest and Stream. New York: Forest and Stream Publishing Co., various issues from 1878.

Herreshoff Marine Museum. Bristol, RI: Collection of half models, photographs, correspondence, boats, and other artifacts.

Herreshoff Marine Museum Chronicle, Nos. 1–18. Bristol, RI: Herreshoff Marine Museum.

Herreshoff, N. G. Correspondence with Henry C. White: Originals privately held.

_____. Correspondence with Henry S. Morgan: Originals privately held.

_____. *Recollections* (notebook handwritten in pencil), 1933–1934.

Meyer, Elizabeth. "Powerful in Every Way." Essex, CT: *Nautical Quarterly* No. 31, Autumn 1985.

M.I.T. Museums. Cambridge, MA: Haffenreffer–Herreshoff Collection, including drawings and offset booklets, the Herreshoff Mfg. Co. construction record, and correspondence. (See also *Guide to the Haffenreffer–Herreshoff Collection.* Francis Hart Nautical Collections. Cambridge, MA: M.I.T. Museum, 1997.)

M.I.T. Museums staff. *Nathanael G. Herreshoff, The Engineering Wizard of Bristol.* An exhibit brochure, 1985.

Motor Boating. New York: The Hearst Corp., various issues from 1908.

Mystic Seaport Museum. Mystic, CT: Collections, including boats, manuscripts, oral history tapes, photographs, models, and drawings.

The Rudder. New York: The Rudder Publishing Co., various issues from 1893.

WoodenBoat magazine, Editors of. "The New York Thirties." *WoodenBoat* No. 35, July/August 1980.

Yachting. New York: Yachting Publishing Co., various issues from 1907.

Yachting magazine, Editors of. *Your New Boat.* New York: Simon and Schuster, Inc., 1946.

Yearbooks of the Beverly Yacht Club. Marion, MA: Privately printed, various years.

Yearbooks of the Cruising Club of America. New York: Privately printed, various years.

Yearbooks of the New York Yacht Club. New York: Privately printed, various years.

Various. Discussions and interviews with ex-employees, yacht owners, family members, and others who were associated in some way with the Herreshoff Mfg. Co., the Herreshoff family, or Herreshoff watercraft.

Various. Studies of extant Herreshoff-built yachts held privately and by museums.

Index

Photographs are indicated by bold page numbers.

Photo Credits

About the Authors

MAYNARD BRAY first came to appreciate Herreshoff boats as they sailed his home waters of Penobscot Bay, Maine. The writings of L. Francis Herreshoff were an early influence as well, and were more firmly committed to memory than the principles of engineering studied at the University of Maine. For Maynard, L. Francis became professor of philosophy and aesthetics, and the great Nathanael Greene Herreshoff, a mentor of unsurpassed skill in efficient and practical structural design.

Bray helped design submarines for General Dynamics and destroyers for Bath Iron Works before resigning in 1969 as the latter firm's Chief Mechanical Engineer to head the ship preservation effort at Mystic Seaport Museum. While no longer at Mystic Seaport, he was connected as a Trustee Emeritus and member of the Watercraft Committee and Yachting & Boating Committee until recently. It is not surprising that ALERION and the rest of the Museum's fleet of Herreshoff-built boats were given special attention over the years of Bray's involvement.

As Technical Editor of *WoodenBoat* magazine, a post he held for a decade, Maynard wrote numerous articles on the building and appreciation, care and repair of classic wooden watercraft. His book *Mystic Seaport Watercraft* came out in 1977 and has, with assistance from two co-authors, been expanded to keep up with the Seaport's ever-growing collection.

The beautiful 33½-foot centerboard cruising yawl AÏDA (HMCo #1002, 1926) has been a cherished member of the Bray family for over thirty-five years. FLICKER (HMCo #674, 1907) is the latest acquisition.

Maynard Bray lives in Brooklin, Maine, with his equally boat-crazy wife, Anne, who is *WoodenBoat*'s Research Director. They have three children—Kathy, Nathanael, and Sarah—and two grandchildren.

THE LATE CARLTON PINHEIRO'S interest in the Herreshoff tradition began about 1950 as the result of his maternal grandmother's employment as cook for Miss Agnes M. Herreshoff at Love Rocks. When Miss Agnes was away from home on family visits or on weekend sails, Carlton was asked to stay with his grandmother as company in the large house. It was at Love Rocks that he first pored over many of the photograph albums whose contents appear in this book. He was also allowed to visit the third-floor model room, which was kept just as N. G. Herreshoff had left it.

It later years, strong friendships developed between Carlton and Sidney's sons, Nat and Halsey Herreshoff. Over the years, they sailed together a good deal, and Carlton and Nat traveled to Europe together. A frequent visitor to Carlton's home was Captain Nat's son Clarence, whose recollections were invaluable to Carlton's study of the family.

For many years, Pinheiro owned and meticulously maintained the Herreshoff 12½-footer KELPIE (HMCo #1148). Originally owned by David P. Wheatland, a college professor who summered in Sorrento, Maine, the Marconi-rigged WE THREE was purchased by a Bristol resident in the early 1960's to replace a 12½ which had been lost in a hurricane in September 1960. Renamed KELPIE and subsequently coming into Carlton's possession, she sailed in Bristol waters until 1983, when she was sold to a family in Brooklin, Maine.

One of Carlton's proudest possessions was the mahogany bed designed by N. G. Herreshoff and built at the Herreshoff Mfg. Co. in 1883 for the designer's use at Love Rocks. Associated with the Herreshoff Marine Museum from 1977 until his passing in 2000, Carlton became the Museum's first curator in 1985. He contributed numerous articles to the *Herreshoff Marine Museum Chronicle* and to local publications. The Bristol native was a 1963 graduate of the University of Rhode Island and taught English at East Greenwich High School for over twenty-five years. He lived in Bristol, close to the Herreshoff Mfg. Co. site. He is survived by his wife Lianne and two sons, Nathanael and Sam.